TREASURY OF CAN
BED AND BREAKFAST

TREASURY OF CANADIAN BED AND BREAKFAST

WILLIAM STREET PRESS

Text and illustrations copyright © 1992
Patricia Wilson

Canadian Cataloguing in Publication Data

Wilson, Patricia
  The Treasury of Canadian Bed and Breakfast

ISBN 0-9695097-1-5

1. Bed and Breakfast, etc. - Canada -
Directories. 1. Title

TX910.C2W54 647'.94713 C83-098359-7

Published by The William Street Press
          RR# 2
          STAFFA, Ontario
          N0K 1Y0

Printed and bound in Canada

Cover Design: Scott McKowen

Contents

7   Introduction to *The Treasury*

8   *Islands* of British Columbia

25   British Columbia

50   Alberta

66   Saskatchewan

70   Manitoba

78   Ontario

154   Quebec

176   New Brunswick

190   Nova Scotia

204   Prince Edward Island

212   Newfoundland

Introduction to The Treasury of Canadian Bed and Breakfast

The Treasury of Canadian Bed and Breakfast is *unique* because we have travelled *across Canada*, coast to coast, to research personally all the places in this book. In this way we can recommend with confidence the bed and breakfasts listed here; *The Treasury* is the *only* Canadian Bed and Breakfast Book that can cheerfully vouch for every home listed.

More and more, people from all over the world are travelling across Canada the Bed and Breakfast way. Since some of the *most interesting* Bed and Breakfast homes are in *out-of-the-way places*, you, the traveller need help to locate these *hidden treasures*; the book provides this service. The style and location of homes will vary as you travel across this great land -- ranch homes; ocean fronts; city mansions; country cottages, to name a few -- yet every *treasure* is special in its own way.

Whether you organize a holiday around a network of these quality Bed and Breakfasts, or simply use one for a week-end get-away, we feel sure that your trip will be more worthwhile; you will be warmly welcomed by *informed* hosts; you will be served an appetizing breakfast, ranging from generous continental to gourmet; you will probably meet other guests with which to exchange anecdotes about your travels; and you will come away feeling that you now really know that area of Canada, much like visiting "family".

We would like to emphasize that these Bed and Breakfast places could not *ask* to be in this book; they were *invited* to come in. Of the many places contacted these are the ones we chose because we felt that every one included here in *The Treasury* would add something special to your travelling enjoyment.

The places in this book are arranged by province, from West to East, and alphabetically by community, under each province.

British Columbia is the one exception to this arrangement as the places on *Vancouver Island* and *Salt Spring Island* are listed alphabetically by community, first, before the *British Columbia mainland*.

The maps of *Western Canada* and *Eastern Canada*, located inside the front and back covers, respectively, show the locations of all the Bed and Breakfast places in this book *and* the page numbers where they are written up.

Finally, we certainly cannot claim to have found *all* the Bed and Breakfast Treasures of Canada. If you happen to discover a *Treasure* in your travels we sincerely invite you to write to us with your recommendations.

Patricia Wilson

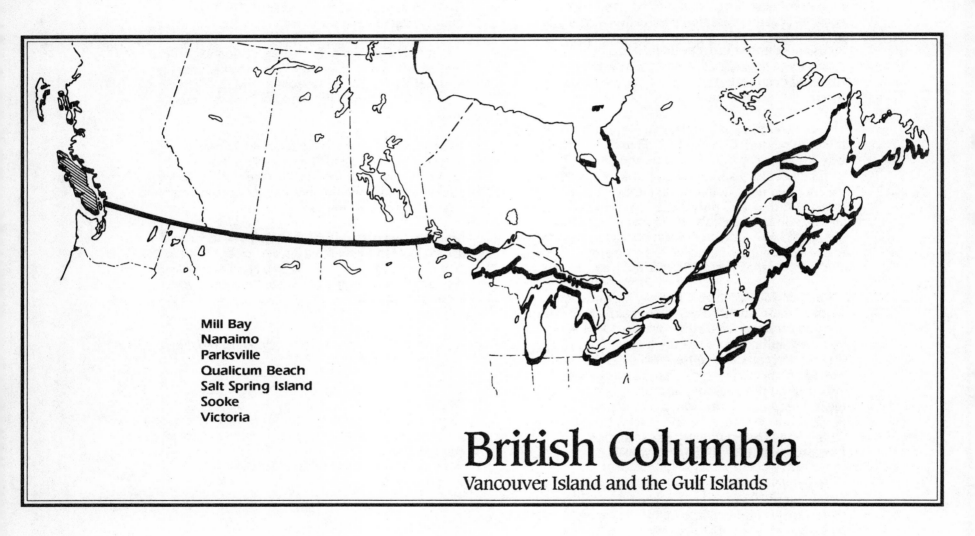

Mill Bay
Nanaimo
Parksville
Qualicum Beach
Salt Spring Island
Sooke
Victoria

British Columbia
Vancouver Island and the Gulf Islands

Weston Lake Inn B&B

You wind up, up the long driveway beside a split-rail fence under tall Douglas firs. Cows graze contentedly in the pasture as you approach this charming country home nestled on a well-tended knoll of flowering trees and shrubs. Wilson, the old English Sheepdog, greets you warmly. The view of Weston Lake is serene and beautiful.

The inn, run by hosts Susan Evans and Ted Harrison, is peaceful and comfortable, an idyllic adult getaway. Three guest bedrooms, with private combination baths, down duvets and fresh bouquets, are each decorated on a theme. The Petitpoint Room, overlooking the lake, is filled with intricate needlework crafted by Ted. The Sailboat Room and the Eskimo Room look out over a stonework water garden.

Inside the inn there is a special fireside lounge with library, satellite TV and VCR exclusively for the use of guests. And outside on a landscaped garden terrace facing the lake is a hot tub where guests can relax and contemplate nature at its best.

Breakfast is a full-course meal served to the sounds of classical music in the antique-filled dining room. Guests are treated to such fare as cream-coated strawberries in season from Susan's organic vegetable garden, French toast adorned with blueberry sauce with a hint of Triple Sec, and eggs benedict a la Weston Lake, the eggs, compliments of the farm's free-range chickens.

Susan and Ted were born on the southern B.C. coast and have travelled the Pacific Northwest by sail, bicycle and kayak. They invite you to share their love of this beautiful area, and the comfort and hospitality of their country B&B.

Salt Spring has an artist community of potters, weavers, painters and writers that have become an integral part of its charm. Ruckle Park, for hiking and picnicking, is just four miles from *Weston Lake Inn Bed and Breakfast.*

WESTON LAKE INN

Susan Evans and Ted Harrison
813 Beaver Point Road, RR1
Fulford Harbour
Salt Spring Island, British Columbia
V0S 1C0
(604) 653-4311

Season: All year
Rates: Single $65 - $80 Double $80 - $95 Additional person $25
Types of Accommodation: 1 Double, 1 Queen and 1 room with a Double and Single
Bathrooms: 2 En Suite and 1 Private detached
Breakfast: Full
Special Information: Adult oriented; Non-smoking home; No guests' pets please; Dog "Wilson" and Cats "Jose" and "Cactus" in residence; Visa and MasterCard accepted; Gift certificates available
Languages: English and French
Handicapped Facilities: Limited
Directions: We are 2 1/2 miles from the Fulford Harbour Ferry Terminal on the road to Ruckle Provincial Park. We are 7 miles from Ganges.

Applecroft B&B

You will receive an enthusiastic welcome from hosts Diane and Bob Hele when you stay at their cozy heritage family farm (circa 1893). There is a sitting room for guests and bright dining room for breakfasts. The rooms are furnished comfortably with antiques. Landscaped gardens, cooing doves from the bird house, make an inviting place to relax and stroll. Every season at *Applecroft* provides a different beauty. Frogs announce springtime with a chorus; crickets the coming of Fall. Carpets of wild flowers colour the banks of the stream, meadows and fields where the goats, geese and other animals graze. The age-old Douglas Firs tower over all to provide a backdrop of majestic peace.

Situated on the main floor is the charming Rose Room with a queen sized four-poster bed with down comforter and a very indulgent-looking double jacuzzi. The Morning Glory Room has a double bed and down comforter and en suite private bathroom. The Lilac Room, overlooking the old orchard and gardens has twin beds and a private bathroom with jacuzzi.

A secluded cottage, perfect for honeymooners and getaways is a hide-away at the edge of the forest. Completely self-contained, it has a soaker tub for two beneath a skylight. Upstairs is a queen sized bed, balcony and forest and valley view.

A generous breakfast includes eggs from the farm, and other home-made treats.

Salt Spring Island itself is another treasure. Ocean beaches, trails, ferries, restaurants, shopping, golf and recreation are all only minutes away.

APPLECROFT B.&B.

Bob and Diane Hele
551 Upper Ganges Road, RR3
Ganges, Salt Spring Island, British Columbia
V0S 1E0
(604) 537-5605

Season: All year
Rates: Single $55 - $75 Double $65 - $85 plus tax
Types of Accommodation: 1 Double, 1 Queen, 1 Twin, and a Cottage with Queen size bed
Bathrooms: 4 Private
Breakfast: Full
Special Information: No guests' pets; No smoking; Visa and Master-Card accepted; Check-in Time 4:30 p.m.; Check-out Time 11:00 a.m.; Reservations recommended
Directions: *Applecroft* is located 2 miles north of Ganges, next to the golf course and tennis courts. Please call for detailed directions.

Green Rose Farm B&B

Green, naturally, is a favourite colour at *Green Rose Farm Bed and Breakfast*. This 1916 farm house has been restored with a pleasing ambience produced by dark green painted floors, white walls and pine woodwork; the overall effect is of uncluttered space and inviting rooms where guests will feel at home. This is carried over into the three guest rooms, all with queen size beds, cozy down quilts and down pillows.

A delicious full breakfast is served in the pleasant dining room. The large living room and the den, both with fireplaces are for the guests' use.

Located a few minutes north of the village of Ganges, on Salt Spring Island, *Green Rose Farm* consists of 17 acres of fields, gardens, orchards and forest. Some of the apple trees are old-fashioned varieties at least one hundred years old.

There is so much to do on idyllic Salt Spring. Blessed with a balmy climate, plenty of sunshine, picturesque scenery, eleven sparkling lakes, and breathtaking views, the island is an artist's paradise. There are many galleries, shops to tour, and places to dine. Besides this, there is Ruckle Provincial Park where one can hike the shoreline or across grassy meadows; other pastimes are riding, canoeing, fishing, and cruising, to mention a few.

GREEN ROSE FARM

Tom Hoff and Ron Aird
346 Robinson Road
RR4, Mansell, C-78
Ganges, Salt Spring Island
British Columbia
V0S 1E0
(604) 537-9927

Season: All year
Rates: $65 and up
Types of Accommodation: 3 Queen
Bathrooms: 1 Private and 1 Shared
Breakfast: Full
Special Information: Adult guests only please; Non-smoking home
Directions: *Green Rose Farm B&B* is 1 1/2 miles north of the main village of Ganges, on Robinson Road, right hand side, green sign.

The Old Farm House

This beautifully restored one-hundred year-old heritage farm home is set among tall trees, orchards and meadows on lovely Salt Spring Island, not far from Ganges village and St. Mary's Lake.

When Gerti and Karl Fuss restored their farm home, Karl with an architect's advice, planned and built the guest-house addition himself, seeking out authentic windows and doors, then refinishing them. Gerti produced the furnishings, and lovely drapes, bedskirts and pillows for the rooms.

At *The Old Farm House* you will be spoiled by European hospitality. Every morning guests from all parts of the world and all walks of life gather around the beautifully set table. Fresh flowers from the garden brighten the room while guests enjoy Gerti's famous gourmet breakfast. Conversation might turn to the subject of the resident "ghost"! Gerti produces volumes of home baked goodies; cinnamon buns, croissants, breads or muffins might introduce a meal that could include smoked salmon souffle, or German apple pancakes; and apple juice freshly pressed from their own apples.

Besides pampering a stream of guests, Gerti and Karl are kept busy with their flower and herb gardens and fruit trees which are a part of the lovely setting for their home. The balmy climate of Salt Spring Island provides an excellent place to grow things.

While staying at *The Old Farm House* tour the Island and take in the picturesque scenery of sparkling lakes, breathtaking ocean views and greenery. Besides recreational opportunities, the Island offers many galleries and craft studios which are interesting places to visit.

The OLD FARMHOUSE

Gerti and Karl Fuss
1077 North End Road
RR4, Ganges
Salt Spring Island, British Columbia
V0S 1E0
(604) 537-4113

Season: All year
Rates: Single $110 Double $110
Types of Accommodation: 1 Double, 2 Queen and 1 Twin
Bathrooms: 4 Private -- combination Tub and Shower
Breakfast: Full
Languages: English and German
Handicapped Facilities: Limited
Directions: Four km north of Ganges on North End Road. At the beginning of St. Mary's Lake.

Pinelodge Farm B&B

PINE LODGE FARM

The first reaction to the interior of *Pine Lodge Farm* is to think of an English baronial castle because here is a "great hall" with a stone fireplace at the one end towering to the ceiling. Above, the upper balcony provides access to the guest rooms. Yet the exterior appears as a large log home.

Your hosts, Cliff and Barbara Clarke, who are also antique dealers, built their massive pine house on 30 acres of rolling farmland and furnished it with their best antiques and oriental rugs.

Only 25 miles north of Victoria, the farm has a trout pond, cows and chickens clucking away in their pens. There are beautiful flower gardens and a trail that descends to lovely woods and fields.

The bedrooms are comfortable and all have antique armoires, as well as other antique furnishings and old prints. All the rooms have private baths and some even have a view of the Channel where the ferries pass coming to and from Vancouver.

There is also a honeymoon cottage with fireplace and hot tub available.

Breakfast comprising of fresh brown farm eggs, in any style, accompanied by bacon, sausage, pancakes and, in season, home grown berries, is served outside or in the dining room, surrounded by antique collections.

There is a golf course in the area and fishing charters can be arranged at Cowichan Bay, which is nearby.

Cliff and Barbara Clarke
3191 Mutter Road
Mill Bay, Vancouver Island
British Columbia
V0R 2P0
(604) 743-4083

Season: All year except for holidays
Rates: Single $50 Double $70 - $80
Types of Accommodation: 2 Double, 4 Queen, 1 Twin
Bathrooms: 7 Private with showers
Breakfast: Full
Special Information: Children welcome; Non-smoking home but smoking permitted outside; No guests' pets
Directions: Coming from Victoria, travel 25 miles to Mill Bay on the Trans Canada Highway. Turn right at the fifth stoplight (Kilmalu Road), then turn left onto Telegraph Road. Go two blocks up and turn right onto Meredith Road and then left onto Mutter Road.

Loon Watch B&B

LOON WATCH B&B

Yes, people *really* can watch loons at *Loon Watch Bed and Breakfast*, but only from October through April. Then they leave to go to the interior lakes for the summer. But there are other creatures to watch -- killer whales, seals, herons and bald eagles, right from the balcony, because *Loon Watch* is situated right on the ocean front of Vancouver Island facing the Inside Passage where cruise ships go by on their way to Alaska and guests can beachcomb, or dig for clams especially at low tide, to their heart's delight.

Loon Watch offers large comfortable bedrooms with a 4-piece bath en suite. Each bedroom has large windows and an entrance onto the balcony which faces the ocean. A full breakfast is served in the dining room and lively conversation is usually part of the fare, as myriads of birds enjoy the morning tidal pools.

This area of Vancouver Island is known for its beaches, parks, boating, scuba diving, salmon charters, and for just relaxing by the ocean and mountains. And from Parksville, one can cross the island through giant forests, past legendary trout lakes to the booming Pacific rim.

John and Dorothy Gourlay
1513 Admiral Tryon Blvd.,
Parksville, Vancouver Island
British Columbia
V9P 1Y3
(604) 752-9698

Season: All year
Rates: Single $45 Double $65 Cot $10
Types of Accommodation: 1 Queen, 2 Twin
Bathrooms: 2 Private
Breakfast: Full
Special Information: Non-smoking home; No guests' pets please; Cat in residence named "Abigail"; Wonderful bird watching; Brant Festival in March
Directions: *Loon Watch* is 4 km north of Parksville, over the French Creek Bridge and turn right onto Columbia (Beach). Continue to the water and turn left on Admiral Tryon.

Blue Willow B&B

The Blue Willow has established English country charm in beautiful Qualicum Beach. John and Arlene England's Bed and Breakfast home is located just minutes from the beach and the village, 45 kilometers north of the Nanaimo ferry terminal on Vancouver Island.

The Blue Willow is a Tudor-style home with leaded glass windows and beamed ceilings set amid a profusion of flowers, shrubs and tall trees. The beautifully decorated guest rooms offer comfort and quiet relaxation; all have private bath or shower. There is also a charming self-contained "studio" available with queen size and single bed, separate from the main house.

Whenever possible, the elegant breakfast is served on the patio; you have a choice of either Continental or full English breakfast fare. Whichever your choice, it is served with West Coast hospitality; breakfast at *Blue Willow* is a special event.

Your hosts, who also have a good knowledge of French and German, and are always ready to offer knowledgeable tips on what to see or where to dine.

Qualicum Beach area offers an abundance of activities. Some suggestions would be swimming, golfing, fishing, or hiking in the Provincial Parks. The Highway to Long Beach on the West Coast of Vancouver Island begins near Nanaimo and this would make an interesting day-trip. Alternatively, guests may simply want to relax and enjoy a cup of tea in the *Blue Willow's* delightful English country garden.

QUALICUM BEACH (near Nanaimo)
Vancouver Island
BRITISH COLUMBIA

BLUE WILLOW B.+B.

John and Arlene England
524 Quatna Road
Qualicum Beach, Vancouver Island
British Columbia
V9K 1B4
(604) 752-9052

Season: All year
Rates: $45 - $60 and up
Types of Accommodation: Queen, Double and Single
Bathrooms: Private
Breakfast: Full or Continental, your preference
Special Information: Prior arrangements should be made for young children or guests' pets; Dachshund in residence; Non-smoking home; Check-in time between 3:00 p.m. and 6:00 p.m.; Check-out time is 10:30 a.m.
Languages: English, French, and German
Directions: On Quatna Road, which runs north and south between Hall Road and Qualicum Road, and is one block west of the Island Highway 19.

Malahat Farm

Malahat Farm Bed and Breakfast Guest House was built in 1910; the home is featured in *101 Historical Buildings of the Sooke Region*. Whether relaxing by the fireplace in your cozy guest room, or sleeping in an old brass bed the ambiance of the past is all around. Ascend the curving staircase to the upper rooms where pastoral views abound. All the rooms have private baths, queen size beds and are decorated with a touch of yesteryear. The rooms are named after the original family, the Andersons who homesteaded the farm in 1896. Examples are "The William Henry Room", a large main floor bed-sitting room, with fireplace, four-poster bed, private bath with claw-footed tub and hand held showers and "Lavinnia's Room", upstairs, decorated in rose and white with brass bed and view of the back pasture, private bath with claw-footed tub and hand held shower.

The tradition of hospitality abounds at *Malahat Farm*. Awaken to the sounds of the country. Taste the goodness of home-made breads, farm fresh eggs, jams and jellies from the fruit trees, and honey from the hives. Smell the aroma of your morning coffee simmering on the old woodstove.

Malahat Farm is 45 acres surrounded by forest -- great for walking.

Parks in the area offer the opporunity to beach-comb, birdwatch, hike, surf and picnic. Salmon fishing can be arranged; kayaking, and sea life tours are available. Sooke has fine dining, "down home" restaurants, quaint tea rooms, and craft stores featuring local artisans. *Malahat Farm* is one hours' drive from Victoria.

- MALAHAT FARM -

George and Diana Clare
Anderson Road, RR2
Sooke, Vancouver Island
British Columbia
V0S 1N0
(604) 642-6868

Season: All year, except Christmas
Rates: $90 and up
Types of Accommodation: 1 Single, 4 Queen
Bathrooms: 4 Private
Breakfast: Full
Special Information: Adult guests only; Non-smoking home; No guests' pets; Dog named "Billie" and Cat named "Faline" at our home -- not in guest house; Farm animals -- cows, geese, chickens, and sheep; 45 acre farm
Directions: Take Highway 14 to Sooke. *Malahat Farm* is 15 minutes west of Sooke on Anderson Road.

The Haterleigh

The Haterleigh, a Bed and Breakfast operated from a designated heritage building, has been lovingly restored. Built in 1901 by Thomas Hooper as his personal residence, the house was moved to its present location in 1911. And it is this location, within strolling distance of the inner harbour and downtown Victoria, that is one of the house's attractions. Another is its architectural style -- beautiful woodwork; outstanding leaded windows; ornate plaster mouldings; and antique furniture grace its rooms.

The bedrooms are all en suite but one, and that one has its own detached bathroom. Architecturally, each is exceptional, from "White Gable" with slanted ceilings and tiny balcony to the "Day Dreams" suite with high ceilings, sitting room, and double jacuzzi. And one suite, the "Secret Garden" has many windows and a deck with a view of the Olympic mountains.

Your hostess, Mary Lane Anderson, serves a delicious breakfast in the dining room.

Victoria, the capital city of British Columbia offers sight-seeing, shopping and restaurants. Visit its world-famous gardens, the Royal British Columbia Museum and many other attractions.

The Haterleigh House

Les and Mary Lane Anderson
243 Kingston Street
Victoria, Vancouver Island, British Columbia
V8V 1V5
(604) 384-9995 or (604) 388-4598

Season: All year
Rates: Summer: Double $70 - $135 Extra person $20 Winter: Double $55 - $115 Extra person $15
Types of Accommodation: 3 Double, 3 Queen, 1 King (1 is a 2 bedroom suite)
Bathrooms: 1 Private detached and 5 En Suite
Breakfast: Full Vegetarian
Special Information: Children by special arrangement; Non-smoking; Two day cancellation policy; No facilities for guests' pets; Cat in residence named "Oreo"; Special weekend rates (2 nights)
Directions: Travel west to the end of Belleville (in front of Parliament); forced left onto Pendray which dead ends in our driveway on Kingston Street.

The Inn on St. Andrews

The Inn on St. Andrews was built in 1913 by Edith Carr, eldest sister of the famous Canadian artist and author, Emily Carr. Built on the Carr property, near the family home, *The Inn* is designated as a heritage property. The house is surrounded by a garden that changes with the seasons; here guests can relax after a busy day sight-seeing in Victoria. There is a sunroom overlooking the east garden, a sun-deck overlooking the west garden, a cosy T.V. room and a larger drawing room.

The tudor-style charm of this residence, with its interesting woodwork and comfortable atmosphere is matched by the welcome and "old-fashioned" hospitality which makes one feel instantly "at home". Joan does everything to make your stay in Victoria as rewarding as possible.

The James Bay location of the home means that it is close to the Victoria Inner Harbour, ferry and seaplane terminals, the Royal British Columbia Museum, the famous Empress Hotel, and downtown shops. A short walk in another direction takes one to the renowned Beacon Hill Park and the Juan de Fuca Strait connecting to off the Pacific Ocean. Joan has prepared a special map of Victoria that provides a "walking tour" for guests; places to see by car; and restaurant locations. In a city noted for expensive accommodation, *The Inn on St. Andrews* is a great value in every way.

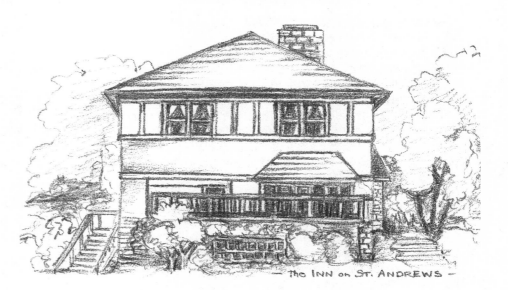

— The INN on ST. ANDREWS —

Joan Peggs
231 St. Andrews Street
Victoria, Vancouver Island
British Columbia
V8V 2N1
(604) 384-8613

Season: All year
Rates: Single $50 Double $65
Types of Accommodation: 1 Double, 1 Queen, and 1 Twin
Bathrooms: 2 Full
Breakfast: Full
Special Information: Children welcome; Non-smoking home
Directions: Between Douglas and Government Streets at Simcoe Street.

Joan Brown's B&B

This Bed and Breakfast is an 1883 mansion built for a former Lieutenant Governor of the province in the Rockland District of Victoria. It is truly a majestic home, impressive entry, high ceilings, many large rooms, beautiful woodwork, a grand staircase, and a solarium (which is one of the guest rooms) that is hung with wisteria in the Springtime.

The bedrooms are large and feature Laura Ashley touches and handmade quilts; all beds are queen or king size. Breakfast is served in the elegant dining room. The grounds and gardens are beautiful and make a pleasant place for guests to relax.

We found your hostess, Joan Brown, a true eccentric, and very full of enthusiasm for bed and breakfast and for Victoria.

The lovely city of Victoria itself has so much to offer. Nearby *Joan Brown's* is Beacon Hill Park and the ocean front for walks. Downtown places to visit are the harbour, the British Columbia Parliament Buildings, the Royal British Columbia Museum and the Empress Hotel (which is famous for afternoon tea -- call ahead). And the city offers gardens, as they can only grow in this temperate climate and a plethora of restaurants. Bon appetit! Some other major attractions in and around Vancouver are the miniature world in the Empress Hotel; Crystal Garden, a glass - enclosed tropical garden; and the world famous Butchart Gardens, open every day of the year.

JOAN BROWN'S B.+B.

Joan Brown
729 Pemberton Road
Victoria, Vancouver Island
British Columbia
V8S 3R3
(604) 592-5929

Season: All year
Rates: Available upon request
Types of Accommodation: Queen and King beds
Bathrooms: Private and Shared
Breakfast: Full or Continental
Directions: *Joan Brown's Bed and Breakfast* is located on Pemberton Road north of Rockland and two blocks from Craigdarroch Castle and Government House.

Laird House

LAIRD HOUSE

Laird House is a charming and inviting 1912 Victoria heritage-style home in quiet and lovely James Bay, an historical residential area just fifteen minutes walk from downtown, ferries, the Royal British Columbia Museum, restaurants and tearooms. Guests love to take an early morning walk along the nearby ocean front promenade, watch the sailboats and marine life, or stroll through beautiful Beacon Hill Park.

Spacious, charmingly furnished guest rooms (one with a fireplace and balcony) come with fruit baskets, fresh flowers, robes, hairdryers and share two guest bathrooms. Complimentary tea, coffee, hot chocolate and cookies are available anytime. Guests are invited to browse the books or sip a sherry by the fire in the panelled sitting room library.

Breakfast is a full, hearty three-course meal, complete with home-made jam, currant scones and muffins.

Ruth Laird has been welcoming guests from around the world into her home for years, and has received the Government of Canada Tourist Ambassador Certificate for exceptional effort, in Canada's tradition of friendship and goodwill towards international visitors. Guests have said "*Laird House* is the best".

Ruth Laird
134 St. Andrews Street
Victoria, Vancouver Island
British Columbia
V8V 2M7
(604) 384-3177

Season: All year
Rates: Single $56 Double from $66
Types of Accommodation: 1 Double, 1 Queen
Bathrooms: 2 Bathrooms with showers
Breakfast: Full
Special Information: Adult guests only please; Non-smokers home; No guests' pets please; Two cats in residence named "Bubba" and "Kitty"
Directions: *Laird House* is located between Douglas and Government at Beacon Street. Near Beacon Hill Park.

Prior House

PRIOR HOUSE B.&B.

Prior House is an historic Edwardian mansion built in 1912 for the Lieutenant Governor of British Columbia of that day. You step in the front door to be steeped in the ambience of rich oak panelling, stained glass windows, and antique furnishings. Carved stone terraces overlook the large garden. Prior House is situated in Rockland, a very prestigious neighbourhood of Victoria, near the famous Government House.

You will be greeted by your gracious hostess Candis Cooperrider, and in the afternoon-evening, guests gather in front of the open-hearth fireplace of the drawing room, library or on the terrace for complimentary tea, treats and friendly conversation.

A sumptuous full breakfast is served in the mansion dining room, or, if you wish, in the privacy of your room with a breakfast tray or breakfast-in-bed.

Each guest room is individually designed; three are suites; all have their own baths and all are marvellous. Most rooms have fireplaces; all have Canadian goose-down comforters and pillows, and fresh flowers. The most romantic is the "Boudoir" with windows that face across the water toward the Olympic Mountains.

Prior House, of course, is close to all that Victoria and area offers visitors -- the British Columbia Parliament Buildings at Royal Museum, the Empress Hotel; Butchart Gardens, open every day, and interesting places to eat. Prior House costs a little more than some Bed and Breakfasts in Victoria, but is good value considering its exceptional amenities.

Candis Cooperrider
620 St. Charles
Victoria, Vancouver Island
British Columbia
V8S 3N7
(604) 592-8847

Season: All year
Rates: $80 - $190
Types of Accommodation: 5 Guest rooms
Bathrooms: 5 Private
Breakfast: Full
Special Information: Visa and MasterCard accepted; Smoking only in gardens, on decks and terraces; Check-in is between 4:00 and 6:00 p.m.; Check-out time is 11:00 a.m.
Directions: *Prior House* is on St. Charles just south of Rockland near the Government House.

Raven Tree Gardens

Raven Tree Gardens Bed and Breakfast offers warm hospitality in a forest setting twenty minutes from downtown Victoria. Here, against the backdrop of the big trees Dennis and Georgina Knight's charming tudor-style home sits on a knoll above beautifully landscaped grounds featuring exquisite Iris gardens, a trout pond and a magnificent "Raven Tree".

Upstairs, charming guest rooms welcome guests. Every afternoon tea is served in the lounge or on the terrace overlooking the garden and pond.

Raven Tree is a perfect setting for camera buffs, birders and naturalists; there are 10 acres of gardens and woodland paths to stroll in peace and quiet.

Raven Tree is close to Victoria and all the city offers, but also close to Sooke where fine dining, tea rooms, arts and crafts stores are a visitors' delight. The ocean, for marinas, salmon fishing, boating, whale watching and water sports is only minutes away. Beaches for casual hiking and beachcombing can be found on Whiffin Spit, which separates the quiet waters of Sooke Harbour from the Strait of Juan de Fuca.

— RAVEN TREE GARDENS —

Dennis and Georgina Knight
1853 Connie Road, RR2
Victoria, Vancouver Island
British Columbia
V9B 5B4
(604) 642-5248

Season: All year
Rates: Double $75 and up Single 15% less
Types of Accommodation: 1 Double, 1 Queen, 4 King, 1 Twin
Bathrooms: 3 En Suite, 1 Private detached
Breakfast: Full
Special Information: Children over 12 years welcome; No guests' pets (Country Club Kennels nearby); No smoking in house; Gardens toured several times per year by Horticultural clubs; 140 varieties of Iris in bloom May 25 - end of June
Directions: From the Airport or Swartz Bay Ferry: take Highway 17 to Highway 1 then to Highway 14 to Sooke. From Victoria: take Highway 1 to Highway 14 to Sooke.

The Weathervane B&B

The Weathervane Bed and Breakfast is an antique and art filled comfortable "Cape Cod" style home renovated in 1989 by Sue and John Cabeldu to accommodate bed and breakfast guests.

Each luxurious room is its own private domain with down quilts and king or queen size beds, private bath and key. The living room is reserved for guests to relax in, read or watch T.V. Here visitor information, maps, books to read and a glass of sherry at the end of the day are all available. Breakfast is served in the elegant dining room each morning; John is a very capable chef.

The Weathervane is located in the prestigious, quiet Rockland area of Victoria, near the Lieutenant Governor's mansion. If you wish to leave your car and explore the city on foot, there is a local bus stop close by to provide transportation downtown.

There is so much to do in and around Victoria, British Columbia's capital city! The blessing of a temperate climate and sunshine make possible the beautiful gardens. Some of the attractions are English Teas, walking tours, Sealand, the Wax works, Undersea Gardens, Miniature World, the Butchart Gardens and a variety of excellent restaurants.

The WEATHERVANE

John, Sue and David Cabeldu
1633 Rockland Avenue
Victoria, Vancouver Island
British Columbia
V8S 1W6
(604) 592-6493

Season: All year
Rates: $75 and up
Types of Accommodation: 2 King, 2 Queen and 1 Single
Bathrooms: 3 En Suite (one with jacuzzi) and 1 Private with shower
Special Information: Children over 10 years old welcome; Non-smoking home; No guests' pets
Languages: English, French, and German
Handicapped Facilities: Wheelchair accessible bedroom on main floor
Directions: From city center take Fort Street (one way). Right on Cook Street, left onto Rockland Avenue

Wooded Acres B&B

WOODED ACRES

The home at *Wooded Acres Bed and Breakfast* was created as a "labour of love" by Elva and Skip Kennedy. This charming log home is nestled among huge trees on over three acres of peace and solitude.

The lounge has a warm snug atmosphere and is enhanced by a rustic stone fireplace. Watch the birds and squirrels while enjoying home-baked specialties for breakfast, with fresh brown eggs from the hen house!

On the second floor, one party of guests at a time enjoys complete privacy. There are two charming bedrooms with queen beds, eyelet-covered down duvets and a private bathroom with old-fashioned claw-footed tub. Relax in your own spa, with candlelight in an adjoining room, open to the wilderness. Robes provided.

This is an ideal location for honeymooners, a family, or two couples travelling together. A thoughtful touch is the ice-box on the landing that is kept replenished.

Metchosin is a "green wilderness" municipality with lots of beaches and parks, all within minutes of Victoria. Guests can explore this unspoiled natural recreation area only 30 minutes from the city centre of the capital city of British Columbia.

Wooded Acres is close to some of the best fishing in the world; and at Race Rocks Ecological Reserve close by one can observe all sea life, including various pods of whales travelling through the area. Boat rentals, charters, golf courses, beaches, parks and dining, from coffee shops to the famous "Sooke Harbour House", are all near.

Elva and Skip Kennedy
4907 Rocky Point Road, RR2
Victoria, Vancouver Island
British Columbia
V9B 5B4
(604) 478-8172

Season: All year
Rates: Single $85.60 Double $90.95 Two Couples (2 rooms) $160.50
Extra person $25 (prices included GST)
Types of Accommodation: 2 Queen
Bathrooms: 1 Full
Breakfast: Full
Special Information: Adult oriented; Children over 10 welcome; Cats and Dog in residence; Smoking area provided; Hot tub open area
Directions: Located in the rural municipality of Metchosin, between Victoria and Sooke. From Highway 14, turn onto Metchosin Road, right onto Happy Valley Road and left onto Rocky Point Road.

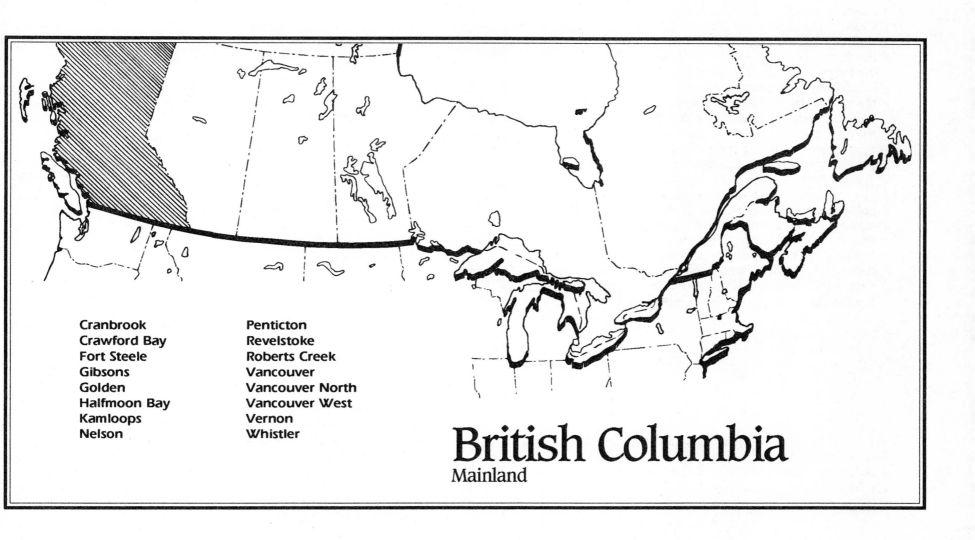

Cranbrook
Crawford Bay
Fort Steele
Gibsons
Golden
Halfmoon Bay
Kamloops
Nelson

Penticton
Revelstoke
Roberts Creek
Vancouver
Vancouver North
Vancouver West
Vernon
Whistler

British Columbia
Mainland

Baker Hill B&B

Ray and Colleen Harlos' Bed and Breakfast is called *Baker Hill* after this historic part of Cranbrook, British Columbia where it is located; built in 1910 *Baker Hill* is in a quiet residential neighbourhood, yet within walking distance of downtown, and close to skiing and golf.

This large comfortable home is beautifully furnished and offers large, quiet guest rooms. Breakfast is served in a friendly, home-like atmosphere in the dining room. *Baker Hill Bed and Breakfast* has a beautiful in-ground swimming pool set at the back of spacious lawns for guests to enjoy; there is also a sauna.

In Cranbrook, you can visit the Railway Museum and Gallery. Here one of the world's vintage trains, some cars of the Trans Canada Limited, have been restored to 1929 elegance. Fish in the Moyie and Jimsmith Lake, below Cranbrook. Then take a side trip to Fort Steele, a turn-of-the-century town, with over sixty restored and reconstructed homes and buildings.

BAKER HILL B.&B.

Ray and Colleen Harlos
305 - 12th Avenue South
Cranbrook, British Columbia
V1C 2S6
(604) 426-2632

Season: All year
Rates: Single $40 Double $55
Types of Accommodation: 1 Double, 1 Queen, 1 Twin
Bathrooms: 2 Private sinks and shower/tub with shared toilet
Breakfast: Full
Special Information: Children by prior arrangement; Non-smoking home; No guests' pets please; Resident Cat named "Pepper"
Directions: *Baker Hill Bed and Breakfast* is on 12th Avenue South just three blocks from Baker Street.

Wedgwood Manor B&B

Wedgwood Manor, dating from the early 1900's, was built on a fifty-acre estate overlooking a small valley at the foot of the Purcell Mountains.

The large guest rooms are furnished with Victorian pieces and each has a distinct personality. Entering this gracious old home is to step back in time. The library lounge, living room, dining room, and front verandah all provide pleasant settings for meeting and mingling with other guests.

Breakfasts are far from ordinary and your hosts, Joan and John, use, as much as possible, fresh food straight from the *Manor* gardens. Evening tea is served in the living room or on the verandah, a tradition established by the very first mistress of the house, Lucy Caroline Wedgwood.

Wedgwood Manor is a quiet hideaway, yet there are many activities and diversions nearby. Directly across from the estate is Kokanee Springs Championship golf course, one of the finest in British Columbia. Crawford Bay Beach is on ninety-mile long Kootenay Lake where one can swim, canoe, and fish for rainbow trout (record is thirty pounds plus). Excellent walking and hiking begins right at the doorstep; guided alpine and nature tours are available locally. Bicycles are available free for the guests to explore local backroads.

Scenic day trips might be the free ferry across Kootenay Lake to visit the hot springs and cavern at Ainsworth, or the historic town of Kaslo; or the city of Nelson for great dining and shopping.

Wedgwood Manor is a marvellous place to shed the rush of city life, and for a honeymoon or romantic getaway; stretch out in a verandah hammock, or, on rainy days, curl up with a glass of sherry and good book before the fire.

- WEDGWOOD MANOR -

Joan and John Huiberts
16002 Crawford Creek Road, Box 135
Crawford Bay, British Columbia
V0B 1E0
(604) 227-9233

Season: April 1 - November 1
Rates: Single $55 Double $69 Twin $75 Honeymoon Suite $75 Extra person $20 (Provincial and Federal taxes extra)
Types of Accommodation: 5 Guest rooms
Breakfast: Full
Special Information: Minimum Stay - 2 nights, July/August; Children (six and older) welcome; Please no smoking or pets; Visa and Master-Card accepted; Golf packages and Ainsworth Hot Springs packages available
Directions: From Nelson: go 20 miles east on Hwy 3A, cross Kootenay Lake by ferry, drive east to Crawford Bay. From Creston: Drive 50 miles north on Hwy 3A along Kootenay Lake to Crawford Bay.

Wild Horse Farm B&B

Orma and Bob Termuende welcome you to their spacious two-storey twelve-room heritage home, *Wild Horse Farm Bed and Breakfast*. The large, rambling log-faced, vine-covered country home with tall chimneys, screened verandahs, and cozy fireplaces was built in the early 1900's by William Astor Drayton of New York; many of the original fixtures are still in use.

Guest accommodations include a well-appointed upstairs bedroom with a queen size canopy bed, and a main floor suite with a private entrance. The suite consists of a corner bedroom with king size bed and a fireplace, a private bathroom and a comfortable sitting room, also with a fireplace.

Guests are invited to enjoy the living room, with its comfortable leather furnishings, antiques, player piano, and games table. Hot coffee or tea is brought to each guest's room while Orma puts the finishing touches on a gourmet breakfast to be served in the dining room.

Wild Horse Farm Bed and Breakfast is set among tall trees, surrounded by spacious lawns and gardens, that are just a portion of an 80-acre estate.

The many beautiful lakes nearby invite fishermen, boaters, and water-sport enthusiasts. Hiking and riding trails abound and, in winter, there are cross-country ski trails right on the Farm. Kimberley and Cranbrook are minutes away and have excellent golf courses, dining and shopping. Alpine skiing areas are close by at Kimberley, Fernie, and Fairmont. *Wild Horse Farm Bed and Breakfast* is located right across the road from Fort Steele Heritage Town, a restored 19th Century town where you can enjoy "living history".

WILD HORSE FARM

Orma and Bob Termuende
Box 7
Fort Steele, British Columbia
V0B 1N0
(604) 426-6000

Season: All year
Rates: Single $48 - $67 Double $58 - $77 Extra adult (12 yrs plus) $13 Extra Child $9
Types of Accommodation: 1 Queen, 1 King en suite, 1 Twin
Bathrooms: En Suite and Shared
Breakfast: Full
Special Information: Children welcome; Smoking in living room only; Farm animals outdoors i.e. chickens, ducks, cattle, and outdoor cat named "Chloe"; Trampoline, Lawn bowling, Tetherball and Volleyball available to guests; Coffee served in guest's room in morning
Handicapped Facilities: Downstairs rooms are wheelchair accessible
Directions: *Wild Horse Farm B&B* is located on Highway 93/95 directly across from Fort Steele Heritage Town.

Ocean-View Cottage

Ocean-View Cottage Bed and Breakfast sits on a mountainside overlooking the Georgia Strait on the Sunshine Coast of British Columbia. This spacious new home of wood and glass is surrounded by decks and set against the quiet of the evergreen forest. Wild flower meadows, dotted here and there by spruce trees plunge downward, sloping toward the water, far below -- a marvellous place for ship-watching.

Dianne Verzyl, your bilingual hostess (English and French) will give you a warm welcome to her spacious comfortable home. Breakfast is served in an area overlooking the ocean. There is also available a new completely self-contained cottage, a little way from the house; set back against the trees, but again with a spectacular view of the Channel and a deck to sit out on.

The Sunshine Coast is the coastal area of British Columbia directly north of Vancouver, reached by ferry from Horseshoe Bay. The Highway follows the coastline and the scenery is magnificent -- the Pacific backed by mountains all the way from Gibsons to Powell River.

There are many things for the visitor to do and see here -- trails to hike; gardens to visit; cruises to take; fishing in season; skiing in winter -- plus galleries, museums, theatres and shops to explore.

OCEAN VIEW B.+B.

Dianne and Bert Verzyl
1927 Grandview Road, RR2, S46, C10
Gibsons, British Columbia
V0N 1V0
(604) 886-7943

Season: All year
Rates: Single $45 Double $55 Cottage $65 Additional person $20
Types of Accommodation: 1 Double, 1 Queen, 1 Twin, Cottage with Double and sofa bed
Bathrooms: 2 Private
Special Information: Non-smoking home; No guests' pets; Children welcome for cottage only
Languages: English, French and Dutch
Directions: Take the ferry from Horseshoe Bay to the Sunshine Coast. *Ocean-View Cottage* is 3 km north of Upper Gibsons. Follow Highway 101 to Lower Road (10 minute drive), turn left onto Lower Road and then left onto Pine and Right onto Grandview Road. B&B sign at Lower Road and Pine.

Country Comfort B&B

Between Glacier National Park and the Rocky Mountains on the east is the town of Golden; in fact Golden is the gateway to Yoho National Park, and the first town after crossing through Kicking Horse Pass coming from Alberta into British Columbia. No wonder this spectacular mountainous region is well-known to campers, hikers, fishermen, and outdoor recreationalists.

If you plan to stop for a few days or just overnight *Country Comfort Bed and Breakfast* is absolutely the best place for this in Golden. Wendell, who used to fly his own tour airplanes over the area and his wife, Shari, who does the daily weather report for the region, are the best people to inform you about this area of British Columbia.

Wendell and Shari's large mainstreet home has seven tastefully decorated guest rooms, some with their own bath, and a special guest lounge with fireplace. The home is conveniently located so guests can walk to restaurants and shopping. A delicious breakfast is served in the dining room by Wendell.

Wendell and Shari Johnston
1005 10th Avenue South, Box 645
Golden, British Columbia
V0A 1H0
(604) 344-6200 or (604) 344-2338

Season: All year except children's Christmas holidays
Rates: From $38 - $84
Types of Accommodation: 2 Queen, 3 Twin, 2 Family rooms with 1 Queen and 2 Twins
Bathrooms: 3 1/2 bathrooms; 2 are private
Breakfast: Full
Special Information: Children welcome; No smoking; No guests' pets; Small children in residence named Ryan, Megan and Robin (children speak French)
Languages: English and French
Directions: *Country Comfort* is at the corner of 10th Avenue and 10th Street.

Burchill's "B&B By the Sea"

Jack and Millie Burchill offer *Bed and Breakfast by the Sea* right on the Sunshine Coast which is on the British Columbia Coastline of the Inside Passage above Vancouver, reached by ferry from Horseshoe Bay.

The Burchills offer a self-contained cottage by the sea with a master bedroom, two double-bunk rooms, kitchen, bathroom with shower and a living room with a large fireplace. Everything you need for breakfast including home-made bread, muffins and jams (made by Jack) is supplied.

Beside the cottage and just below the front deck is a saltwater pool overlooking the ocean. Guests can follow the steps to the beach below and swim or row the Burchill's boats.

From the cottage or the deck there is an ever-changing panoramic view of the Malaspina Straits and Texada Island across the channel.

Visitors come to the Sunshine Coast to relax by the oceanfront. But, if they want to be busy, there are many choices: hiking, swimming, fishing, golfing, beachcombing, dining, shopping, scaling a waterfall, exploring the Glacier Fjord of Princess Louisa Inlet, visiting the roaring tidal rapids of the Skookumchuck, or digging up butter clams. There are art galleries and museums to visit, live theatre performances, or sunset charter cruises.

BURCHILL'S B&B by the SEA.

Jack and Millie Burchill
RR1 Donley, Site C-17
Halfmoon Bay, British Columbia
V0N 1Y0
(604) 883-2400

Season: All year
Rates: Available upon request
Types of Accommodation: Self-contained cottage
Breakfast: Full
Special Information: Children welcome; Non-smoking home; No guests' pets please; Wire Haired Fox Terriers named "Peggy" and "Paul" in residence
Directions: *Burchill's "B&B by the Sea"* is 50 kms north of Langdale and 23 km north of Sechelt. Please call for detailed directions.

Barb's Place B&B

When you travel through the High County of British Columbia, Kamloops is a logical stopping-over place. Set back on a quiet suburban street is *Barb's Place Bed and Breakfast*. The house is modest and welcoming as are your hosts Bob and Barb Harcott. There is a pleasant backyard garden for sitting out in. Also Barb has a separate suite that is ideal for families, two couples travelling together or people who like more room.

At the end of the Coquihalla Highway over the mountains or the scenic Fraser Valley Route #1 from Vancouver, you will discover that Kamloops has more to offer than just a stopping-over place between Vancouver and Calgary.

The city of Kamloops is the centre of this region's best fly fishing; you can catch a float plane here and head for a fly-in fishing adventure. Trail-riding and backpack hiking tours of the High Country can be arranged.

Kamloops is the meeting place of highways and river systems, and is also the retail centre of the High Country. Steeped in history and culture, this bustling city offers visitors many things to see and do. The Kamloops Museum and Archives, located centrally downtown, will introduce you to the notable history and people of this pioneering city.

— KAMLOOPS —

Bob and Barb Harcott
1124 Schriener Street
Kamloops, British Columbia
V2B 5W5
(604) 376-8080

Season: All year
Rates: Double $45 Queen $45
Types of Accommodation: Single, Double, Queen, and Suite
Bathrooms: Private and Shared
Breakfast: Full
Special Information: Non-smoking
Directions: *Barb's Place Bed and Breakfast* is located in residential Kamloops. Please call for detailed directions.

Park Place B&B

Park Place Bed and Breakfast is situated on a picturesque acre located on the North Thompson riverfront, yet only five minutes from downtown Kamloops.

All the bedrooms are easily accessible on the ground level and a full country breakfast is served in Lynn and Trevor's sunny solarium with a view of the river flowing by and of Mount Paul. There is also a solar-heated inground swimming pool for guests to use.

Kamloops is the meeting place of the Highways and river systems of central British Columbia and is also the retail service centre of the High Country. Visit the Secrvepemc Museum and learn all about native culture or the Kamloops Museum and Archives which will introduce you to the notable history of this pioneering city. Kamloops has an Art Gallery and a strong Western Canada Theatre Company.

Visitors can explore the Thompson River aboard the historic paddle wheel riverboat, the Wanda Sue. Kamloops is also recognized for its recreational achievements. Visitors and residents alike enjoy the several beautiful parks in and around this active city. Fishing, swimming, hiking, horseback riding, tennis, golfing and boating are all popular summertime pursuits, while wintertime offers excellent downhill and cross-country skiing.

PARK PLACE B.+B.

Lynn and Trevor Bentz
720 Yates Road
Kamloops, British Columbia
V2B 6C9
(604) 554-2179

Season: All year
Rates: Single $35 and up Double $45 and up
Types of Accommodation: 1 Single, 2 Double
Bathrooms: 1 Shared
Breakfast: Full
Special Information: Not suitable for small children; Smoking and pets (on leash) permitted outdoors; Air-conditioned
Directions: To reach *Park Place Bed and Breakfast* take the 5th right turn off of Westsyde Road. Please call for detailed directions.

Mountain View B&B

Ten minutes from downtown Nelson, *Mountain View Bed and Breakfast* at the top of Taylor Drive looks out through picture windows at the mountains and Kootenay Lake.

This charming addition to the main home is a complete self-contained luxury apartment with private entrance. At the end of the day, cocoon beneath a cosy goose-down duvet. Awaken refreshed by crisp mountain air and, perhaps, catch a glimpse of the regular visitors -- deer and squirrels.

Sue provides a tasty home-made continental breakfast for you to enjoy at the dining table or informally in the wicker furnished solarium.

Complimentary coffee, tea and juice are available at anytime.

Mountain View is a perfect "home away from home" while you experience the Kootenays. Nelson, so rich in natural beauty, also has a Heritage Walking Tour covering 25 of the more than 350 heritage buildings that reflect the bonanza of the past -- most restored to their origianl splendor. Visit the mining and history museums for more about Nelson's glory days. Then, for the here-and-now, visit Lakeside Park to go boating or windsurfing where paddle wheelers once churned upstream on Kootenay Lake. Hot springs are located nearby and many recreational activities abound.

MOUNTAIN VIEW B+B.

Sue and Bob McLure
RR1, 2181 Taylor Drive
Nelson, British Columbia
V1L 5P4
(604) 825-4674

Season: All year
Rates: Single $80 Double $95
Types of Accommodation: 1 Double Suite
Bathrooms: 1 Private
Breakfast: Continental
Special Information: Children 12 and over welcome; Non-smoking home; No guests' pets please
Handicapped Facilities: Wide Doorways and large shower
Directions: *Mountain View Bed and Breakfast* is 4 miles east of Nelson on Highway 3A.

Panorama Place B&B

When you visit Penticton, between Okanagan Lake and Skaha Lake on the river channel that joins the two, stay at the place with the view!

Panorama Place Bed and Breakfast is a suburban house located within walking distance of two malls and Skaha Lake. But what a suburbia! Located in a quiet hill area away from the main thoroughfare, one of the best things this bed and breakfast has going for it is the view of the mountians that rise from both sides of Okanagan Valley. From the second floor balconies (there is one at either end of the house), guests can sit and enjoy the panoramic view; and summer mornings, Lorraine will serve a delicious breakfast here outside in the cool morning air, or in the formal dining room.

Guests rooms, bathroom, and living room with TV are located on the ground floor. Outside the grounds are landscaped with rock gardens and a small patio for sitting out in.

Penticton is a favourite destination anytime of the year because it is located between two lakes in the Okanagan Valley; it is blessed with a warm dry climate; and, in winter, alpine skiing at Apex Alpine is only thirty minutes away.

The hillsides around the Penticton region are covered with vineyards and one can spend an afternoon touring the five wineries in the region. In season, this is also a great peach and apple growing area.

PANORAMA PLACE

Lester and Lorraine Fieber
80 Greenwood Drive
Penticton, British Columbia
V2A 7P7
(604) 493-6476

Season: All year
Rates: Single $35 Double $45
Types of Accommodation: 2 Queen
Bathrooms: 1 Shared
Breakfast: Full
Special Information: Smoking on decks and patio; Neighbor's cat often in residence; Not really suitable for children, but small children could be accommodated; Air-coniditioning
Languages: English and some German
Directions: Travelling north or south on Highway 97 turn east onto Green Avenue which turns into Greenwood Drive.

Holten House B&B

Deborah and Calvin Jackson welcome you to share in one of Revelstoke's oldest historical homes and to enjoy a full home cooked breakfast elegantly served in their home's spacious dining room. The luxuriously decorated comfortable bedrooms are all accompanied by private bathrooms.

Holten House was built in 1897 for the bride of one of Revelstoke's prominent businessmen. Elaborate Victorian trim adorns both interior and exterior; the design of the elaborate wrap-around verandah being a most interesting example. *Holten House* is within easy walking of downtown Revelstoke.

Deborah and Calvin have restored the house using period patterns and designs, accented by original hardwood floors and a growing collection of antique furniture. The parlour, complete with fireplace provides guests with a sitting area, especially for reading and games.

Revelstoke itself is a tourists' paradise. This majestic mountain setting nestled among the Selkirks, the Columbia River, Lakes, Mount Revelstoke itself would make one want to spend several days at least. Within half an hour there are mountain trails, parks, beaches, wild life, an 18-hole riverside golf course, shopping and cultural presentations by the city's Summer Street Festival.

HOLTEN HOUSE

Deborah and Calvin Jackson
1221 First Street West, Box 2631
Revelstoke, British Columbia
V0E 2S0
(604) 837-5287

Season: May 15 - October 15
Rates: Starting at $65
Types of Accommodation: 1 Double, 2 Queen
Bathrooms: 3 Private
Breakfast: Full
Special Information: Adult guests only; Non-smoking home; No guests' pets please
Directions: From North or South on Trans Canada Highway turn east onto Victoria Road, continue until Wales Street, turn south (right); proceed one block to first turn (left/west). *Holten House* is halfway down block on left side.

L&R Nelles Ranch B&B

The L&R Nelles Ranch Bed and Breakfast is a working horse ranch, set amid the majesty of the Selkirk Mountains just outside of Revelstoke and only two miles off the Trans Canada Highway.

Bed and Breakfast guests are greeted by the warm, down-to-earth hospitality of your hosts, Larry and Rosalyne Nelles. The fresh mountain air and comfortable accommodations assure you of a good night's sleep. You will wake up, refreshed, to breathtaking scenery and a hearty ranch breakfast.

The Ranch offers wilderness trail rides on excellent, well-trained horses. Riding in the wilderness you will experience the clear mountain air and streams and some of the most magnificent scenery in the world. Experienced and inexperienced riders alike, can fulfill their "cowboy dreams"! Larry is also very knowledgeable about skiing around Revelstoke.

There is a family museum on the premises called "Jennie's Dolls and Treasures" that has been lovingly assembled and is well worth viewing.

Revelstoke is a busy refurbished town with much to interest visitors, from the Sunday Farmer's Market to the free musical concerts given in the Grizzly Plaza.

On either side of town are Lake Revelstoke and Upper Arrow Lake created by dams on the Columbia River. There is an 18-hole riverside golf course, Mount Revelstoke itself, endless ski runs on vast mountainscapes, parks and beaches and a friendly little city at the heart of it, all within this spellbinding alpine setting.

L & R NELLES RANCH

Larry and Rosalyne Nelles
Highway 23 South, Box 430
Revelstoke, British Columbia
V0E 2S0
(604) 837-3800

Season: All year
Rates: Available upon request
Types of Accommodation: 4 Guest rooms and 1 Family room
Bathrooms: 3 Shared
Breakfast: Full
Special Information: Families with children welcome; Mountain wilderness trail rides
Directions: Located 2.2 km off the Trans Canada Highway on Highway 23 South.

The Piano Keep B&B

Vern and Gwen Enyedy moved to Revelstoke in 1988 to pursue their dream: to create a piano museum, tea room and bed and breakfast. In order to do this they purchased and are restoring a 17-room heritage home which they named *The Piano Keep*. Here, Vienna-born Enyedy -- piano technician, restorer, and trader by profession; pianist, artist and designer by desire -- has assembled one of Canada's finest piano collections where one "can hear the music the way the great composers heard it". Here also Vern and Gwen offer, on a separate floor, three very charming bed and breakfast rooms with baths. A delicious full breakfast is served, if possible, outside on the second floor balcony. Gwen's dream of a tea room is in the works for this coming season.

Vern also poured his energy into the community and co-ordinated the city's first Summer Street Festival, bringing a stream of performers and events to Grizzly Plaza. Now culture is blooming in Revelstoke.

Besides culture, Revelstoke offers the majesty of the mountains. The recreational facilities, parks, beaches, the "endless" ski runs on vast mountainscapes, the 18-hole riverside golf course, the refurbished downtown, are all close by.

From the town of Revelstoke, one can be unwinding along a mountain trail within half an hour -- far from the busy world beyond the mountains.

The PIANO KEEP

Vern and Gwen Enyedy
815 Mackenzie, Box 1893
Revelstoke, British Columbia
V0E 2S0
(604) 837-2120

Season: All year
Rates: Single $55 Double $65 and up
Types of Accommodation: 2 Double, 1 Queen
Bathrooms: 3 Private
Breakfast: Full
Special Information: Non-smoking home; No guests' pets please; Not suitable for small children or those who have difficulty negotiating stairs
Directions: From Highway 1 follow Victoria to MacKenzie turn right and go to 7th Street. *Piano Keep* is between 7th and 8th on MacKenzie.

Country Cottage B&B

Located in the tiny hamlet of Roberts Creek, just above Gibsons, this charming cafe au lait-coloured farm house with red trim is set behind a perennial garden, beside fruit trees and vegetables. The sheep who are contentedly grazing in the pasture are the pets who provide the wool for the sweaters that Loragene handknits.

The pleasing interior look of this bed and breakfast has been lovingly created with warm wood, subdued colour, handloomed rugs, welcoming fireplace, and collectibles. When you visit, Loragene could have weaving in progress on the loom set up in the front room.

The breakfasts are prepared by Loragene on a kitchen woodstove and served with special care in the traditional country kitchen.

Honeymooners and anyone else seeking a getaway will find the perfect place in the romantic little cottage behind the white picket fence across the yard from the farmhouse. It has a painted iron bed, sofa, and is self-contained with kitchen, cable TV, and a woodstove. The wood floors, rugs and decor echo the charm of the main house.

The Sunshine Coast is a marvellous place to take a holiday -- spectacular mountain and ocean scenery combined with the opportunities for swimming, fishing, theatre going, and galleries and shops to visit.

Loragene and Philip Gaulin
General Delivery
Roberts Creek, British Columbia
V0N 2W0
(604) 885-7448

Season: All year
Rates: Single $40 - $55 Double $50 - $65 (and up) Extra person $15
Types of Accommodation: 2 Double
Bathrooms: 1 En Suite and 1 Private
Breakfast: Full
Special Information: Dog and two cats in residence; No guests' pets; Children ten and over welcome; No smoking
Languages: English and French
Directions: *Country Cottage Bed and Breakfast* is on the Sunshine Coast at Roberts Creek, off Highway 101 above Gibsons.

English Bay Inn B&B

"There is nothing which has yet been contrived by man, by which so much happiness is produced as a good inn." (Samuel Johnson, 1776).
Thus you will be delighted to discover the *English Inn Bed and Breakfast* tucked away snugly between two high-rises in a quiet corner of Vancouver's West End, an unexpected hideaway right in the heart of the city.

The English Bay Inn is only a short, one-block stroll to Stanley Park and the seawall that meanders at the water's edge along English Bay. You can easily walk downtown along the tree-lined streets, past the fashionable shops of Robson Street.

Owner, Bob Chapin, will give you a warm welcome over a cup of tea while you chat in front of the living room fire. A full breakfast is served by the fire in the Gothic style dining room. Here guests can relax and linger over morning coffee.

Five cozy bedrooms, all with private bathrooms are furnished with family heirlooms and antiques, luxurious queen size beds, fresh flowers, bath robes, and duvets dressed in smooth sauve Ralph Lauren linens. Three of the bedrooms overlook the small, peaceful backyard garden offering welcome solace in an urban setting. And the cozy two-room suite, perfect for romantic seclusion, features a sitting room with garden view, loft bedroom with skylight, stained glass window, fireplace, sleigh bed and six-foot whirlpool bath.

ENGLISH BAY INN

Bob Chapin
1968 Comox Street
Vancouver, British Columbia
V6G 1R4
(604) 683-8002

Season: All year
Rates: Double $110 - $195
Types of Accommodation: 5 Queen
Bathrooms: 5 Private
Breakfast: Full
Special Information: Adults only; No smoking; No guests' pets please
Directions: Take the Pacific West exit from Granville Bridge. Travel west toward Stanley Park along Pacific Street and Beach Avenue to Chilco Street. Turn right on Chilco to Comox Street. Turn right. Second building from the corner of Chilco and Comox on the right hand side.

Locarno Inn on the Beach

Locarno Inn on the Beach Bed and Breakfast is a modern wood and glass home set into the hillside, directly across from the park, beach and ocean, with large windows giving a magnificent view of sea and mountains.

Sigrid, who also speaks German, has a pottery on the premises and is a connoisseur of primitive and south-east Asian art. Her marvellous art collection is a feast for the eyes; everywhere one looks there is something unique to see. A delicious breakfast is served in the interesting dining area. Comfortable living room furniture provides a place for guests to relax. The second floor is given over to guests; the rooms are comfortable with pine furniture and handmade quilts. The view is either of the ocean or garden.

Swimming, sailing, tennis, and Jericho Nature Park are all just a five minute walk away. The University of British Columbia is located in this area of Vancouver. Exploring the city by transit is easy because the bus stops at the front and it is fifteen minutes to downtown.

Vancouver offers much: Stanley Park and the sea life Aquarium, famous for the resident killer whales; historic Gastown, full of boutiques and galleries; Chinatown to give you a taste of another country; and Granville Island for shopping, dining, theatre and the Market. Vancouver is also a city of gardens, which are all well worth visiting, and the first trip to Vancouver would not be complete without a visit to Grouse Mountain for a city panoramic view and to the suspension bridge at Capilano Canyon!

LOCARNO INN on the BEACH

Sigrid Wittman
4550 N.W. Marine Drive
Vancouver, British Columbia
V6R 1B8
(604) 224-2177

Season: All year
Rates: Available upon request
Types of Accommodation: Double, Queen
Bathrooms: Shared
Breakfast: Full
Special Information: Restricted smoking; No guests' pets; Dog and Cat in residence; Breakfast served 7:30 - 9:30 a.m.
Languages: English and German
Directions: *Locarno Inn on the Beach* is directly across from the Locarno beach, near 4th Avenue. Please call for detailed directions.

41

Storwick House

Storwick House is situated in the quiet old residential area of lovely Shaughnessy. This home is easily reached by car and only 15 minutes from the airport. *Storwick House* is also ideal for guests without a car because there is bus service one block away. Vancouver offers a variety of experiences for travellers; beautiful Stanley Park with its magnificient old redwoods, and marine life Aquaruim; Gross Mountain for the view, restaurant dining, and skiing; beautiful gardens such as Queen Elizabeth Park; China Town; and the boutiques, restaurant and theatre experience of Granville Island, to name a few.

The upstairs floor of this gracious home which includes three large, bright rooms, two with double beds, and one with twin beds and a full guest bathroom is reserved for guests. *Storwick House* also offers the main floor den and a TV for guests' use; there is a delightful flower garden, patio and sundeck on which guests can relax, or enjoy their morning coffee. A full breakfast is served in the bright sunroom or outside on the sundeck, weather permitting.

- STORWICK HOUSE -

Mrs. J.A. Wickens
1576 Nanton Avenue
Vancouver, British Columbia
V6J 2X2
(604) 738-9865

Season: All year
Rates: Single $40 - $45 Double $50 - $60
Types of Accommodation: 2 Double, 1 Twin
Bathrooms: 1 Shared
Breakfast: Full
Special Information: No smoking; No guests' pets please; Check-in time by 9 p.m.; Check-out time by 11:00 a.m.
Directions: *Storwick House* is located near Granville Street and W. King Edward Avenue. Please call for detailed directions.

West End Guest House

The West End Guest House Bed and Breakfast offers the perfect combination to make your Vancouver holiday special -- ambiance and location.

Built at the turn-of-the-century for the Edwards family, the home has been completely refurbished; while preserving the original Victorian flavour with fixtures, decor and furnishings, Casablanca ceiling fans and baths en suite have been added. A very special breakfast is served in the bright, airy dining room. The guest rooms are furnished with beautiful brass and goose down beds, cozy duvets and lovely linens. Complimentary refreshments are offered to guests and the front parlour and verdandah are used by guests for relaxing.

The West End Guest House is a popular place for Romantic holidays and getaways. Located in the heart of Vancouver's West End, this bed and breakfast inn is only one block south from cosmopolitian Robson Street, well-known for many fine restaurants, fashion boutiques and specialty shops. Stanley Park, with miles of waterfront, giant redwood forest walkways, beaches, gardens and sea life Aquarium lies six blocks west.

Vancouver has much to offer the visitor: it is a city of Gardens; tour the Vancouver Museum, the MacMillan Planetarium and the Vancouver Art Gallery. Visit Chinatown, restored Gastown; the Granville Island Market, shops and galleries; and you can always take a bus to visit Capilano Suspension Bridge or Grouse Mountain, overlooking all of Vancouver in its sea to mountain splendor.

WEST END GUEST HOUSE

The West End Guest House
1362 Haro Street
Vancouver, British Columbia
V6E 1G2
(604) 681-2889

Season: All year
Rates: Available upon request
Types of Accommodation: 7 Guest rooms
Bathrooms: 7 Private en suite
Breakfast: full
Special Information: Smoking is restricted to outdoor areas only; No guests' pets; Check-in 3:00 - 6:00 p.m.; Check-out 11:00 a.m.; Visa and MasterCard accepted; Cancellation Policy: 72 hours prior to date of arrival
Directions: *West End Guest House* is located on Haro Street one block south of Robson Street, between Jervis and Broughton Streets.

Laburnum Cottage B&B

Laburnum Cottage Bed and Breakfast is hidden away in a quiet corner of North Vancouver surrounded by forest at the foot of Grouse Mountain, Hollyburn Mountain and Mount Seymour, providing a fabulous setting that is only minutes away from the city (only two blocks from major bus routes), Grouse Mountain, Capilano Canyon and the Horseshoe Bay Ferry that connects with the "Sunshine Coast" and Vancouver Island.

Laburnum Cottage is five minutes from tennis courts, par 3 nine-hole golf and the ski slopes of Grouse Mountain.

Inside this charming home, with a country Victorian flair, there are three bright, extremely comfortable guest rooms; each has lovely carpeting, a beautiful bath and a view of the garden. Set amid the award winning English garden with a meandering stream, a little red bridge, pool and fountain, are two beautifully appointed cottages. One, Laburnum Cottage, for which the *B&B* is named, is a self-contained haven with romantic brass bed and soothing atmosphere -- ideal for Honeymooners or the "Getaway" holiday. The other has a bright summery atmosphere; both look out on garden and forest.

Delphine is a gracious, entertaining hostess; it is lovely to spend a few moments relaxing on the patio or in the cool of the garden having afternoon tea. Delphine will serve you a full breakfast every day with that extra gourmet flair!

From the snow-capped distant mountains to the salt-water beaches, geographically Vancouver has so much beauty to offer. A few places of interest in this stunning city are Stanley Park and the sea wall; the historically-preserved district of Gastown; the formal gardens and magnificent botanical conservatories; and the sophisticated architecture.

LABURNUM COTTAGE B.&B.

Delphine Masterton
1388 Terrace Avenue
North Vancouver, British Columbia
V7R 1B4
(604) 988-4877

Season: All year
Rates: Single $75 Double $95 - $110 Extra for Triples and Quads
Types of Accommodation: 1 Double, 4 Queen, 1 Twin, and 1 Triple all with private baths (2 cottages)
Bathrooms: 4 Three-piece baths and 1 Full bath with tub
Breakfast: Full
Special Information: Non-smoking (smoking on patio and deck only); No guests' pets, cat in residence.
Handicapped Facilities: Ground floor cottage sleeps 2- 6 people with a kitchen and full bath
Directions: Take Lions Gate Bridge to North Vancouver; go north on Capilano Road to Paisley Road (turn right), right again on Philip Avenue; follow south to Woods Drive and Terrace Avenue.

Beachside B&B

Situated right on the ocean at the end of a quiet well-treed cul de sac, this bed and breakfast offers a beach at the doorstep, yet is handy to all Vancouver has to offer.

Hanging plants, old brick, and terra cotta roof, antique stained glass windows offer tranquil ambience amid cool ocean breezes. Ships pass by, en route to Vancouver's harbour. All the bedrooms are comfortable, and one special en suite faces the ocean. Full breakfast is served in the dining room with floor to ceiling windows overlooking the sea.

Gordon and Joan Gibbs, your gracious hosts, can provide historical, economic and geographic background about Vancouver; if you need travel information they are more than happy to oblige. An added bonus is the seaside whirlpool that they invite guests to enjoy and a fruit basket and fresh flowers add an extra welcome to each guest room.

Of course, because the location is Vancouver, all this is set against the spectacular backdrop of the mountains, the city's exciting cultural events, parks, gardens, world renowned aquarium, and fisherman's paradise. The location is near a bus route, minutes to Stanley Park and downtown, near a public golf course and close to skiing.

BEACHSIDE B.+.B.

Gordon and Joan Gibbs
4208 Evergreen Avenue
West Vancouver, British Columbia
V7V 1H1
(604) 922-7773

Fax: (604) 926-8073
Season: All year
Rates: Double $95 and up
Types of Accommodations: 3 Twin bedrooms
Bathrooms: 3 Private
Breakfast: Full
Special Information: Non-smoking home; Resident Bichon Frise Dog
Directions: From Lions Gate Bridge travel west along Marine Drive to Ferndale. South on Ferndale and left on Evergreen to the end of the cul de sac.

Castle on the Mountain

The view from a *Castle on the Mountain* is spectacular. Here, on the sunny southern exposure of Silver Star Mountain, 10 minutes from an excellent ski area and 10 minutes from the city of Vernon, this Bed and Breakfast overlooks the Okanagan Valley, city, lakes, and the mountains beyond. This Bed and Breakfast combines the peace and ruggedness of the mountain environment with the luxury of five rooms, beautiful works of art, and a Picture and Framing Gallery in a Tudor-style mansion, designed and built by Eskil and Sharon Larson.

Guests can enjoy the large covered balcony area, have tea or coffee and a tour through the Gallery and Studio. Featured artists are R. Reubert oil paintings, water colours by Anne Gordon and Wood and Floart sculptures by Eskil.

The entire ground floor is for guests; this includes a living room area where one can relax by the fire, and a kitchenette and two bedrooms with their own baths. There are two more guest rooms on the second floor with even more marvellous views, especially from the turret-shaped many-windowed bedroom. Outdoors, there is a hot tub to soak in, picnic area with bonfire pit and space to hike in.

Vernon, itself, is a great place to visit at any time of the year. Spring brings the sweet smell of the fruit blossoms; summer is the time for swimming and the sun; winter of course, is the time to come and ski.

CASTLE on the MOUNTAIN

Eskil and Sharon Larson
8227 Silver Star Road
S10, C12, RR8
Vernon, British Columbia
V1T 8L6
(604) 542-4593

Season: All year
Rates: Single $45 - $55 Double $55 - $75 Extra person $10
Types of Accommodation: 3 Double, 1 King or Twin
Bathrooms: 2 Private and 1 Shared
Breakfast: Full
Special Information: Visa and MasterCard accepted; Smoking outside only; Check-in before 8 p.m.; Check-out 11 a.m.
Handicapped Facilities: Wheelchair accessibility
Directions: *Castle on the Mountain* is 10 km east of Hwy 97 on 48th Avenue (Silver Star Road).

The Falcon Nest

The Falcon Nest Bed and Breakfast is named after its resident falcon and its vantage point high above the Okanagan Valley with a view of Lake Okanagan and the city of Vernon.

Your hostess, Emmy Kennedy, is an artist and traveller who offers her large contemporary cedar home with its spacious, comfortable rooms to bed and breakfast guests. The living room is an inviting place to sit, relax or read in front of the fireplace. There is a solarium with a hot tub where one can relax and have a breathtaking view of the valley and lakes. Generous international gourmet breakfasts are served in a choice of areas. Aesthetically appointed rooms all exhibit attentive hospitality and vary from accommodations for ski groups to the honeymoon suite complete with jacuzzi tub.

The Falcon Nest is enroute to Silver Star Ski Hill and there are trails for hiking and cross-country skiing right at the back door.

The city of Vernon, located in the beautiful Northern Okanagan, is blessed with a moderate climate throughout the year and most of the snowfall in winter is in the Mountains, popular ski places. Agriculturally known as a fruit-growing area, culturally and recreationally Vernon has theatre, scenic parks, fishing, boating and horseback riding.

FALCON NEST

Emmy Kennedy
RR8, Site 7A, Comp. 1
Vernon, British Columbia
V1T 8L6
(604) 545-1759

Season: All year
Rates: Rates available upon request
Types of Accommodation: Double, Twin, Dormitory, and Suites
Bathrooms: Private and Shared
Special Information: Reservations recommended; Smoking outside only; Visa accepted; Check-in time after 1:00 p.m.; Check-out time 11:00 a.m.
Languages: English, German and Italian
Directions: *The Falcon Nest* is just north of the city of Vernon close to the Silver Star Ski Area. Detailed directions upon request.

Alta Vista Chalet B&B

Alta Vista Chalet Bed and Breakfast is a spacious three-storey home where guest comfort is the main objective. Tim and Yvonne Manville offer warm hospitality in their Bed and Breakfast Inn located equidistant from the ski centres at both Whistler Village or Whistler South. They offer free pick-up from the bus or train and village shuttle bus stops in front of the chalet.

Alta Vista on the Valley Trail in a quiet forest setting overlooks beautiful Alta Lake. Nearby Lakeside Beach has swimming, picnic tables, barbeques and canoe, kayak, and windsurfer rentals for use in the lake. It is a 15 minute walk along the Valley Trail, beside the golf course to the village.

The guest rooms at *Alta Vista* have queen or twin beds, either lake or forest views, warm pine furnishings, down comforters and most with private baths. Two of the rooms are larger with an additional sofabed, TV and one of these has a fireplace.

Gourmet breakfasts are served in the spacious dining room furnished with early American pine. A guest lounge leads onto a sundeck with Jacuzzi hot tub; there is an adjoining games room with TV, VCR and guest fridge. Complimentary afternoon tea is served in the lounge or on the sundeck.

Whistler, of course, is world-renowned for winter skiing and *Alta Vista Chalet* offers special ski package rates and secured ski storage. But there are many things to do in the Whistler area during other seasons: Mountain biking; a River Raft float trip; horseback riding; touring the mountain parks and lakes; custom alpine hiking tours for a top-of-the-world sunset, to name a few.

ALTA VISTA CHALET

Tim and Yvonne Manville
3229 Archibald Way
Whistler, British Columbia
V0N 1B3
(604) 932-4900

Fax: (604) 932-4933
Season: All year
Rates: Winter $85 and up Summer $69 and up
Types of Accommodation: 5 Queen, 3 Twin
Bathrooms: 6 Private and 2 Shared
Breakfast: Full
Special Information: Non-smoking home; Dog "Joseph" in residence; No guests' pets; Dinners offered on request; Packed lunches; Honeymoon, Anniversary and Ski packages; Golden Age discount off regular room rates; Cancellation Policy: summer 14 days, winter 30 days; Visa and MasterCard accepted
Languages: English and French
Directions: Off Highway 99 (2 km south of Whistler), turn west onto Hillcrest Drive, into Alta Vista area. Turn right onto Alpine Crescent and left onto Archibald Way.

Chalet Luise

Whether you come to Whistler in the Winter or the Summer, *Chalet Luise* offers deluxe accommodation in an immaculate Swiss-style mountain home with wood and plaster exterior. There is a guest lounge with fire side, a patio and a sauna, a jacuzzi and ski room. All bedrooms have private, en suite bathrooms and down quilts. Some have balconies. The breakfasts are a highlight, most breads are home-baked by your hostess, Luise.

Chalet Luise is located within walking distance of the village, ski lifts, Lost Lake Park and cross-country ski trails.

Whistler is well known as a winter ski place. But a summer holiday in Whistler has much to offer too; mountain biking, river rafting, canoeing, windsurfing and sailing. Custom hiking tours are available; take the gondola or chairlift 3,000 feet above Whistler Village where you can see for miles and watch the sunset. Or plan a conducted Alpine Trek into Garibaldi Park's alpine region; this begins from the summit of Whistler's gondola and takes you to flowered mountain meadows, glaciers and emerald lakes. Other sight-seeing trips can be arranged to such places as Nairn Falls, where the river surges through narrow gorges and rips around sharp bends to drop into a shower of spray below.

After a day of exploring or skiing relax in the jacuzzi or in front of the fire at *Chalet Luise*.

CHALET LUISE

Eric and Luise Zinsli
7461 Ambassador Crescent, Box 352
Whistler, British Columbia
V0N 1B0
(604) 932-4187

Fax: (604) 938-1531
Season: All year
Rates: Summer: Single $59 Double $69 - $85
       Winter: Single $85 Double $95 - $119
Types of Accommodation: 4 Double, 3 Twin
Bathrooms: 7 Private; 3 with tub/shower, 4 with shower
Breakfast: Full
Special Information: Non-smoking; Children from 3 years and up welcome
Lanuages: English and German
Directions: About 1 km North of Whistler village, turn right into White Gold on Nancy Green Drive and then right on Ambassador Crescent. Go 2 blocks to *Chalet Luise* at 7461 Ambassador Crescent.

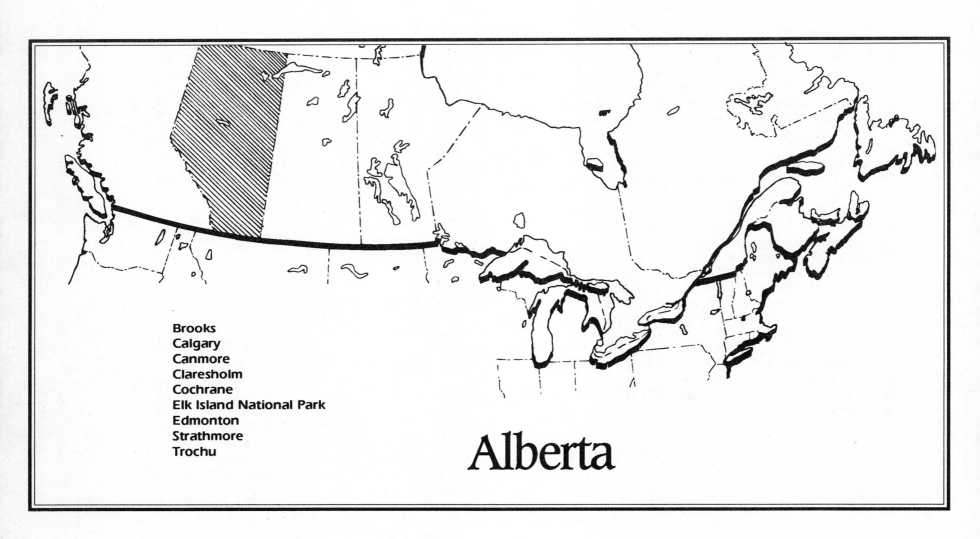

Brooks
Calgary
Canmore
Claresholm
Cochrane
Elk Island National Park
Edmonton
Strathmore
Trochu

Alberta

Douglas Country Inn

The Douglas's, recognizing the need for a bed and breakfast in their area, built an *Inn* specifically for that purpose. Here, in a peaceful country atmosphere, they serve a full breakfast to overnight guests in the beautifully appointed dining room of their new *Inn*; lunches can be arranged, and there is a one-sitting dinner available, served Monday to Saturday at 7:00 pm, by reservations only. Dinner is available to the general public also, and the dining room is licensed.

The *Douglas Country Inn* has on-site facilities where sportsmen can clean and freeze their birds and fish. Kennels are located on the property as well. Hiking trails have recently been completed.

The sitting room, with fireplace, is available for guests' relaxation, and, just down the hall, is a TV room. Each of the seven beautifully appointed, air-conditioned guest rooms includes a private bath and complimentary sherry.

Within a half hour's pleasant drive from *Douglas Country Inn* are several world class tourist attractions. The Dinosaur Provincial Park is a World Heritage Site. Near Brooks are located the Alberta Horticultural Research Centre; Kinbrook Island Provincial Park; Tillebrook Provincial Park; Brooks and District Historical Museum; E.I.D. Historical Park and Museum; Crawling Valley Reservoir; and a Petting Ranch.

This area is known particularly for hunting and fishing (summer and winter). There are also places for golfing, hiking, photography and Bird Watching.

DOUGLAS COUNTRY INN

Doral and Ilene Douglas, Innkeepers
Box 463
Brooks, Alberta
T1R 1B5
(403) 362-2873

Season: All year
Rates: $60 - $85 Senior and Corporate Discounts available
Types of Accommodations: 1 Double, 5 Queen, and 1 Twin
Bathrooms: 7 Private
Breakfast: Full
Special Information: No facilities for young children; Completely non-smoking
Directions: *Douglas Country Inn* is 4 miles north of the town of Brook and the Trans Canada Highway, on Highway 873.

Bide-A-Wee™ B&B

Bide-A-Wee Bed and Breakfast is a spacious, executive home located in an exclusive cul de sac situated in the centre of a golf course. In the summer months, mature trees and lush foliage keep the golf course separate and provide tranquil privacy for the large court yard with fire pit for evening gatherings with guests.

Traude and Jim, early retired business professionals, offer warm hospitality, and willingly share their knowledge about points of interest to experience while in Calgary. They offer a special Canadian Thanksgiving, Christmas, and New Year's stay-over celebration package and would be happy to send a colour brochure.

Bide-A-Wee has an indoor pool, jacuzzi and recreation room with a pool table for guest use. There are four spacious bedrooms, each with en suite bath and waffle-foam topped queen size mattresses. The home has air-conditioning in summer and fireplaces for the cooler weather. A full breakfast is served and also a complimentary beverage in the evening.

The location is within walking distance to the C-Train Station, bus route, several finer shopping centres, boutiques, and many excellent restaurants. It is minutes by car to Fish Creek Park, Heritage Park, Canada Olympic Park, Calgary Zoo, the Calgary Stampede (held in July each year), downtown, Glenbow Museum and Prehistoric Park. From here there is easy access to the University of Calgary, McMahon Stadium, Jubilee Auditorium, Calaway Park, the Kananaskis Country Ski Trails, mountains and wilderness areas.

BIDE-A-WEE B.+B.

Traude and Jim Senger
4 Willow Park Green S.E.
Calgary, Alberta
T2J 3L1
(403) 271-1321

Season: All year
Rates: Single $45 Double $50, $55 or $60
Types of Accommodation: 4 Queen
Bathrooms: 3 En Suite and 1 Private
Breakfast: Full
Special Information: MasterCard and Visa accepted; Smoking in designated area; Sorry, no children or guests' pets
Languages: English and German
Directions: Take MacLeod Trail to Willow Park Drive (at approx. 107 Avenue) and proceed 7 blocks east to Fairmount Drive. Turn right and continue 3 blocks south to Willow Park Green. Turn left to the first house on the left.

52

The Robin's Nest B&B

The Robin's Nest sits in the quiet of the Rocky Mountain foothills. Just 20 minutes out of Calgary this marvellous location is peaceful and relaxing with a panoramic view of mountains and evening sunsets.

Your hosts, Dorothy and Bill Jackson have done much to make this an ideal place to stay. This environmentally conscious non-smoking home offers tastefully appointed rooms. Separate entrance, bath, recreation and sitting area are decorated with western heritage memorabilia, including that of their involvement in the famous Calgary Stampede.

The Jacksons also offer you the choice of staying in a nostalgic country cedar log cabin. Ideal for families and those who like to be close to nature or for an inspirational getaway. A haven for writers and artists.

Awaken to the birds' songs and the aroma of fresh baking. *The Robin's Nest* kitchen will prepare picnic baskets and backpack lunches. The house specialty is rainbow trout.

There are interpretive nature trails through the secluded woods around the beaver pond; watch for deer and moose; enjoy the wild flowers; see the Scottish Highland cattle and sheep grazing on the hillside pastures; then come back to a crackling fire or have a buggy ride with the Fjord ponies.

The Jacksons are a pioneer ranch family. Bill's grandfather came west in 1882 working on the railroad, then homesteading on the property where the Jacksons still live.

There are many things to do in the area. *The Robin's Nest* is located close to Millarville Farmer's Market, trail riding on horseback in the mountains, hiking, cycling, fishing, golfing and ballooning. Dorothy and Bill will be glad to assist guests in making arrangements.

The city of Calgary, home of the Calgary Stampede each July, Spruce Meadows Equestrian Centre, Kananaskis Country and Banff are all within easy driving distance.

CALGARY
ALBERTA

Bill and Dorothy Jackson
Box 2, Site 7, RR8
Calgary, Alberta
T2J 2T9
(403) 931-3514

Season: All year
Rates: Single $35 and up Double $55 and up
Types of Accommodation: 2 Double, 1 Twin
Bathrooms: 2 Bathrooms with tub and shower
Breakfast: Full
Special Information: Children welcome; a Birders' B&B
Directions: *The Robin's Nest* is southwest of Calgary on Highway 22 between Priddis and Millarville.

Rosedale House B&B

Rosedale House Bed and Breakfast is a large estate home built in the mid 1980's. Careful attention was given to ensure that it blended architecturally into this old, established Calgary neighbourhood of Rosedale, where quiet tree-lined streets are just a short distance from downtown Calgary. The house has over 5,000 square feet of living area and 1,200 square feet has been dedicated exclusively to bed and breakfast guests for their enjoyment.

Rosedale House features extensive oak woodwork and country style decorating throughout. Guests are encouraged to make themselves at home and may retire to the privacy of their guest lounge, or to join in the various family activities.

Tastefully decorated suites are available; each with a private bath, queen sized beds, a bar sized refrigerator and independent heating controls. The private guest lounge has a fireplace and a billiard table. A two-person jacuzzi is available in an adjacent room where guests can unwind after a busy day. Complimentary home-cooked full or continental breakfast, whichever is preferred, is served in the spacious dining area.

As a family, the Gills enjoy camping, cycling, and exploring Alberta, particularly the Rocky Mountains, and are happy to share with guests their favourite spots in and around Calgary.

Within walking distance, besides downtown shopping and business district, are Riley Park Gardens; Princes Island Park; Confederation Park and Golf Course; Jubilee Auditorium; southern Alberta Institute of Technology Campus; and many good restaurants.

ROSEDALE HOUSE B. & B.

Glen and Terri Gill
1633 - 7A Street N.W.
Calgary, Alberta
T2M 3K2
(403) 284-0010

Season: All year
Rates: Single $35 - $45 Double $50 - $65 Each additional person $15
Types of Accommodation: 2 Suites with Queen size beds
Bathrooms: 2 Private en suite
Breakfast: Full or Continental, your preference
Special Information: Reservations required; Brochure available; Jacuzzi tub for guests
Directions: *Rosedale House Bed and Breakfast* can easily be found just off the Trans Canada Highway (16th Avenue North) in the small downtown Calgary community of Rosedale.

Turgeon's B&B

Turgeon's Bed and Breakfast is a comfortable, air-conditioned bungalow, surrounded by a rose and flower garden, in a quiet residential district. Here Denis and Eileen Turgeon offer "real" Western Hospitality. Guests may relax on the brick patio or enjoy a game of darts or cribbage in the family room.

The guest rooms are cheerful and comfortable. A family room on the lower level with TV and fireplace is available for guest use. Breakfast choices are many -- cereal, fresh muffins, pancakes, sausages and homemade preserves.

Turgeon's Bed and Breakfast is within 1 block to the Calgary Transit Bus Line connecting with the Light Rail Transit to downtown -- so you can park your car and forget it. They are also a short distance to McMahon Stadium, the University of Calgary and two major shopping centres.

Denis and Eileen will help you plan your day; Calgary has much to offer -- the Botanical Gardens and Prehistoric Park located at the Calgary Zoo; Canada Olympic Park; Heritage Park; Glenbow Museum; Calgary Tower; Calgary Centre of Performing Arts; Calgary Stampede held in July of each year; and the town of Bragg Creek (known for its' potters; artists and restaurants).

From Calgary one can take day trips to places such as Drumheller, the home of the world famous Tyrrell Museum of Paleontology; Dinosaur Valley in Red Deer River; Badlands; Head-Smashed-In-Buffalo Jump; Fort MacLeod Museum; and Kananaskis Provincial Park.

TURGEON'S B&B.

Denis and Eileen Turgeon
4903 Viceroy Drive N.W.
Calgary, Alberta
T3A 0V2
(403) 288-0494

Season: All year
Rates: Single $30 Double $45
Types of Accommodation: 1 Double, 1 Queen
Bathrooms: 2 Shared
Breakfast: Full
Special Information: Adults only please; Restricted areas for smoking; No guests' pets; A Cocker Spaniel named "Buffy" and Siamese Cat named "Suki" in residence - both very friendly; Air-conditioning; Dinner available at nominal cost with prior arrangements; Laundry facilities available at nominal cost
Directions: *Turgeon's Bed and Breakfast* is situated between Highway 1 and Highway 1A. Please call for detailed directions.

Jac'n Sarah's B&B

Jac'n Sarah's beautiful mountain town home is only one block from the main street of Canmore, yet nestled in quiet woods bordering the Bow River. Just behind the house one can take quiet mountain walks or strenuous hikes.

There are two beautiful guest areas, each with its own loft. The Guest Suite contains a kitchenette area and a TV. There are two queen beds, with one double bed in the loft. The Skylight Room boasts a large opening skylight on the main area, with a smaller one in the loft. This room contains one queen bed, with two single beds in the loft. For single guests there is a comfortable bed in the den with an adjacent half bathroom.

With the outside stairway, guests are able to be as private or sociable as they wish. The decks with a large hammock and comfortable chairs provide great relaxation amid gorgeous surroundings. The living room invites good conversation. Jac and Sarah's books, maps and knowledge of the area can help guests plan a satisfying itinerary.

Breakfasts are light or hearty with fresh fruit salad, juice, and Sarah's home-baking, a part of either choice.

The fact that Sarah is a Marriage Commissioner, performing civil marriage ceremonies in this mountain area adds an interesting dimension to the bed and breakfast experience.

In 1988 the Winter Olympics came to Canada and the Canmore Nordic Centre was constructed. Here guests can picnic, hike or ride many scenic mountain trails in the summertime, or cross-country ski in winter.

Canmore has a golf course. Banff National Park and the Kananaskis Country are only minutes away. World renowned alpine skiing is an hour away at Lake Louise. Calgary, for a day trip, is only one-hour east.

JAC 'N SARAH'S B.+B

Jac and Sarah Segstro
10 Riverview Place, Box 1067
Canmore, Alberta
T0L 0M0
(403) 678-2770

Season: All year
Rates: Guest Suite $70 Skylight Room $60 (rates are based on double occupancy in the High Season) Single $40 Additional person $10
Types of Accommodation: Guest Suite: 2 Queen and 1 Double Skylight Room: 1 Queen and 2 Single; 1 Single
Bathrooms: Shared full bathroom and Private half bathroom
Breakfast: Full or Continental, your preference
Special Information: Non-smoking home; Friendly dog and cat in residence
Languages: English, Dutch, and some French and German
Handicapped Facilities: Limited to single room on main floor
Directions: Phone for complete directions.

Spring Creek B&B

Spring Creek Bed and Breakfast is a spacious new home located in a quiet corner of Canmore on Spring Creek near the Three Sisters Mountain. Out the window guests may see wildlife grazing nearby on the meadow along Spring Creek, and beautiful mountain scenery. Yet, the centre of this town, located on the Bow River, is walking distance away. Banff National Park and Kananaskis Country is within minutes by car; Calgary or Lake Louise are about one hour away.

The beautifully appointed spacious bedrooms all have private baths and, of course, views. There is a sitting room with a TV, especially for guest use. A full breakfast is served, either in the dining room or the cheerful breakfast area in front of large glass windows that give a splendid view of the outdoors.

The 1988 Olympics put Canmore on the map when the Canmore Nordic Centre was constructed and some of the Winter Games were held there; there are many trails to hike or cross-country ski. Area downhill skiing can be found at Sunshine, Lake Louise, Norquay and Nakiska. Nearby golf courses are at Canmore, Banff and Kananaskis. This is a renowned area for fishing and mountain climbing. Helicopter Tours, horseback riding, whitewater rafting or just relaxing on the deck or balcony round out some of the other activities available.

SPRINGCREEK B&B.

Frank and Dora Guy
1002 - 3rd Avenue, Box 172
Canmore, Alberta
T0L 0M0
(403) 678-6726

Season: All year
Rates: Winter: $55 and up Summer: $65 and up
Types of Accommodation: 3 Queen
Bathrooms: 3 Private
Breakfast: Full
Special Information: Adult guests only please; Non-smoking home; No pets
Directions: Located in Southeast Canmore on Spring Creek at the corner of 1st Street and 3rd Avenue.

Anola's B&B

Discover the wide open spaces, beauty and solitude of the prairies; stay on a 3,800 acre Southern Alberta grain farm, a perfect getaway for rest and relaxation.

The guest accommodations have a separate entrance at ground level into the ranch house. Relax in the hot tub or curl up with a best seller.

Anola serves warm muffins and tea on arrival and a hearty farm style breakfast in the solarium.

For perfect privacy guests may choose to stay in *Anola's* lovingly restored guest cottage, with antiques and a wood-burning stove. Totally self-contained, the cottage has a full bath with an old-fashioned cast iron bathtub. Romantic and private, the country cottage guest house is the perfect spot to spend a special night. Cuddle up in front of a glowing fire or snuggle under *Gramma's* quilts in the ambiance of charming, country decor. A delicious breakfast will be delivered right to your door.

Claresholm, is located at the union of two lifestyles -- where the fertile wheatlands of the Great Plains meet the foothills; to the west is the world of cattle, cowboys and wide open spaces. To the east, the rolling acres of grain. Nearby, the Head-Smashed-In-Buffalo Jump Interpretive Centre documents the buffalo hunting culture of the Plains Indians from ancient times to the arrival of the Europeans.

CLARESHOLM (North of Lethbridge)
ALBERTA

ANOLA'S B.&B.

Anola and Gordon Laing
Laing Farms Ltd.
Box 340
Claresholm, Alberta
T0L 0T0
(403) 625-4389

Season: April 1 - November 1, other with advance reservations only
Rates: Single $35 Cottage $95
Types of Accommodation: 2 Twin and a Cottage with 1 Double and a hide-a-bed
Bathrooms: Ranch House has 1 Shared bathroom, Cottage has a private bathroom
Breakfast: Full
Special Information: Non-smoking home; Dog in residence named "Diamond"; No guests' pets please
Directions: *Anola's Bed and Breakfast* is 15 km East of Claresholm on Highway 520; 1.5 km North.

Angle Acres B&B

Angle Acres Bed and Breakfast is on a ranch just outside of Cochrane, Alberta. Here guests can enjoy the quiet, country atmosphere and the mountain view. Guests at the ranch can enjoy hiking, and horseshoes. Horses are welcome in the corral and hay is available. There are horseback riding facilities nearby.

Available are two double and one twin guest room and always a gift candy on the pillow. There is a piano, pool table and TV room for guests to use.

A full breakfast is served and guests meet over evening tea. Margie also prepares packed picnic lunches by prearrangement.

The historical town of Cochrane is the site of the first Alberta ranch where a Western Heritage Centre is being established. Located on the bluff above the original Cochrane Ranch is the statue of a pioneer rancher on his horse.

The town of Cochrane is nestled at the base of the Big Hill along the banks of the Bow River, a setting of unsurpassed beauty and, ideally located just twenty minutes west of Calgary on the scenic Bow Valley Trail (Hwy 1A). Cochrane is less than an hour from Kananaskis Country, Banff National Park and the majestic Canadian Rockies.

Cochrane is a delightful town with many restaurants, interesting craft and gift shops, a golf course, swimming pool, and bike trail.

— ANGLE ACRES —

Margie and Jim Houghton
Box 531
Cochrane, Alberta
T0L 0W0
(403) 932-5550

Season: May 15 - October 1
Rates: Single $35 Double $45 Families $60 - $80
Types of Accommodation: 2 Double, 1 Twin
Bathrooms: 2 Full, and a 1/2 bathroom
Breakfast: Full
Special Information: Non-smoking; Children welcome; Corrals for horses
Handicapped Facilities: Limited; can accommodate people with walkers but not wheelchairs
Directions: Please phone for directions or request a brochure with map on it.

Hillside Haven B&B

Hillside Haven, nestled on the western slope of the Big Hill in the town of Cochrane (where you may Discover The Natural West), is ideally located just twenty minutes west of Calgary on the scenic Bow Valley Trail (Hwy 1A) and is less than an hour away from Kananaskis Country, Banff National Park and the majestic Canadian Rockies.

Your hosts Jean and Doug Heath, having enjoyed wonderful bed and breakfast experiences throughout Western Canada, were pleased to open their home as a B&B. They have resided in Western, Central and Northern Canada and were two and three-quarters years in Nairobi, Kenya.

Hillside Haven is air-conditioned with the Hexagonal living areas constructed around a two-level stone fireplace which also provides the main support for a soaring beamed ceiling. The living, dining and kitchen areas surround the fireplace with many windows facing the mountains. Guests are also welcome to use the family room on the lower level where the T.V. and music centre are located.

Two attractive guest rooms are located in the rectangular wing of the home furnished with comfortable beds and libraries. There are two bathrooms to be shared by guests.

Guests will be welcomed with refreshments and shown their rooms and entertainment areas. Upon returning from a tour of the town and visits to craft shops, restaurants, etc., they will find their bed turned down and soft welcoming lights glowing. Tea, coffee cake or cookies are served before retiring.

A full breakfast is served, usually including a selection from fresh fruits, juices, muffins, egg dishes, casseroles, sausage or bacon; Doug makes delicious waffles served with maple syrup, glazed bananas or berries, and creme de fracchi.

HILLSIDE HAVEN B+B

Jean and Doug Heath
528 - 4th Avenue North
Cochrane, Alberta
T0L 0W2
(403) 932-2531

Season: All year
Rates: Single $50 Double $60
Types of Accommodation: 1 Double, 1 Queen
Bathrooms: 2 Shared 4-piece
Breakfast: Full
Special Information: Adult guests only please; Non-smoking home; No guests' pets please; Air-conditioning
Languages: English and Ukrainian
Directions: From Highway 1A, turn north on Fourth Avenue at the Pedestrian lights.

Chez Suzanne B&B

When you are visiting Edmonton and you need a comfortable place to stay in a convenient location *Chez Suzanne Bed and Breakfast* is a fine choice. This roomy suburban home is located in a quiet area, yet only five minutes by car from the West Edmonton Mall. A choice of neighbourhood restaurants are about a five minute walk away and your hosts, Paul and Suzanne, will gladly help you decide what to do and see while you are in Edmonton. As you can guess from its name *Chez Suzanne* is a bilingual (English and French) Bed and Breakfast.

The guest area is on the ground floor with its own lounge area. The lounge has a fireplace, books, games, television and VCR, all for guest use. There is a coffee station and fridge where guests may help themselves to complimentary tea or coffee at any time. Suzanne, a gourmet cook, serves breakfast in the cheerful dining area.

Edmonton, of course, is well known for many things. Strongly recommended are: Fort Edmonton Park, Devon Botanical Gardens, the Ukrainian village and Muttart Conservatory. Edmonton also hosts Jazz, Theatre, Heritage, and Street Performers Festivals in the summer. And of course, not to miss is the West Edmonton Mall, the world's largest shopping complex and indoor amusement centre. Spanning the equivalent of forty-eight city blocks, the Mall is a fascinating blend of fashion, fun and fantasy. Here you'll discover the world's largest indoor amusement park, an 18-hole miniature golf course, the world's largest indoor waterpark, submarine rides, dolphin shows and much more.

Edmonton is also the gateway to Jasper in the magnificent Canadian Rockies and the beautiful Northern Wilderness.

CHEZ SUZANNE B&B

Paul and Suzanne Croteau
18603 - 68 Avenue
Edmonton, Alberta
T5T 2M8
(403) 487-2071

Season: All year
Rates: Single $35 Double $45 Family (4) $70
Types of Accommodation: 2 Single, 2 Double
Bathrooms: 1 Private and 1 Shared
Breakfast: Full or Continental, your preference
Special Information: Children welcome; Our Cat "Prince" lives with us; Dinner and picnic lunches offered on request
Languages: English and French
Directions: From West Edmonton Mall: South on 178 Street to 69 Avenue; turn right to 184 Street; turn left to 66 Avenue, then right to 185 Street. Turn right again and follow large Crescent (about 2 blocks). *Chez Suzanne Bed and Breakfast* is half way up -- look for a large, green and white home.

Virginia's B&B

Virginia's Bed and Breakfast offers the hospitality that one looks forward to when staying with a good friend. Enjoy the warmth of Virginia's home located on the South Side of Edmonton, a few short blocks from Highway 2 (the main access to the city from the South). *Virginia's B&B* is very secluded. Located on a quiet street, this interesting modern home is designed so that the windows face the lovely treed lawn and garden area behind the house. Weather permitting, breakfast is served on the deck in this park-like setting; otherwise in the dining room.

The house has wooden and beamed ceilings and is decorated with co-ordinating chintz and small print wallpaper in guest fireside room. The fireside room has many collectibles and a Victorian country atmosphere; it is a place to relax and curl up with a good book, or for a visit.

Edmonton, a city of just over half a million, is an all-season destination. It is nationally known for professional hockey and football, and theatre.

Plan a leisurely stroll through the Old Strathcona section of Edmonton. This early 1900's area has been restored and has many unique gift, craft, antique and clothing shops.

The West Edmonton Mall is the world's largest shopping complex and indoor amusement center. Spanning the equivalent of forty-eight city blocks it contains the world's largest amusement park, and 18-hole miniature golf course, indoor water park, submarine rides, dolphin shows and over 800 stores for shopping and services. Edmonton is the gateway to Jasper and the Canadian Rockies to the West.

VIRGINIA'S B&B.

Virginia Zelent
5815 - 107th Street
Edmonton, Alberta
T6H 2X6
(403) 434-5282

Season: All year
Rates: Queen with en suite: Single $48 Double $53
Double bedroom: Single $35 Double $40
Types of Accommodation: 1 Double, 1 Queen
Bathrooms: Private and Shared
Breakfast: Continental during week; Full on weekends
Special Information: Adults only; Non-smoking home; No guests' pets please; No pets or children in residence; Air-conditioning in family (fireside) room and living/dining room; Complimentary soap for stays of two days or more from Virginia's Soap Co.
Languages: English and limited German
Directions: From Highway 2 coming from the South. Turn left on 51 Avenue; drive to 106 St. and turn right. Proceed North to where 107 and 106 Street meet at an angle, (just before school on right) turn left on 107 Street and drive approx 1 block. Home is on left side of street.

Birdwood B&B

Nestled in the woods, close to Elk Island National Park, is a bird-lover's paradise -- a "Bird and Breakfast" bed and breakfast called *Birdwood*.

Bob and Jan Carroll left the city behind to establish their secluded country getaway.

Guests are treated to a cozy, rustic barn-like cabin with all the necessary amenities. Known as the "Bird's Nest", the two-level cabin features a comfortable queen size bed and pull-out sofa, a private bath and showers and cooking facilities. A home-style breakfast is served in the bright sunny kitchen of the main house, or you may have breakfast served in the "nest".

The location is ideal for the summer and winter outdoor enthusiast; you can hike, cycle, cross-country ski, or just relax. There is a spacious backyard, a barbecue pit and picnic table outdoor; meals and picnics prepared on the premises.

Bob, the resident bird watching expert, offers guided day trips in the region.

Besides being close to Elk Island National Park, *Birdwood* is close to Beaverhill Lake, Cooking Lake, Blackfoot Grazing Wildlife and Provincial Recreation Area, the Ukranian Cultural Heritage Village and the city of Edmonton.

ELK ISLAND NATIONAL PARK
(Near Edmonton)
ALBERTA

BIRDWOOD B&B

Bob and Jan Carroll
RR2
Fort Saskatchewan, Alberta
T8L 2N8
(403) 998-0082

Season: All year
Rates: Single $45 Double $55 Additional person $10
Types of Accommodation: Loft apartment with Queen and Twin beds
Bathrooms: Private with shower
Breakfast: Full
Special Information: Children welcome; Non-smoking home; No guests' pets please; a Birders' B&B; Dinners and other meals offered on request
Directions: *Birdwood Bed and Breakfast* is 45 km east and north of Edmonton.

Sproule Heritage B&B

The Sproule Heritage Bed and Breakfast property consists of a large stately house and barn, 14.5 km, east of Strathmore, an impressive landmark set well back from the Trans Canada Highway. The land was first settled by the Harry Scheer family from Illinois in 1909. Bountiful crops and encouraging grain prices between 1915 and 1920 inspired the Sheers to contract the Hornstrom Brothers of Calgary (former of Sweden) to build their 3-storey house and well-equipped barn on a grand scale. In 1985, the Sproules purchased the buildings and, with assistance from the Alberta Heritage Foundation, have been gradually restoring them.

The house was chosen in 1987 by Hallmark, a United States greeting card company, as the location for their costly Christmas Commercial because it was a "marvellous warm old house - a house to come home to for Christmas".

Bed and Breakfast visitors to the *Sproule Heritage* place enjoy the restored historic buildings as much as Vera and Winston. The large comfortable rooms feature beds with quilts designed by Vera; breakfast served in the large bright kitchen or dining room is enhanced by Vera's home-baking.

The Sproule Heritage Bed and Breakfast is near to Rosebud, where Summer theatre has been established and close enough to Calgary for visitors to take an interesting day trip to the city, and return again in the evening to the peace of the Alberta Countryside.

SPROULE HERITAGE B.&B.

Winston and Vera Sproule
Box 1534
Strathmore, Alberta
T0J 3H0
(403) 934-3219

Season: All year
Rates: Single $32 Double $43 (GST included in rate)
Types of Accommodation: 1 Double, 1 Queen, and 1 Twin
Bathrooms: 1 Shared
Breakfast: Home-baked
Special Information: Adult guests only please; No guests' pets please; Non-smoking home (open verandah for smokers); Dinner offered on request
Languages: English, Russian, Ukrainian
Directions: Located on Trans Canada Highway 7.6 km west from Junction 561 or 4.8 km east of Junction 21.

St. Ann Ranch B&B

St. Ann Ranch Trading Co. Bed and Breakfast is the historic thirty-room original ranch mansion that once was the home for the St. Ann Ranch Trading Co. The Ranch was settled in 1905 by a group of aristocratic Cavalrymen from Brittany, France. A major French settlement soon developed around the site; gardens, grain fields and flowers were planted in the area; a stopping place, a post office, school, and Catholic Church followed. Purebred horses and cattle were raised on the ranch. The North West Mounted Police arrived in 1907; the Sisters of Euron in 1909; the Grand Trunk Pacific Railway in 1910. The settlement thrived until the W.W.I. in 1914 when most returned to France to defend their homeland; only five returned.

Your hosts, Louis and Lorene Frere are direct descendants of those first pioneer ranchers; Lorene has researched extensively the history of the early life of the area, including over 600 photographs, diaries and letters, all available for viewing.

Exclusively for bed and breakfast guests are rooms furnished with period antiques, a private guest entrance, library, T.V. room, breakfast room, patio, and parlour with a fireplace. Lorene operates a tea room on the premises; home-baked Saskatoon and rhubarb desserts are specialties.

St. Ann Ranch Trading Co. Bed and Breakfast is ideal for a peaceful or romantic getaway. The original 1904 pioneer log cabin has now been restored as a honeymoon suite or country weekend retreat; this is a pioneer experience - coal oil lamps, wood stove, etc. An original two-bedroom home on the property, also 1904, has been restored to period. This early clapboard home with wrap-around verandah has period bathroom with claw-foot tub, and common area sitting room.

Trochu has a nine-hole golf course; Santa's workshop; a home-made gift and craft place; Trochu Valley Museum, featuring exhibits of Indian and Dinosaur artifacts; and the Trochu Arboretum.

St. Ann Ranch Trading Co.

Louis, Lewis, and Lorene Frere
Box 249
Trochu, Alberta
T0M 2C0
(403) 442-3924

Season: All year
Rates: Single $45 Double $55 - $65 Log Cabin $75
Types of Accommodation: Double, Queen, and Twin
Bathrooms: 1 Private, 3 Shared, and an outside toilet for the cabin
Breakfast: Full
Special Information: Adult accommodation only; No smoking; No guests' pets please; Dinner on request; 48 seat Tea House open May 1 to end of September; Birders' paradise!
Languages: English and some French and German
Handicapped Facilities: The kitchen, two bedrooms, the bathrooms and the porches and deck are handicapped accessible
Directions: *St. Ann Ranch Trading Co. Bed and Breakfast* is 60 miles southeast of Red Deer and 50 miles Northwest of Drumheller.

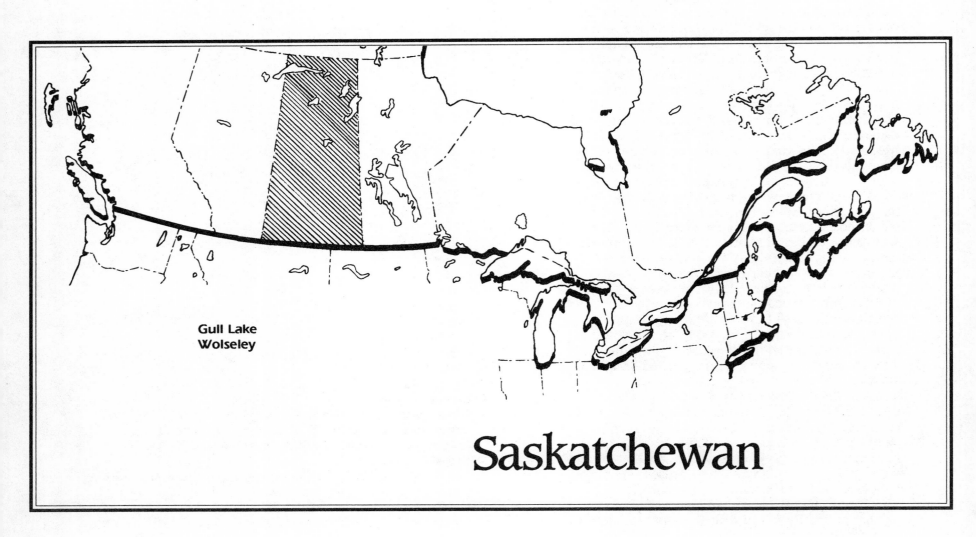

Gull Lake
Wolseley

Saskatchewan

Wounded Knee B&B

Come visit *Wounded Knee* in picturesque Carmichael, Saskatchewan, just one and half mile off the Trans Canada Highway. You will be warmly welcomed at this small hobby farm where Dick and Judy Wells raise sheep, and goats and keep a resident Border Collie named "Kiltie MacTavish".

There are three comfortable bedrooms off a large family room on the lower level; the guest shower and bathroom are also there. Besides bed and breakfast, excellent home cooked meals are available, prepared from a variety of home-grown food.

Your hosts enjoy music, gardening, nature and sports. They welcome families with children and hunters in season.

To the South lie the "Bench Hills" and to the North the great Sand Hills of Saskatchewan. The whole area abounds in wildlife and excellent hunting of ducks, geese, Hungarian Partridge, Prairie chicken, Prong Horn antelope, mule and white tail deer -- a hunters paradise! Forty miles West enjoy the beauty of Cypress Hills Park and nearby the town of Gull Lake offers a swimming pool, golf course, and miniature golf.

WOUNDED KNEE B+B.

Dick and Judy Wells
Box 527
Gull Lake, Saskatchewan
S0N 1A0
(306) 672-3651

Season: All year
Rates: Supper and Bed and Breakfast: Single $30 Double $50
Bed and Breakfast: Single $25 Double $40 Children under 12 $20, rates do not include E&H tax (rates subject to change)
Types of Accommodation: 2 Queen, 2 Twin
Bathrooms: 1 on the lower level (shower) and 1 on the ground level (bath tub)
Breakfast: Full
Special Information: Children welcome; Air-Conditioning; Meals and box lunch on request; Guests' pets welcome
Directions: Turn south off Trans Canada Highway 1 at Carmichael sign. Travel 1 1/2 miles to the "Old White School", turn west (right) and *Wounded Knee* will be the first house on your left.

The Banbury House Inn

The Banbury Inn in Wolseley is dedicated to giving gracious, hospitable accommodation. Built in 1906 by Edwin A. Banbury, the founder of the Beaver Lumber Company, this elegant Edwardian house was moved in 1985 over a specially-built road to today's site, beside the authentic French restaurant, Le Parisien. Here it was designated a Heritage Site and sits on three acres of beautifully landscaped lawns and trees. This tranquil location unites with the best of turn-of-the-century architecture. A painstaking restoration has captured the original interior splendor for guests to enjoy.

Exquisite guest rooms and honeymoon suites, each spacious, gracious and unique, feature antique furniture, rich draperies and tapestry imported from Britain. Each room has baths with corner showers en suite -- one suite has a jacuzzi.

Breakfast is served in the dining room with its beautiful fireplace; the guest lounge has a fireplace also.

There is a golf course and tennis court nearby. Wolseley has a lake, one of Canada's longest swinging bridges, and Saskatchewan's oldest courthouse.

Together with Le Parisien restaurant, *the Banbury House Inn* is Saskatchewan's "grande dame" of accommodation.

The BANBURY HOUSE INN

Ernest Boeheme
104 Front Street
Wolseley, Saskatchewan
S0G 5H0
(306) 698-2239 or (306) 698-2801

Season: All year
Rates: $40 - $120
Types of Accommodation: 9 Queen
Bathrooms: 9 En Suite
Breakfast: European ($5/person)
Special Information: Check-in time is 4:00 p.m.; Check-out time is 12:00 p.m.; Cater to bus tours, weddings, and meetings; Visa, Master-Card, and American Express accepted; Reservations recommended
Directions: *The Banbury House Inn* is east off the Trans Canada Highway 1 at 104 Front Street. Please call for detailed directions.

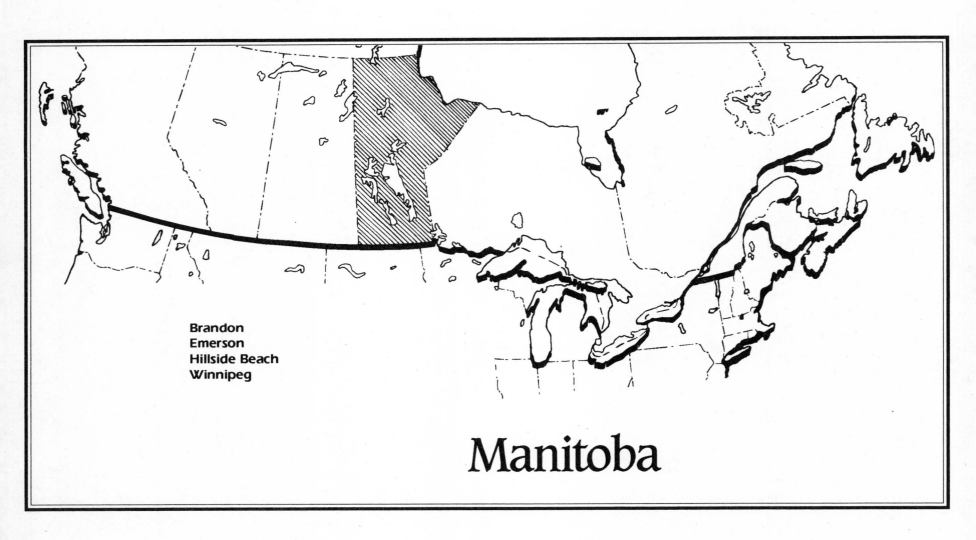

Brandon
Emerson
Hillside Beach
Winnipeg

Manitoba

Gwenmar B&B

Joy and Keith Smith welcome you to *Gwenmar*. Hundreds of bed and breakfast guests have visited with them in the past twelve years. We know you'll enjoy their full breakfasts including homemade bread, jams and jellies; walks in the beautiful valley of the Little Saskatchewan River, the spacious grounds and huge gardens; fantastic sunsets and total peace and quiet.

Gwenmar was the summer home of Manitoba's Lieutenant Governor, J.D. McGregor (1929-34) where he occasionally entertained royalty. Rumour has it that Winston Churchill once slept in the main guest room; you are invited to come try it out for yourselves!

Gwenmar has two bathrooms and four large bedrooms. There is a huge veranda for relaxing and visiting. Most guests come, leave their things, and then have dinner in Brandon, returning in the evening for a chat before retiring.

Nearby attractions include Brandon (40,000 population) for good shopping; the Commonwealth Air Training Plan Museum; waterslide; writer Margaret Laurence's home at Neepawa; Souris suspension bridge; and the International Peace Gardens.

GWENMAR B.+B.

Joy and Keith Smith
RR3, Box 59
Brandon, Manitoba
R7A 5Y3
(204) 728-7339

Season: All year
Rates: Single $25 Double $40, special rates for children
Types of Accommodation: 1 Double, 2 Queen, and 2 Twin
Bathrooms: 2 Shared (1 room with a sink in it)
Breakfast: Full
Special Information: Children welcome; Guests' pets welcome but we have Dogs in residence; Dinner can be arranged
Handicapped Facilities: Limited
Directions: We are four miles off the Trans Canada Hwy, Northwest of Brandon. Please phone for detailed directions.

Bryce House B&B

Bryce House was built in Italianate Victorian style in 1881 by John Bryce, an early builder in Emerson; this home was one of a very few in Western Canada to be built in this style.

The rooms are spacious and comfortable; one bedroom is large enough to accommodate three people. Sharon-Ann has furnished the home with antiques and is gradually restoring it to its original grandeur.

A full breakfast is served in the elegant dining room consisting of bacon or sausage, eggs and hashbrowns, or something simpler, if preferred.

Bryce House sits on spacious well-treed grounds in the small, peaceful town of Emerson, on the banks of the Red River, close to the Canada-United States Border. The Emerson Townhall and Courthouse has been designated a Provincial Heritage site. A five minute drive will take you to Fort Dufferin, the original home of the Northwest Mounted Police and it was from here they moved west to Fort MacLeod to open up Saskatchewan and the western territories for settlement. There is a hiking trail from Emerson into Fort Dufferin.

Deer, many bird species and small animals can be seen on any given day in the area.

BRYCE HOUSE B&B.

Sharon-Ann Ewens
99 Assiniboine Street, Box 455
Emerson, Manitoba
R0A 0L0
(204) 373-2110 (evenings and weekends)

Season: All year
Rates: Single $25 Double $35 Triple $45
Types of Accommodation: 2 Double, 1 Single
Bathrooms: 1 Shared
Breakfast: Full or Continental, your choice
Special Information: Children welcome; No guests' pets please; Dog and 2 Cats in residence (Charlie, Ben and Jenny); Dinners offer on request
Directions: Once in Emerson, follow Fourth Street North past bend in the road, *Bryce House B&B* is the first house on the left.

Hillside B&B

If you enjoy the sweet smells of spring, or the clear, clean water lapping white sandy beaches, or golf courses with long green fairways then you will enjoy the "Beaches" in the summer.

Watch smoke rise lazily from cottage chimneys as you breathe in the fresh air and glide by over the crisp snow on your cross-country skies or snow machine; this is winter at the "Beaches".

Autumn invites you on long walks through masses of colour, the air strong with the smell of aspen. You can stand at the edge of the lake and watch Canada Geese start their long flight South, while ducks take their last swim.

At anytime of the year you can visit a Viking-styled nondenominational Church and mingle there with the second and third generations, descendants of the pioneer families who settled this area.

Hillside Bed and Breakfast is located right in the middle of this natural paradise. Your hosts, Carol and Jim, offer two bedrooms, one with a double antique bed and the other with a queen size, surrounded by serene teakwood walls.

A snow machine is available for guest use in winter, and in warm weather there are bicycles for riding over the many paths and trails. You will find a warm welcome at *Hillside Bed and Breakfast*, just one hour from Winnipeg.

HILLSIDE BEACH B+B

Carol and Jim Hall
Lot 8, Hillside Point Road
General Delivery
Traverse Bay, Manitoba
R0E 2A0
(204) 756-3967

Season: All year
Rates: Single $36 Double $42
Types of Accommodation: 2 Double
Bathrooms: Shared
Breakfast: Full
Special Information: Non-smoking home; Reservations recommended
Directions: *Hillside Bed and Breakfast* is one hour north of Winnipeg. Please call for detailed directions.

Hawchuk's B&B

HAWCHUK'S B&B.

Helga and Steve Hawchuk, an artist and a River-boat Captain, respectively, have created a "home-away-from-home" for Bed and Breakfast guests in their sprawling Tudor-style house right on the Red River in Winnipeg, Manitoba. Their brick home is airy and spacious. Silk flowers, paintings and other handiwork brighten every room. Floor-to-ceiling windows look out onto a garden of fruit trees and bushes including apples, pears, apricots, raspberries, strawberries, gooseberries and blueberries, with the river flowing past. During summer, flowers bloom in a variety of colour; these gardens are perfect for wedding pictures, and this Bed and Breakfast is an ideal Honeymmoners' or Anniversary accommodation.

The guest rooms have their own private bath and each has a different theme for decor -- there is the Victorian Room and the Nautical Room, for example.

A sumptuous home cooked breakfast is served offering a variety of delicious foods; guests may choose home-made bread, waffles, jams, jellies, fruit and muffins. There is an indoor barbeque and meat smoker and Helga loves cooking, and guests may make prearrangements for dinner.

The Winnipeg City centre is just 15-20 minutes away. *Hawchuk's Bed and Breakfast* is close to tennis and golf, near Birds Hill Park, the Folk Festival and Lower Fort Garry.

Steve and Helga Hawchuk
22 Everette Place
Winnipeg, Manitoba
R2V 4E8
(204) 339-7005

Season: All year
Rates: $49 and up
Types of Accommodation: 3 Single and 1 Queen
Bathrooms: Private and Shared
Breakfast: Full
Special Information: Children welcome; no smoking home; No pets please, Dinners offered on request
Languages: German, French, Ukrainian, and English
Directions: Go north on Main Street, past Kildonan Park, about 7 minutes, turn right on River Glen Crescent at traffic light,(just inside Perimeter), go to Mirabelle (2nd Street), turn right and follow to the end of Street. *Hawchuk's Bed and Breakfast* is at the end of the cul de sac.

Riverside B&B

Located right on the banks of the Red River, close to shopping and museums, with a Bus Stop right at the front door, *Riverside Bed and Breakfast* offers a pleasant stay in a quiet three-story home.

If you make arrangements, Walter or Mary will pick you up or drop you off at the airport or train station.

Their river location means your hosts can offer you, by prearrangement, a personally conducted cruise on the Red River; leave right from their back yard in their 22 or 40-foot boat, weather permitting.

A full breakfast is served with a morning view of the Red River. Comfortable guest accommodation is provided on the second floor; some rooms have a river view.

While staying at *Riverside* you are welcome to browse in our Wedding Boutique, right on the premises.

Winnipeg has many interesting summer festivals including Folklorama, Octoberfest and Winnipeg's French speaking people conduct the Festival du Voyageur in February. Music lovers can be enlivened by the Winnipeg Symphony Orchestra or The Royal Winnipg Ballet; the Contemporary Dancers are among the best in modern dance in North America. The Exchange District, Winnipeg's historic restoration area of turn-of-the-century buildings, provides some of Winnipeg's finest shopping, dining and entertainment; the open market, Old Market Square, offers old time bargains and flavour every summer Saturday and Sunday.

Walter and Mary Pedersen
476 St. Marys Road
Winnipeg, Manitoba
R2M 3K6
(204) 233-3218

Season: All year
Rates: Single $30 Double $40
Types of Accommodation: 1 Double and a Suite with 2 Double beds and 1 Single
Bathroom: 1 Shared
Breakfast: Full
Special Information: Children welcome; Non-smoking home; air-conditioning; Will pick guests up at the Airport and Train Station
Languages: Ukrainian, Danish, Japanese, some German, and English
Directions: St. Marys Road is part of Highway 1 going through the city of Winnipeg. *Riverside Bed and Breakfast* is at 476 St. Marys Road.

Voyageur House B&B

Voyageur House Bed and Breakfast is situated in the historic French Canadian area of St. Boniface, in Winnipeg, Manitoba.

Bob Drenker, who was instrumental in the construction of the Museum of Man and Nature is able to direct guests to any area of the City. Bob and Isobel have information and maps showing all the tourist attractions in the area.

A separate air-conditioned suite is available for guests; three double rooms with sitting room where TV can be enjoyed beside the fireplace. Full bath with shower and kitchen makes this an ideal setting for families. Pickup at transporation centres. Laundry facilities and bicycles are available.

There are many things to do and see in Winnipeg; the Convention Centre; Manitoba Theatre Centre; Winnipeg Art Gallery; Assiniboine Park and Zoo; Winnipeg Arena and Stadium; the Forks Market; St. Boniface Cathedrale; downtown shopping; and River Boat Excursions.

VOYAGEUR HOUSE B+B.

Bob and Isobel Drenker
268 Notre Dame Street East
Winnipeg, (St. Boniface)
Manitoba
R2H 0C6
(204) 231-1783

Season: All year
Rates: Single $35 Double $45
Types of Accommodation: 3 Double
Bathroom: 1 Shared 4-piece
Breakfast: European
Special Information: Children welcome; Non-smoking home; Air-conditioning; Dog named "Max" in residence
Languages: English, French and German
Directions: Go East and cross Provencher Bridge into St. Boniface. Call for further directions.

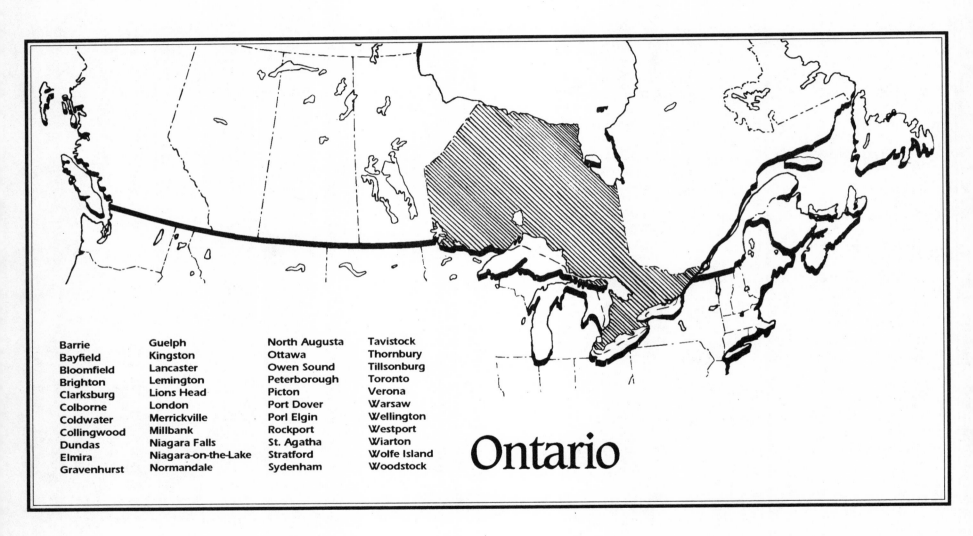

Barrie	Guelph	North Augusta	Tavistock
Bayfield	Kingston	Ottawa	Thornbury
Bloomfield	Lancaster	Owen Sound	Tillsonburg
Brighton	Lemington	Peterborough	Toronto
Clarksburg	Lions Head	Picton	Verona
Colborne	London	Port Dover	Warsaw
Coldwater	Merrickville	Porl Elgin	Wellington
Collingwood	Millbank	Rockport	Westport
Dundas	Niagara Falls	St. Agatha	Wiarton
Elmira	Niagara-on-the-Lake	Stratford	Wolfe Island
Gravenhurst	Normandale	Sydenham	Woodstock

Ontario

Bunker's Inn

Bunker's Inn, is an integral component to this New England colonial "saltbox". The main architectural design has been featured in *Country Living* and *Early American Life* magazines. The *Inn* is located on a quiet, forested street in the rural village of Anten Mills.

Country elegance has been combined with modern comfort to create an unusual quality bed and breakfast establishment. The *Inn* features a luxurious suite with separate entrance, private whirlpool bath, colour TV, and second storey walk-out balcony. Consideration for allergy sufferers was incorporated in the overall design, including ceramic flooring, cotton fabrics and non-toxic accessories. Smoking or pets are not permitted

The Bunker's serene haven is not only frequented by weary travellers and recreationalists, but numerous honeymooners and anniversary couples have stayed at their "getaway". Guests are served a plentiful and nutritious breakfast of fresh fruits, a specialty such as omlettes or pancakes, and a selection of home-made condiments.

Within the village of Anten Mills, guests can cross-country ski, hike, or cycle on existing trails that wander through the many acres of adjacent reforestation lands. This secluded village is central to the major centres of Barrie, Orillia, Midland, and Collingwood. Your hosts will be glad to help you seek out local places for skiing, golfing, marine and water recreation, antique and craft shopping, museums and fine dining.

Harry and Nancy Bunker
3 Ghibb Avenue, Anten Mills (Barrie), Ontario
Mailing Address: RR2, Box 5, Minesing, Ontario
L0L 1Y0
(705) 722-0429

Season: All year
Rates: Single $52 Double $58
Types of Accommodation: 1 Queen
Bathrooms: Private 3-piece
Breakfast: Full
Special Information: Adult guests only please; Non-smoking home; No guests' pets please; Reservation confirmed upon 50% deposit
Directions: Take Highway 400 to Barrie. Exit on 98 (Stayner/Wasaga Beach - Highway 26/27). Travel 15 km north on Highway 27 (Bayfield Street) to Horseshoe Valley Road (County Road 22). Turn left for the village of Anten Mills, 3.5 km. Turn left (south) onto Vespra Concession 7, down to the fourth street, Ghibb Avenue, and turn right.

The Robins' Nest

The Robins' Nest, built in 1903, was originally a general store, and even served as a bank. The Robins bought the building in 1983, and after a complete restoration, now offer their home as a bed and breakfast and adjoining craft shop where they feature unique gift items, collectibles, and antiques.

The guest bedrooms all feature period furniture, county decor, handmade quilts and are all named after Ruth and Paul Robins' ancestors. A double whirlpool is available -- great for those aching muscles after a day on the ski slopes or sightseeing in the area. There is a sitting area for guests with reading material and television. The home is centrally air-conditioned.

Breakfast is an enjoyable time, with lots of friendly conversation. The breakfast fare is hearty with something special such as homemade scones.

Craighurst is just a half mile from the Horseshoe Valley Road for downhill winter skiing. There is golfing in the area as well. Barrie, close by, is right on Lake Simcoe. Guests can explore the shopping and restaurants, and, in summer, the Gryphon Theatre offers professional live stage productions at the Georgian College Theatre.

The ROBIN'S NEST

Paul and Ruth Robins
RR1, (Craighurst)
Barrie, Ontario
L4M 4Y8
(705) 726-7838

Season: All year
Rates: Single $40 Double $50
Types of Accommodation: 3 Guest rooms
Bathrooms: 2 Shared
Breakfast: Full
Special Information: Dog and Cat in residence; Air-conditioned
Directions: Take Highway 400 extension north from Barrie to Horseshoe Valley Road (about 20 km); turn right to flashing light at Highway 93 (Craighurst Valley Centre). Turn left 1 km. *The Robins' Nest* is at the railway crossing.

Brentwood on the Beach

Although the address is Zurich and the location is St. Joseph's Shores on Lake Huron, *Brentwood on the Beach* is just down the road (Highway 21) from the beautiful, unspoiled village of Bayfield.

This very large modern home is built on the bluffs overlooking Lake Huron's beaches. There are not many places that offer so much encouragement for relaxing and escaping the stresses of life the way *Brentwood on the Beach* does. Imagine a warm friendly, atmosphere, the vista of Lake Huron, privacy if desired, the luxury of swimming in the lake and relaxing on the sandy beach; or in an indoor pool, sauna and whirlpool, that are in the heart of this home.

Breakfast is served in the sun room overlooking Lake Huron. Guests usually organize their evening plans to include enjoying world-renowned sunsets. There is over 150 feet of glass that looks out over the lake. In March, *Brentwood* is on the migrating path of Tundra Swans.

Comfortable, beautifully decorated guest rooms, a very special honeymoon suite, two large lounges, sunroom, patios, large porch, and lakeside balcony all add to the appeal of *Brentwood on the Beach*.

Find an Ideal Winter Getaway here with cross-country skiing nearby. Evenings, curl up by one of the two fieldstone fireplaces. There are board games, puzzles, chess, cribbage, ping pong, and a library of books for guests to borrow and enjoy.

Joan Cassidy, your hostess, a former flight attendant, does everything possible to pamper her guests.

Besides the proximity of the little Harbour village of Bayfield, noted for interesting boutiques and galleries, *Brentwood* is near several golf courses, summer theatres, marina, a choice of restaurants, Grand Bend, and Pinery Provincial Park.

BRENTWOOD on the BEACH

Joan Cassidy
St. Joseph Shores 1, RR2
Zurich, Ontario
N0M 2T0
(519) 236-7137

Season: All year
Rates: Single $65 Double from $85 - $175 Extra person $20
Types of Acommodation: 1 Single, 3 Queen, 1 King, 1 Twin
Bathrooms: 4 Private and 2 Shared
Breakfast: Full
Special Information: No guests' pets; Air-conditioing; Smoking on the patios and porches
Languages: English and German
Directions: Take Highway 21 for 8.4 km (5.4 mi.) north of Highway 83 or Highway 21 for 0.7 km (1/4 mi.) south of Highway 84. Follow kilometers or mileage carefully and you will be at the entrance to St. Joseph Shores Phase 1. *Brentwood on the Beach* is the third house on the left on the lake side, an orange brick house (sign on lamp post).

Clair on the Square B&B

Clair on the Square Bed and Breakfast is a beautifully restored 1857 yellow brick home furnished with antiques, in unspoiled Bayfield, on the high banks of Lake Huron's shores.

The pretty guest rooms, decorated with chintz and art have their own baths. Delicious full breakfasts, with home-baking and Clair's preserves, are served in the large dining room overlooking the lovely garden. Elegant fixed menu dinners are served (by reservation to groups) at "The Dinner Party" which caters to people who enjoy exquisite food served in an elegant, yet informal atmosphere. Fresh fruits and vegetables are served from Clair's garden in season.

The delightful village of Bayfield is known for its many shops and boutiques, most of which are located in restored Nineteenth Century buildings; here one can browse for unique clothing, books, antiques, arts and crafts; stop at one of the excellent eating places; or just relax on a bench under the huge trees that line Main Street.

Theatre lovers will be attracted to productions being held at nearby Grand Bend or Blyth. Romantics and others will wish to watch the sunset over Lake Huron from Pioneer Park overlooking the lake or take a horse and buggy ride through town from Clangregor Square. There are scenic footpaths leading down the buffs to the river and beach. Boaters will enjoy the convenience of the large sheltered Harbour and Marina. There are wildlife areas, birdwatching, and cross-country skiing locally. Clair has several old bicycles for guests to use to explore the village.

This is truly an unspoiled corner of Canada -- step back in time.

BAYFIELD (South of Goderich)
ONTARIO

CLAIR on the SQUARE

Clair Soper
12 Clangregor Square, Box 158
Bayfield, Ontario
N0M 1G0
(519) 565-2135

Season: Summers, weekends in off-season by reservation
Rates: Single from $65 Double from $75 Double with Private bath from $95
Types of Accommodation: Single, Double, and Twin
Bathrooms: 1 Private and 2 Shared
Breakfast: Full
Special Information: Non-smoking home; No guests' pets please
Languages: English, French and Latin
Directions: *Clair on the Square* is on the west side of Clangregor Square, south end of Main Street in Bayfield.

Cornelius White House

The Cornelius White House, named after a Dutch settler, owner of the property in the early 1800's, is on the edge of Bloomfield, a quiet, quaint village in Prince Edward County on the Loyalist Parkway, near West Lake and Sandbanks Provincial Park.

Bonnie and Frank Evans have restored and refurbished their home in European style with many Dutch accents, reflecting the years they spent in Europe while Frank was enlisted with the Canadian Armed Forces. The six-over-six paned windows and central gothic demonstrate the heritage style of their yellow-brick home.

Bloomfield, although in an industrious farming area, has many antique shops, artisans and interesting eating places. The main attraction of Prince Edward County is its beautiful sandy beaches and clear water. There are excellent opportunities for windsurfing, fishing, scenic cycling and, in winter, cross country skiing.

CORNELIUS WHITE HOUSE

Bonnie and Frank Evans
8 Wellington Street, Box 347
Bloomfield, Ontario
K0K 1G0
(613) 393-2282

Season: All year
Rates: Single $40 Double $50 - $85
Types of Accommodation: Suite with private bath and 3 Guest rooms
Bathrooms: Private and Shared
Breakfast: Full
Special Information: "Kiki" the cat in residence; No smoking; No guests' pets
Directions: *Cornelius White House* is on Highway 33 south of Highway 401 (off Wooler Road) at 8 Wellington Street in the village of Bloomfield.

Applecrest House

Applecrest House Bed and Breakfast sits high on a hill, secluded among tall maples and apple orchards, overlooking Lake Ontario and Presqu'ile Provincial Park.

The large, 1868 red-brick home has high-ceilinged spacious rooms, furnished with family heirlooms. A rosy morning glow from the lovely red glass window above the front stairwell will greet you as you descend the stairs in the morning. The guest bedrooms are lovely, furnished and decorated with Victoriana. The atmosphere is one of peace and quiet.

Breakfast, served at the big kitchen table, is bountiful and Eleanor is known for her special recipes.

Applecrest House is close to the excellent sand beach at Presqu'ile where there are also nature walks, places for launching a boat and for picnicking. In winter there are cross-country ski trails. Birding is exceptional. The whole of scenic Prince Edward County is rich in antiques, arts and craft shops. The Trent-Severn Waterway for boating is close by.

APPLECREST HOUSE

Eleanor Muir
Box 1106
Brighton, Ontario
K0K 1H0
(613) 475-0538

Season: All year
Rates: Available upon request
Types of Accommodation: Single, Double, Twin
Bathrooms: Private and Shared
Breakfast: Full
Special Information: Non-smoking home; No guests' pets please; No drinking
Directions: Brighton is on Highway 2, 90 miles east of Toronto. Take Highway 401 Exit 509 south to Brighton. From the main traffic light in Brighton go west on Highway 2 for 1 km and then north on Simpson Street. *Applecrest House* is the second driveway on the right at the top of the hill.

Hillside B&B

Imagine an 1880 Victorian home situated on a hill overlooking the village of Clarksburg on three and a half beautifully treed acres, surrounded by terraced lawns, graced by a natural stream. Add to this the interior: spacious high-ceilinged rooms; fireplaces; deep wood trims and chandeliers; large comfortable guest bedrooms; period furniture; a full breakfast served around an elegant Victorian dining table by Karen, your hostess. Indulge in a variety of breakfast fare, highlighted by home-baking and homemade preserves. And also, to complete the picture a friendly welcoming atmosphere provided by caring hosts. This is *Hillside Bed and Breakfast*.

Only minutes from all the best downhill skiing in Ontario in Winter, *Hillside Bed and Breakfast* is located right in the village of Clarksburg, next to Thornbury, on the Southern shores of Georgian Bay. Since this is a renowned apple-growing area, Spring is blossom time and Fall harvest time. Georgian Bay is very close for fishing, boating and the beach. Clarksburg is at the head of the beautiful Beaver Valley, handy to hiking on the Bruce Trail. There is theatre to attend and antique places for browsing.

HILLSIDE B·B

Karen and Norm Stewart
Box 72
Clarksburg, Ontario
N0H 1J0
(519) 599-5523

Season: All year
Rates: Single $40 Double $50
Types of Accommodation: Single and Double
Bathrooms: Shared
Breakfast: Full
Special Information: Smoking outside only please
Directions: From Highway 26 turn south at the lights in Thornbury, follow Bruce Street to Clarksburg about 1.4 km and heading up the hill from the village look for the *Hillside Bed and Breakfast* sign on the stone pillar corner of Brook Street. From Beaver Valley (County Road 13) drive north from Kimberley to Clarksburg.

The Maples B&B

The Maples Bed and Breakfast is situated well back from Highway 2, just east of the village of Colborne, on three and a half acres, featuring trees and gardens. Your hosts, Margaret and Roger Lee, after an early retirement, completely renovated this two-storey century brick home; it is beautifully refurbished with cheerful white woodwork, and wedgwood blue broadloom.

The curving staircase in the front hall leads up to the guest bedrooms which are airy, and cheerfully decorated with old-fashioned miniature papers and white priscilla tie-back curtains. We have three double rooms for guests, two rooms have queen size beds and one a double. All the rooms are large enough to have sitting areas.

Guests are welcome to enjoy the wide verandah or take a leisurely ramble. A full breakfast is served in the gracious dining room.

The Village of Colborne is midway between Toronto and Kingston and the home of the "Big Apple". There are many antique and craft shops in the area. The white sandy beaches of Presqu'ile Provincial Park are just minutes away.

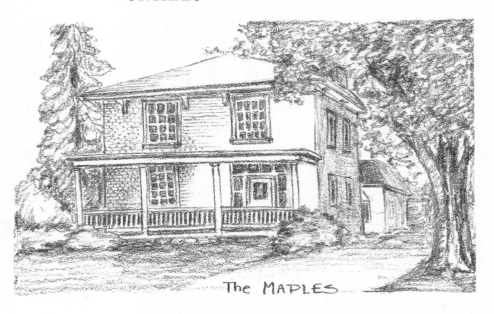

The MAPLES

Roger and Margaret Lee
119 King Street East, Box 743
Colborne, Ontario
K0K 1S0
(416) 355-2059

Season: May - October, other by reservations
Rates: Available upon request
Types of Accommodation: 1 Double, 2 Queen
Bathrooms: 1 Shared
Breakfast: Full
Special Information: Non-smoking home; No guests' pets; Children over two welcome
Directions: Situated on Highway 2, on the east side of the village of Colborne. From Highway 401 take the Percy Street Exit (Interchange 85) into the village to King Street (Highway 2), turn left and follow along King Street till you see *The Maples* sign, also on the left.

Inn The Woods

This spacious newly-built colonial home is located in the heart of ski country on the fringes of Copeland Forest in the scenic Medonte Hills.

Mary and Bob Pearson offer clean, bright comfortable rooms, and a guest lounge with satellite TV. Outdoors there is a large eight-person whirlpool spa for guests to enjoy. A full country breakfast is served in the dining area.

Mt. St. Louis and Horseshoe Valley Ski Resorts are only five minutes from *Inn The Woods Bed and Breakfast*, for winter sport.

In summer there is much to do in the area also. The scenery of the beautiful, rolling Medonte Hills is especially beautiful; there are places to hike or birdwatch, and the Wye Marsh Wildlife Centre is within a twenty-minute drive. At Midland, also not far, the Martyr's Shrine at Sainte-Marie-Among-the-Hurons is worth visiting; it is a restored Seventeenth Century Jesuit Mission. There are three golf courses in the area and the beach is not far for swimming, boating and fishing. Orillia and Midland are near enough for shopping and dining.

Your hosts will be glad to inform you about what there is to do in their area and give directions to places of interest.

INN THE WOODS

Mary and Bob Pearson
RR4
Coldwater, Ontario
L0K 1E0
(705) 835-6193

Season: All year
Rates: Single $45 Double $55 and up Winter Special: 2 Nights and 2 Breakfasts and Dinners $80 per person
Types of Accommodation: 2 Queen, 1 King, and 1 Twin
Bathrooms: 2 Full and 1 Two-piece
Breakfast: Full
Special Information: Children welcome; Dog named "MacDougall" and Cat named "Smokey" in residence; Dinners offered; A birders' B&B
Languages: English and Sign Language
Handicapped Facilities: Limited
Directions: Access from Highway 400 to Horseshoe Valley Road. Turn right and drive through Craighurst past Horseshoe Valley Resort. Turn left on 6th Concession of Medonte, approximately 2 miles on left side before railway tracks.

Pretty River Valley Farm Inn

The Pretty River Valley Farm Inn is nestled amid 120 acres of plateaus and forest in the scenic Blue Mountains overlooking the Pretty River Valley. This log and board and batten home sits among apple orchards; so the Springtime is beautiful with blossoms and the Autumn is harvest time.

Guest rooms are elegant and distinctive, furnished with traditional Canadian pine, which is in keeping with the decor; each room has en suite bath and woodburning fireplace. Several guest rooms have in-room whirlpool baths.

You will awake to the sounds of nature and the aroma of freshly brewed coffee, and the home-baking that is part of your deluxe continental breakfast.

Later, stroll up the hills of the farm and enjoy the serenity of the higher plateaus, and be captivated by the panoramic vista, especially when the fall colours come, of the hills and the valley below. At the end of the day relax in the bubbling whirlpool before retiring to your room with its own cozy fireplace.

At *Pretty River Valley Farm Inn* there is something to do in every season. Hike the Bruce Trail any season; watch, in Spring, the salmon and trout spawn in the local streams; in Summer, swim, water-ski, or windsurf at Wasaga Beach, nearby; in Autumn, pick your own apples right at the farm; in Winter, downhill or cross-country ski at local resorts and conservation areas.

PRETTY RIVER VALLEY FARM

Steve and Diane Szelestowski
RR1
Nottawa (Collingwood), Ontario
L0M 1P0
(705) 445-7598

Season: All year
Rates: Single $55 and up Double $65 and up
Types of Accommodation: 6 Bedrooms and 2 Suites
Bathrooms: 8 Private
Breakfast: Deluxe Continental
Special Information: Children over 8 years welcome; No guests' pets please; Non-smoking home; Air-conditioned
Directions: Staying on Highway 24 at Duntroon go 3 km north towards Collingwood; take first left (Sideroad 30/31) for 8 km to farm on left.

Glenwood B&B

Glenwood is an historic home built in 1827 overlooking the forested Dundas Valley and beautiful Spencer Creek. The home is set well back in this wild setting, close to the Bruce Trail, conservation parklands and cross-country ski trails; yet with easy access to downtown Dundas, Hamilton and Highway 401.

Glenwood was renovated by John and Margaret Carey to provide three airy bedrooms, and a TV lounge and bathroom for bed and breakfast guests. There is a big verandah facing the woods and creek for relaxation. The flavour of the past has been retained by restored pine floors, period furnishing, pleasant chintz and country decor. Breakfast is offered in the cheerful dining area at a long harvest table.

The famous Royal Botanical Gardens and Dundurn Castle, a Nineteenth Century, 35-room mansion restored to its former splendor, are close by -- as are downtown Hamilton for shopping and Theatre, and the Copps Coliseum.

Dundas is a picturesque busy town nestled in a valley between the Niagara Escarpment and Cootes Marsh at the Eastern end of Lake Ontario, right beside the city of Hamilton.

GLENWOOD B.+B.

John and Margaret Carey
42 Osler Drive
Dundas, Ontario
L9H 4B1
(416) 627-5096

Season: All year
Rates: Single $45 Double $45 7 nights $300
Types of Accommodation: 2 Queen, 1 Twin
Bathrooms: 1 Shared 4-piece
Breakfast: Full
Special Information: Non-smoking home; No guests' pets; Cat in residence named "Krystal"; Air-conditioner in 2 guest rooms; Hosts retired; Lots of birds; Adults preferred; No small children
Directions: From Hamilton take Main Street West to Osler Drive into Dundas, past the University Plaza and South Street traffic lights. Follow Osler around curve in road for 300 feet and *Glenwood B&B* is the fourth house on the right.

The Teddy Bear B&B Inn

The Teddy Bear B&B Inn is an Edwardian (1907) schoolhouse that has been converted into a charming heritage bed and breakfast home.

Hospitality abounds as Gerrie and Vivian Smith welcome you to their beautiful countryside vacation inn, enhanced with Canadiana, collectibles, antiques, and memorabilia. Guests are welcome to share in their hosts interest and enthusiasm for genuine Mennonite quilts, hand crafted rugs and wallhangings, horse and buggy scenery, their gift shoppe, and lovingly restored furnishings in delightfully decorated rooms. If you are at all interested in teddy bears, then you will be interested in Gerrie and Vivian's collection; some are for sale.

There are three comfortable guest rooms and a choice of double, twin or king size beds. For more privacy or longer stays there is a self-contained apartment available; good for families. All the guest rooms have TV's, as does the guest lounge. Complimentary refreshments are available; there is a golf course in the area.

Elmira is right in the heart of Pennsylvania German country; one of Canada's earliest settlements, as the Mennonites came to the area in the early 1800's. Set amid the rich farmlands of the Conestoga and Grand Rivers, the area is a centre for Mennonite craftsmen, and the Elmira Maple Syrup Festival each Spring. Kitchener-Waterloo, famous for the two large Mennonite Markets, is close by.

TEDDY BEAR B.&B. INN

Gerrie and Vivian Smith
Wyndham Hall, RR1
Elmira, Ontario
N3B 2Z1
(519) 669-2379

Fax: (519) 669-3271
Season: All year
Rates: Single $55 Double $65 Family rate in apartment
Types of Accommodation: 2 Double, 1 Twin (King)
Bathrooms: 2 Private and 1 En Suite
Breakfast: Deluxe Continental or Full, guests' preference
Special Information: Children welcome; Non-smoking home; No guests' pets please; Dog "Ramzi" lives in a separate part of the house; Dinners by reservation; Air-conditioning in 2 of the rooms
Directions: *Teddy Bear Bed and Breakfast Inn* is northwest of Elmira, just beyond the village of Floradale on Township Road 6 which is a continuation of County Road 19. Floradale is 1.6 km west of Elmira and 4.8 km north on County Road 19 and Township Road 6.

Allen's B&B

Allen's Bed and Breakfast is a cheerful modern, centrally air-conditioned home located on a quiet street. Gull Lake is a few minutes walk in one direction, and downtown Gravenhurst, shops and restaurants are a few minutes walk in the other.

Guest rooms are pretty and comfortable and there is a lounge where guests may sit and watch TV. The lounge, large screened-in sunrooms, deck and dining area, where Karen serves breakfast, all overlook the interesting garden; here a giant protruding Muskoka rockface has been transformed into a "Muskoka rock garden".

Gravenhurst on Muskoka Bay is the "gateway to Muskoka", an area of over 1,600 lakes which in early times were used as the transportation links to help open up the area for settlement. Today, the restored steam ship, the 105-year-old Segwun, still tours the lakes for tourists all the summer season.

Other local attractions include professional summer theatre; the restored birthplace of Dr. Norman Bethune, the beloved medical doctor to the people of China; and the Concert Band on the Barge.

Karen Allen
581 David Street East, Box 2276
Gravenhurst, Ontario
P0C 1G0
(705) 687-7368

Season: May - Thanksgiving, Winter by reservation
Rates: Single $35 Double $45 - $50
Types of Accommodation: 1 Double, 1 Queen and 1 Twin
Bathrooms: Private and Shared
Breakfast: Full
Special Information: Non-smoking home; No guests' pets please (due to allergy); Air-conditioning; Large screened-in sunroom with access to garden
Languages: English and Danish
Directions: From Highway 11 North and South take Gravenhurst Exit 169 to Bethune Drive, turn east on David Street to 581. From Toronto (South), turn right at the third street entering Gravenhurst. From the North, turn left at the third street from traffic lights (station). Beerstore at the corner of Bethune and David.

Cunningham's B&B

Cunningham's Bed and Breakfast is a modern tri-level home set back on a hill among the trees on a quiet cul de sac close to Lake Muskoka (when the leaves are off the trees one can see the lake from the window). Staying in this modern electrically heated home is like staying in the country in town: everything is within walking distance; yet you are tucked into the seclusion of a Muskoka landscape.

The guest bedrooms are large and comfortable and interestingly furnished. Leona and Dave serve a home cooked breakfast in the spacious dining area and guests are welcome to enjoy the sun (Muskoka) room, family room and TV.

From *Cunningham's* one can walk to all the sights of Gravenhurst. The restored steam ship, RMS Segwun begins her tour of the Muskoka lakes here; the Bethune House, birthplace of Dr. Norman Bethune, medical hero to the people of China, has been restored by the town of Gravenhurst. Also, in the summertime there is professional theatre at the town Opera House, and Sunday Evening Band Concerts on the Barge in Gull Lake Park. In Winter, this area is a great place to cross-country ski, and skate on Muskoka Bay.

CUNNINGHAM'S B.&B.

Leona and Dave Cunningham
175 Clairmont Road, Box 574
Gravenhurst, Ontario
P0C 1G0
(705) 687-4511

Season: May - October, Winter by chance
Rates: Single $30 Double $45 - $55
Types of Accommodation: 2 Queen, 1 Twin
Bathrooms: 2 Four-piece and 1 Two-piece
Breakfast: Full
Special Information: Non-smoking home; No guests' pets; Special diets on request
Directions: From the Post Office in the centre of Gravenhurst travel west (Highway 169) four blocks on Bay Street. At the stop sign continue past the "Dead End" sign onto Clairmont Road and straight ahead to 175.

Milnes' B&B

John and Marg's warm, friendly welcome make bed and breakfast guests feel instantly at home in their two-storey white-frame home situated on a shady street in the middle of Gravenhurst. Everything is a few minutes walk away -- downtown, restaurants, summer theatre, the public park and the beach.

Milnes' Bed and Breakfast is surrounded by tall trees and there is a view of the beautiful backyard garden to enjoy during breakfast. There are three comfortable guest bedrooms on the second floor with decor that reflects the Milnes' travels and with cheery hardwood floors.

Gravenhurst is nestled between Gull Lake and Muskoka lake. The town is home to the Muskoka Festival, a professional theatre tradition each summer. The Grand Old Lady of the Lakes (Age 105) the RMS Segwun, is a fully operational steam ship that gives a one-of-a-kind tour on the area lakes. Gravenhurst is the birthplace of Dr. Norman Bethune and Bethune House has been restored for visitors.

John and Marg Milne
270 Hotchkiss Street, Box 1431
Gravenhurst, Ontario
P0C 1G0
(705) 687-4395

Season: May - October, Winter by chance
Rates: Single $25/$35 Double $45
Types of Accommodation: 1 Single, 1 Double and 1 Twin
Bathrooms: 1 Shared
Breakfast: Full
Special Information: Restricted smoking; No guests' pets
Directions: From the Toronto-Dominion Bank near the town centre, turn west on Hotchkiss Street to 270 in the second block.

Willow Manor

It gives a joyous feeling to come upon such a pleasant oasis right in the city. The lovely old limestone home that is *Willow Manor* sits facing out over spacious lawns framed by majestic pines. Jack and Lyn have encouraged the resident song birds to claim this as their territory too, by planting special "song bird" gardens. Springtime will bring a magnificent show when the hundreds of bulbs they have planted along borders of the property bloom. Thyme, sage, and other savory herbs make a fragrant carpet by the paths of the dooryard. Window boxes, hanging baskets, tall pink hollyhocks, and green climbing ivy all contrast against the grey limestone walls.

The spacious bright rooms have deep window sills, soft pastels and inviting period furnishings. In the living room a glowing fireplace, oriental carpets, botanical prints, antique gilt mirrors, and floral bouquets are the backdrop for the turn-of-the-century square baby grand piano.

Guests are pampered at *Willow Manor* by the luxury of powder dusted crisp linens, fat European duvets, terrycloth robes, and heated bathroom floors. For example, in one of the guest bedrooms you will be welcomed by bedside flowers, a fire burning in the fireplace, and hand-made truffles. In the morning you will awaken to the aroma of coffee outside your door. After a leisurely whirlpool bath, you may choose to enjoy breakfast in the comfort of the highback silk chairs in the formal dining room or, weather permitting, poolside. Fresh fruit, juice, muffins, and home-made granola are standard fare. Special dishes, such as Belgian waffles with whipped cream and a warm fruit compote, are often served.

Guelph is a University town worth exploring, 45 minutes west of Toronto, and 20 minutes east of Kitchener, close to the well-known Aberfoyle Antique Market and the beautiful Elora Gorge.

WILLOW MANOR

Jack and Lyn Edwards
408 Willow Road
Guelph, Ontario
N1H 6S5
(519) 763-3574

Season: All year
Rates: Available upon request
Types of Accommodation: Single, Double, Queen and King
Bathrooms: Private
Breakfast: Full
Special Information: Non-smoking home; No guests' pets please; Reservations recommended
Directions: In Guelph, off the Hanlon Expressway (Highway 6) at Willow Road; go two doors west.

Chart House

Across from Olympic Harbour, in what once was the old village of Portsmouth, *Chart House* welcomes bed and breakfast guests. This Designated Historic Kingston home was built in 1848 by Mr. Patterson, who was the owner of the first area brewery.

Chart House Bed and Breakfast is a beautifully renovated red brick home, with Georgian casements and a classical portico, surrounded by a white iron fence. The four pretty guest rooms, with some period furnishings, each have a private sink, and share two four-piece baths.

The front sitting room has a welcoming fireplace. A full country breakfast including cereal, fresh fruit, bacon or sausage, farm fresh eggs, and home-baked muffins is served on the patio overlooking the "English Country" garden, in warm weather. Otherwise breakfast is served in the beautiful formal dining room.

Chart House is within walking distance of Queen's University. Kingston is an interesting historic waterfront city, located where the St. Lawrence River and Lake Ontario converge. Massive stone Martello Towers, originally built in the 1840's to fortify Kingston, still stand along the shoreline and now house museums. Kingston is the city of 1,000 Islands and scenic boat tours; there is a toll free car ferry from Kingston to the largest island, Wolfe Island, which connects Kingston by another ferry to the United States. In the city itself there are many museums and restored Historic homes to visit, such as the home of Canada's first Prime Minister, John A. MacDonald.

CHART HOUSE

Clare and Tom Campbell
90 Yonge Street
Kingston, Ontario
K7M 1E6
(613) 546-9026

Season: All year
Rates: Single $55 Double $65
Types of Accommodation: 3 Double, 1 Queen
Bathrooms: 2 Four-piece
Breakfast: Full
Special Information: Children welcome; Smoking in designated areas; Bicycles available
Languages: English and French
Directions: *Chart House* is on the waterfront off King Street. Phone for detailed directions.

95

Gardiner House

Gardiner House Bed and Breakfast is one of Kingston's oldest homes; built in what once was the old village of Portsmouth, in 1818 to 1819 by James Gardiner, an English immigrant farmer, *Gardiner House* has been officially designated an Heritage Building.

Barbara and Bruce have taken care that the restoration and furnishing of their Georgian brick home reflect the period in which it was built. The two bedrooms have comfortable beds, working fireplaces, and terry robes for the trip to the bathroom that is used exclusively by bed and breakfast guests.

The original kitchen is now a sitting room with the restored cooking fireplace and bake oven as a focal point. Here guests may relax, read, listen to music, or watch TV. A generous Continental breakfast is served in the dining room, or, in warm weather, in the garden. Besides English, German is spoken.

Gardiner House is situated in west-central Kingston overlooking a park, and Portsmouth Olympic Harbour, close to restaurants, and the public beach.

There is much to do while you visit Kingston, the city of 1,000 Islands, where the St. Lawrence joins Lake Ontario. Boat tours begin at Kingston's waterfront for exploring the islands and car ferrys go to the larger ones. Wolfe Island connects Kingston by ferry to the United States.

Kingston is the home of Queen's University and the Agnes Etherington Art Centre; Old Fort Henry, once the principal defense of Upper Canada and now an active military museum; and many Historic homes and museums.

GARDINER HOUSE

Barbara Pusch and Bruce Antliff
9 Kennedy Street
Kingston, Ontario
K7M 2G8
(613) 544-0933

Season: All year
Rates: Single $55 Double $70
Types of Accommodation: 2 Single, 1 Queen
Bathrooms: Shared
Breakfast: Continental Plus
Special Information: Non-smoking home; Two cats in residence
Languages: English and German
Directions: Travel on Highway 401 to Kingston, Exit Sir John A. MacDonald to King Street, turn right a long block to Gardiner Street; turn right a short block to Kennedy Street; turn left onto Kennedy Street, *Gardiner House* is the third house from the corner.

Harkaway House

Harkaway House, on the outskirts of Kingston, is set back on ten beautiful well-treed acres, with a stream winding through the lawns and gardens that surround the buildings. Guests are welcome to explore the grounds, swim, or just relax by the pool.

This Century home has been renovated in such a way as to dramatically expose the beamed ceilings and limestone walls in certain parts of the interior.

There are three guest suites: The" Bloom Room" has a pretty flower decor, two single white painted iron beds and an en suite bath. The "Manse" offers a queen size bed, and bath en suite with beautiful light streaming through the stained glass windows. The "Captain's Quarters" features a four-person jacuzzi in a self-contained bathroom, queen size waterbed and an extensive library.

Breakfast is hearty, home-cooked and served each morning from 7:30 to 9:30 a.m. Complimentary coffee, tea and juice are always available. Each evening guests are invited for complimentary port and sherry on the screened-in porch under one of the large old oak trees.

Kingston, home of Queen's University; the Royal Military College; Old Fort Henry; and many Museums is an historic city, once the capital of Canada. It's waterfront location at the convergence of the St. Lawrence River and Lake Ontario makes it a marine centre for sailing, and other water sports, and cruises up the St. Lawrence through the "Thousand Islands".

Chris and Jim Harkness
2500 Princess Street
Kingston, Ontario
K7M 3G4
(613) 544-3407

Season: All year
Rates: Available upon request
Types of Accommodation: 2 Single, 2 Queen (one is a waterbed)
Bathrooms: 3 En Suite
Breakfast: Full
Special Information: Visa, Cash or Traveller Cheques; Pool available for guest use; Honeymoon Package
Directions: *Harkaway House* is located on Highway 2 or 2500 Princess Street on the western outskirts of Kingston.

Rankin Guest House

Rankin Guest House is approximately 140 years young, named after its original builder Andrew Rankin. One block away is one of the homes where our first Prime Minister, Sir John A. MacDonald, lived.

Rankin Guest House was completely restructured and redesigned in 1985. The entire project took more than two years to complete. All of the rooms in the house now open into a central three-storey atrium.

The Honeymoon Suite comprises the entire third floor and consists of two elegant rooms. The air-conditioned bedroom has a queen size bed and en suite bathroom. The other half of the suite is a luxurious spa, complete with a six-foot round jacuzzi, built-in massage table, private deck and three-piece bathroom. On the lower level there are two more bedrooms, each unique in its style and finishings. One has its own fireplace and the other has an appearance of a country cottage.

Rankin Guest House is for the romantic and young at heart who want the comfort of a country cottage, the privacy of a secluded spa and the luxury of a fine hotel. It is the closest bed and breakfast to the Kingston downtown core -- only two blocks from Princess Street, (the main street), and three blocks from the waterfront. Shops and historical sites are within easy walking distance.

Kingston, at the gateway to the Thousands Islands, is an interesting historical city, once for a brief time, the capital of Upper Canada. It is the home of Fort Henry, the Royal Military College and Queen's University.

RANKIN HOUSE

Garth and Marianne Walker
11 Rideau Street
Kingston, Ontario
K7K 2Z5
(613) 544-4499

Season: All year
Rates: Single $50 Double $60 - $70 Honeymoon Suite $140
Types of Accommodation: 2 Double, 1 Queen
Bathrooms: 2 Private and 1 Shared
Breakfast: Full
Special Information: Air-conditioning in Honeymoon Suite; Non-smoking home
Languages: English, Dutch and some French
Directions: *Rankin Guest House* is the closest B&B to the Kingston downtown core. Our address is 11 Rideau Street, two blocks from Princess Street and three blocks to the waterfront. Please call for detailed directions.

Glengarry County B&B

The Highet's *Glengarry County* home is the original English style bed and breakfast in this area. Their Century home faces the banks of the winding Raisin River, and sits in front of ten acres of evergreen woods. The house is surrounded by spacious lawns, shrubs and flower beds and there is a large inground pool behind the house where guests can swim or just relax.

Marjorie serves tea to guests most afternoons between 4:00 and 5:00 p.m. in the large screened porch where one can enjoy the tranquility of the river. The upstairs is reserved for guests, the two double guests rooms have a quaint, old-fashioned decor that suits the house; there is a shared guest bathroom and sitting room for guests on the second floor also. A traditional full English breakfast is served in the comfortable period dining room, or on the screened porch in pleasant weather.

The Highet's *Glengarry County Bed and Breakfast* is only twenty minutes from Cornwall and the International Bridge to the United States. Montreal is one hour east and Ottawa one and one-half hours north.

— GLENNGARRY B. & B —

Marjorie and Malcolm Highet
RR1
Lancaster, Ontario
K0C 1N0
(613) 347-3550

Season: May - October
Rates: Single $35 Double $45
Types of Accommodation: 1 Double and 1 Queen
Bathrooms: 1 Shared
Breakfast: Full
Special Information: Restricted smoking; Dog named "Brahms" and Cat named "Pollyanna" in residence; Dinners on advanced request
Directions: From Highway 401, take the Alexandria-Lancaster Exit North to Lancaster. Go west on Pine Street 3.2 km. *Glengarry County Bed and Breakfast* is the second house before the bridge with the name on the mailbox.

Home Suite Home

Aggie and Harry Tiessen believe that "people who like people" is what bed and breakfast is all about. The main rule at *Home Suite Home*, according to the Tiessens, is "just make yourself at home and enjoy your stay".

Harry, former Leamington area farmer (and Aggie was a medical secretary) found and set up their home, especially for bed and breakfast in 1986, in the centre of town. Here Aggie offers air-conditioned guest bedrooms with comfortable beds, pretty wallpaper; co-ordinating country style decor and hand-made quilts; and charming dried flower wreaths accenting the walls. This traditional home, built in the 20's, has that "home-away-from-home" welcome. Sip tea on the screened-in verandah or enjoy a swim in the large inground pool; on cooler evenings there will be a fire in the fireplace for cosy relaxation. A full breakfast is served between 5:30 and 9:30 a.m. at guests' convenience.

The bird-watching season is a busy time of the year. People come from all over to view the bird migration at Point Pelee, the most southerly tip of the Canadian mainland. Here birds gather before taking off across Lake Erie for parts north in the spring, and south in the fall. This area is known for the butterfly migration in fall, 22 birding spots, and a big tower at Holiday Beach, where one can watch the hawk migration. Leamington is also located at the entrance to Point Pelee National Park, which has an interpretive centre, transit trains, nature trails, picnic grounds and miles of beaches; there is an especially built mile-long boardwalk through the marshes area, with a wildlife observation tower. Bicycles and canoe rentals are available.

Leamington is known as "the Tomato capital of Canada" and the "biggest tomato" in the world is the local tourist booth. There are fine shops and restaurants, including two dinner theatres, and many area roadside fruit and vegetable stands.

HOME SUITE HOME —

Harry and Agatha Tiessen
115 Erie Street South
Leamington, Ontario
N8H 3B5
(519) 326-7129

Season: All year
Rates: Single $40 Double $50 Double with private bath $60
Types of Accommodation: 1 Single, 2 Double, 1 Twin
Bathrooms: 2 Four-piece
Breakfast: Full
Special Information: Non-smoking home; No guests' pets please; Air-conditioning
Languages: English and German
Directions: Turn south at main intersection on Erie Street in Leamington. *Home Suite Home Bed and Breakfast* is in the fifth block, a sign is on the front lawn.

Wakerobin Woods

When Katharine and Russell Ferguson purchased their 140 acre farm on the Bruce Peninsula, they thought that they might restore the original old pioneer homestead. However, they changed their mind and decided that the old barn, because it was more solid, would convert into a better, and certainly more unique home! They chose to make use of the spacious barn interior by creating a multi-level open concept.

Part of the conversion plan was the two double rooms for guests, one on the main floor and one in a loft position. Turn-of-the-century furniture, quilts, and handmade rugs thrown on the refinished wood floors complete the rooms. A foil to the rustic is the very modern bathroom that serves the two guest bedrooms.

The Fergusons' own produce is used to prepare guests' breakfast; this includes home-made bread and other baking; maple syrup, eggs, garden vegetables, and fruits in season.

Wakerobin Woods is quiet and secluded, surrounded by pasture, woods, and apple orchards, but not difficult to reach as it is just a jog off the main highway (#6) that spines up the Bruce to Tobermory, where one catches the Chi-Cheemaun, the car ferry to Manitoulin Island.

If you arrive in the autumn you could find Katharine and Russell making apple cider from their apples. Delicious!

The farm is close to sandy beaches, spectacular sections of the Bruce Trail for vigorous hiking or casual walking, Federal and Provincial parks, cross-country ski trails and the special flora and fauna of the Bruce Peninsula.

WAKEROBIN WOODS

Katharine and Russell Ferguson
RR1
Lions Head, Ontario
N0H 1W0
(519) 793-4266

Season: All year
Rates: Single $27.50 Double $40
Types of Accommodation: 2 Double
Bathrooms: 1 Shared
Breakfast: Full
Special Information: Dog "Sophie" and Cat "Jesse" in residence; Dinners offered on request
Directions: Please telephone for directions.

The Rose House

The Rose House is a lovely 125-year-old residence located on a tree-lined avenue in an area of fine historic London homes; yet only two blocks from Dundas Street, the main street of the downtown area.

Doug and Betty Rose's centrally air-conditioned, white stucco home, with crisp striped awnings, is surrounded by mature trees, and flower beds and lawn. The guest rooms are beautifully decorated and have period furnishings. Each room has its own unique personality. A full nutritious breakfast is served in the homey kitchen from 7:30 until 9:00 each morning. If you prefer more privacy, a room with bath en suite is available. Quality, comfort, charm, and location are the outstanding features of this attractive older home.

The Rose House is very centrally located; enjoy a short stroll along old London streets to downtown shopping, fine restaurants, the London Art Gallery, movie theatres, and the Grand Theatre, for live productions. Excellent public transportation will take you to the University of Western Ontario, or Fanshawe College.

London has many special events: the London International Air Show, when jets soar the skies; the London Balloon Fiesta, a spectacle rising softly aloft through morning mists; and the Big Band Festival. Eldon House is a monument to our Victorian past; the Museum of Indian Archaeology provides a "hands on" dig on the Western edge of the city. Orchestra London reaches out to music lovers of all ages with its performances of the classics, chamber works, and popular concerts.

The Banting House Museum, honouring the discoverer of Insulin, is a little over a block from *Rose House.*

The ROSE HOUSE

Douglas and Betty Rose
526 Dufferin Avenue
London, Ontario
N6B 2A2
(519) 433-9978

Season: All year
Rates: $30 - $45
Types of Accommodation: 2 Double, 1 Twin
Bathrooms: En Suite 4-piece and Shared 4-piece
Breakfast: Full
Special Information: Adult guests only; Non-smoking home; Air-conditioning; Off-street parking
Directions: From Highway 401 take Wellington Road north to Dufferin Avenue. Turn east on Dufferin Avenue and we are a few short blocks down.

Rideau Bank B&B

Rideau Bank Bed and Breakfast sits right on the Rideau Canal waterway, that links Ottawa and Kingston, at the foot of the Merrickville Locks; the back lawns and gardens slope down to the water, where there are free docking facilities for guests who arrive by boat.

This large red brick turn-of-the-century home, fronted by beautiful flower beds, is surrounded by spacious property where guests are free to roam; to sit on the large wrap-around front verandah; or to take in the sun on the dock, by the water. It is a pleasure to watch the silvery moonlight, reflected on the water, from the screened-in back porch over-looking the river.

The house has been restored and the lovely vibrant colours chosen for each room and period furnishings echo Aline's French Canadian heritage. A full breakfast is served in the dining room and many great conversations take place over afternoon tea.

Merrickville is a picturesque little village with many fine buildings which remain much as they were in the mid-1800's. There are delightful antique and craft shops; parks; pubs and fine dining within easy walking distance. The Blockhouse Museum, originally built as a fort in 1826 at Merrickville, with a moat and drawbridge, is now a museum of the early days of this district. Ottawa is forty-five minutes away.

MERRICKVILLE (South of Ottawa)
ONTARIO

RIDEAU BANK.

Aline Caldwell
423 Main Street East, Box 609
Merrickville, Ontario
K0G 1N0
(613) 269-3864

Season: All year
Rates: Available upon request
Types of Accommodation: Single and Double
Bathrooms: 2 Shared
Breakfast: Full
Special Information: Docking facilities
Directions: *Rideau Bank Bed and Breakfast* is located right on Highway 43 (Main Street East) on the east side of town. From the center of town head east toward Kemptville. *Rideau Bank Bed and Breakfast* is about 1/2 mile from the center of town right on the Rideau River.

Honeybrook Farm B&B

Bed and Breakfast or enjoy a complete holiday in this beautiful split granite stone 1866 farm home located by the Nith River. Jack and Alveretta are the third generation of Hendersons to live here; in times past the farm was well known for its production of raspberries, maple syrup and honey which were sold at the nearby Kitchener Market. In 1980 Jack and Alveretta began their "labour of love" to renovate and restore the family home. Now they invite guests to share the customized comfort they have worked so carefully to create.

Honeybrook Farm Bed and Breakfast has spacious guest bedrooms and two guest bathrooms, all thermostatically controlled. The home is comfortably furnished with beautiful family heirlooms and antiques and has the lovely, deep window sills characteristic of old stone houses. A generous country breakfast is served in the cheerful dining area by the stone fireplace which is part of the country kitchen.

Alveretta offers a delicious varied menu for breakfasts and other meals served in the elegant dining room by prearrangement. Laundry facilities are available for guests.

Transportation to and from local terminals may be prearranged. Jack and Alveretta are experienced travellers and are extremely knowledgeable about their area, St. Jacobs, and Kitchener-Waterloo's Mennonite heritage; tours of the area may be conducted on request. A wilderness area near the river provides ample habitat for fifty or more wild birds for watching.

Honeybrook Farm Bed and Breakfast, besides being close to Kitchener-Waterloo, is only twenty minutes from Stratford Theatres.

MILLBANK (West of Kitchener-Waterloo)
ONTARIO

HONEYBROOK FARM

Jack and Alveretta Henderson
RR1
Millbank, Ontario
N0K 1L0
(519) 595-4604

Season: All year
Rates: Single $30 Double $45 and up
Types of Accommodation: Single, Double
Bathrooms: 2 Complete
Breakfast: Full
Special Information: Adult guests only; Non-smoking home; No guests' pets; Cat in residence but not allowed in when guests present or in the summer; Gourmet dinners offered on request; Partially air-conditioned; a birders' B&B
Languages: English and a little French
Directions: From Kitchener-Waterloo off Waterloo Regional Road 11 on Wellesley Road 20 South; From Stratford, off Perth Road 7 onto Mornington Concession 4 and 5. Telephone for reservations and directions.

Park Place B&B

Park Place Bed and Breakfast is a grand century-old Queen Anne style home which has been designated historic. The house is situated on a large, well-treed corner lot on the River Road facing the Niagara Gorge and in the distance across the River, the United States.

This beautiful home has high ceilings, original parquet floors and period furnishings. The entire family strives to make guests feel welcome and comfortable. Breakfast is served in a formal dining area with silver, fine china, crystal and linen. Special diets are cheerfully accommodated. There is a patio and large front porch to relax on. Two of the guest rooms may adjoin, which is ideal for families. The shuttle bus service to the Falls and the rest of the city is available at the front door.

Niagara Falls is one of the great natural wonders of the world, the thunder of Niagara draws tourists from all over the world; it also draws honeymooners, and what better place to stay than a heritage Bed and Breakfast with a panoramic view.

There is so much to do in the area. One can take the elevator to the bottom of the gorge to the edge of the Whirlpool Rapids. In the Springtime there is a Blossom Festival when the Niagara Parks burst with bloom. The "Maid of the Mist", a tough little tour boat, takes tourists right up the Niagara River to the foot of both Falls, where the noise is deafening and the spray like tropical rain.

PARK PLACE B.+B.

Carolyn and Gary Burke
4851 River Road
Niagara Falls, Ontario
L2E 3G4
(416) 358-0279

Season: July - September, by arrangement in off season
Rates: Available upon request
Types of Accommodation: Single, Double, Family
Breakfast: Full
Special Information: Special diets can be accommodated; No smoking in house, but allowed on patio and front porch; Pick-up guests at bus or train station
Directions: Take the QEW Highway to the Rainbow Bridge; continue to Clifton Hill; turn left and go to River Road; turn left again and drive 1.9 km to the house on the corner of River Road and Ellis Street.

A Rose and Kangaroo

A warm reception awaits guests at this 1910 spacious brick home on the River Road overlooking the Niagara River Gorge. A majestic, century-old oak tree and enormous Manitoba maple shade the front yard. From the beautiful wrap-around verandah there is a clear view of the Gorge and the United States across the Niagara River. A few minutes walk from *A Rose and Kangaroo* will take you to the major attractions of this area; the American and Canadian Falls.

Virginia Rose was raised in the Niagara Peninsula and Laurence is from Australia -- hence the "Rose" and "Kangaroo" a theme repeated in the sign on the front lawn which is shaped like the animal from "down under"!

There are four comfortable guest rooms; guests are invited to lounge in the spacious living room with fireplace, TV, and a piano. A full Canadian breakfast is served each morning in the large dining room.

Besides the splendor of the Falls, there are tours, museums, numerous parks, historic sites, golf courses, wineries, shops, theatres and restaurants that travellers can enjoy. The Furnells have been in the travel business and can be of great help in planning your time in the area, arranging for tours, or providing transportation to and from rail or bus depots.

Laurence and Virginia Furnell
5239 River Road (Niagara River Parkway)
Niagara Falls, Ontario
L2E 3G9
(416) 374-6999

Fax: (416) 358-2861
Season: All year
Rates: Single $30 and up Double $45 and up (seasonal)
Types of Accommodation: 1 Single, 3 Double, 1 Queen
Bathrooms: 1 Private En Suite, 1 Shared En Suite, and 1 Private
Breakfast: Full
Special Information: Children welcome; Pets welcome; Smoking in lounge and on front porch; Declawed Calico Cat named "Max" in residence; BBQ facilities; Air-conditioning; Niagara Gorge is good for bird-watching; Bike rentals
Languages: English, Ukrainian, daughter speaks French and Australian
Directions: *A Rose and Kangaroo* is between Rainbow and Whirlpool Bridges, right on Niagara River Parkway, on same road as Niagara Falls.

Belle Rive

Belle Rive Bed and Breakfast is a charming turn-of-the-century Edwardian home in a wonderful location in Niagara-on-the-Lake, kitty-corner to the Oban Inn and with a view of the golf course and lake from the front windows. The shops and theatres are just steps away.

Belle Rive has three beautifully decorated spacious, air-conditioned rooms. A delicious breakfast is served by your host, Leeanne Weld, in the dining room; featuring seasonal fruits, fresh baked goods, and a selection of hot dishes. Part of the dining room decor are the conversation pieces "polo sticks", and costume set designs from Shaw productions which have been in the family for many generations.

The serene, waterfront setting of Niagara-on-the-Lake has Old World charm, exclusive boutiques, fine dining and first class Theatres of the Shaw Festival, that brings people back year after year. The first capital of Upper Canada (Ontario) from 1791 to 1796, this is one of the best preserved Nineteenth Century towns in North America.

Niagara-on-the-Lake is located in a wine-growing area and several wineries in the area offer tours and tasting. Other area places to visit include Fort George National Historic Site and Niagara Falls.

BELLE RIVE

Harriet Lee and Leeanne Weld
156 Gate Street, Box 68
Niagara-on-the-Lake, Ontario
L0S 1J0
(416) 468-7551

Season: May - End of September/October
Rates: Double $85 Master $105 Master with 3 people $125
Types of Accommodation: 2 Queen, 1 Twin
Bathrooms: 1 En Suite and 1 Shared
Breakfast: Full
Special Information: Non-smoking home; No guests' pets; Children welcome; Air-conditioning
Directions: Turn left off Queen Street (main street in Niagara-on-the-Lake) onto Gate towards the lake. *Belle Rive* is at 156 Gate Street on the corner.

Blaney House

Blaney House Bed and Breakfast is an early Canadian colonial style historic home, circa 1816. Located in the heritage district of Niagara-on-the-Lake, it is steps from main street shops, restaurants and the Shaw Theatres.

Blaney House has been restored to its original graciousness and furnished with period antiques. Distinctive breakfasts are served in the elegant dining room overlooking the rose-filled back garden.

Upstairs are two spacious bedrooms with semi-private bath. The "Colonial Room", with double brass bed, is accented with antique pine furnishings. The "Victorian Room", an oversized bed-sitting room featuring white wicker and wrought iron, offers the option of twin beds or a king. The downstairs room has a lovely, queen size brass bed with partial canopy, en suite bathroom and its own dressing room. Each guest room has comfortable seating and reading areas.

Niagara-on-the-Lake, originally named Newark, dates from 1790 and was the original capital of Upper Canada (Ontario). It is one of the prettiest and best preserved towns in Canada. Its beautiful setting, at the mouth of the Niagara River, on Lake Ontario is very close to the United States; the Rainbow Bridge to New York State is just down river at Niagara Falls.

Because of its history, Niagara-on-the-Lake has many historical sites of interest. One of these is Fort George, a National historic site dating from 1797. A stroll along the main street, Queen Street, of Niagara-on-the-Lake brings you to an Apothacary Museum, a restored 1866 shop; and interesting gift and craft shops and boutiques.

Niagara-on-the-Lake is situated at the head of the Niagara Peninsula, an important fruit-growing area, and one of Canada's main wine-growing areas. Several wineries for tours and tasting are located around Niagara-on-the-Lake.

BLANEY HOUSE B.+B.

Betty Blaney
177 Victoria Street, Box 302
Niagara-on-the-Lake, Ontario
L0S 1J0
(416) 468-5362

Season: All year
Rates: $65 - $85
Types of Accommodation: 1 Double, 1 Queen and 1 Twin or King
Bathrooms: En Suite and Shared
Breakfast: Full
Special Information: Adult guests only please; Non-smoking home; No guests' pets please; Central air-conditioning; Free off-street parking
Directions: From the main street (Queen) turn north (towards the Lake) on Victoria Street, the *Blaney House* is the third house on the west side.

Brockamour Manor

BROCKAMOR MANOR

Brockamour Manor, circa 1818, is a lovely old Georgian House, which was once, long ago, the family home of General Isaac Brock's fiancee. Its romantic historic past can still be felt in its gracious presence. Set in a park-like environment under majestic old trees, and surrounded by flower beds and neat walks, it provides quiet, elegant accommodation for Bed and Breakfast guests who come to historic old Niagara-on-the-Lake.

The large guest rooms are almost as they would have been in a past era, with fireplaces, and baths en suite. A full and varied gourmet breakfast is served in the formal dining room or on the cool summer porches. Picnic baskets can be available by prearrangement.

Brockamour Manor is located within walking distance to the quaint old town shops, the Shaw theatre, bicycle trails and beautiful parks.

Niagara-on-the-Lake is one of the prettiest, best preserved towns in Canada. Rich in history, it is also the site of the famous Shaw Festival, attended from April to November by theatre lovers from around the world. The Festival is named to honour and present, along with other works, the plays of one of the world's greatest dramatists, George Bernard Shaw.

For the history buff the town has plenty to offer, as it was the locale for some of the battles of the War of 1812-1814. Fort George in Niagara-on-the-Lake, and Fort Niagara, across the Niagara River in Youngstown, New York, both still stand as reminders of this struggle between the British and the Americans.

The town is twenty minutes drive to the Canadian cities of St. Catharines and Niagara Falls, and thirty minutes to the Artpark Theatre in Lewiston, New York, U.S.A.

Verna and George Stewart
433 King Street, Box 1488
Niagara-on-the-Lake, Ontario
L0S 1J0
(416) 468-5527

Season: All year
Rates: $60 - $125
Types of Accommodation: 1 Single, 4 Queen, 1 Twin
Bathrooms: 3 En Suite and 1 Shared
Breakfast: Gourmet
Special Information: Non-smoking home; No guests' pets please; Cat in residence named "Blue"
Directions: *Brockamour Manor* is at the corner of King and Mary Streets in Niagara-on-the-Lake.

Lyons House

Lyons House, circa 1835, is unlike most early Niagara-on-the-Lake houses, in that it is set back from the street and surrounded by a large English style garden with daffodils, tulips, peonies, roses, flowering trees and shrubs. A lovely white wisteria hangs along the whole east wall of the house.

The front of the house is most interesting; the seemingly shuttered windows are in fact a "Regency deceit" designed to balance the facade. The lovely front entrance has an eight panelled door, sidelights and graceful loyalist fanlight.

Indoors you will find original pine floors, fireplace, and grand, high moulded ceilings on the main floor. An elegant stairway with scrolled handrails leads to the guest bedrooms; one room has a queen size bed en suite; the second, twin beds with a private bathroom just across the hall. A hearty cooked breakfast with home-made scones, muffins and jams is served in the sunny dining room.

Lyons House Bed and Breakfast is located in the old town of Niagara-on-the-Lake just a few minutes' walk from theatres, restaurants and shopping. Tennis courts, the Common, and historic sites are steps away. Bring your bicycles and enjoy the recreational trail from Niagara-on-the-Lake to Niagara Falls.

Niagara-on-the-Lake is renowned for the Shaw Festival, superb professional theatre which takes place from April to November each year in three local theatres. It is also an historic town, being central to the early Loyalist settlement and the battles of 1812-1814. It is just across the Niagara River from the United States and close to Niagara Falls, and the nearest international bridge.

Sheila and Eric Broughton
8 Centre Street, Box 1298
Niagara-on-the-Lake, Ontario
L0S 1J0
(416) 468-2586

Fax: (416) 468-5353
Season: Spring, Summer and Fall
Rates: Available on request
Types of Accommodation: Queen, Twin
Bathrooms: En suite and Private
Breakfast: Full
Special Information: Reservations recommended; Non-smoking home; Private parking for five cars; Check-in time after 1 pm.
Directions: Centre Street is three blocks south of Queen Street, the main street of Niagara-on-the-Lake.

Villa McNab

Villa Mcnab Bed and Breakfast is a truly romantic, Spanish-style villa, in the heart of the Niagara Peninsula, close to Niagara-on-the-Lake. Set among an acre of lawns and trees this unique bed and breakfast home is located in an area of vineyards and fruit trees. Bob even makes wine from local grapes.

Once you enter *Villa Mcnab*, the impression is tropical luxuriance! The house is built around a large central glass-roofed swimming pool. Beautiful blooming tropical plants hang, resplendent, about the poolsides. The roof adjusts, according to temperature, but in this ideal protected environment the plants' growth can almost equal that of their native home; hence beautiful bougainvillea and huge cacti!

Luxurious guest bedrooms open off a hall all along one side of the villa, at the end of which is the many-windowed, cedar lined hot tub spa room, and the sauna, great places to relax after a swim. All the guest rooms have private baths and TV's. There is a guest sitting room, and, in winter, the fireplace will have a log blazing.

A full English or imaginative continental breakfast is served pool-side. Your hosts, Bob and Beryl, after receiving guests at their stately Inn-home in England for eleven years know how to pamper you.

Villa McNab is within a few minutes driving distance of Niagara-on-the-Lake, the Shaw Festival, and all the other attractions of this historic town. Because *Villa McNab's* amenities are so special, it is well worth the little extra distance. Also, it is right in the heart of Canada's main wine-growing area; ask your hosts about the wine tasting tours, and other attractions in their area!

Bob and Beryl Owen
1356 McNab Road
Niagara-on-the-Lake, Ontario
L0S 1J0
(416) 934-6865 (and Fax)

Season: All year
Rates: High Season $75 - $95 Low Season $65 - $75
Types of Accommodation: 2 Queen, 1 Twin
Bathrooms: 3 En Suite
Breakfast: Full or Continental
Special Information: Smoking in pool area only; Air-conditioning; Resident dog named "Amber; Guests' pets by arrangement; Visa and MasterCard accepted
Languages: English and limited French
Directions: From the Queen Elizabeth Way leave the Q.E.W. at Niagara Street Exit at St. Catharines and head North. Travel along Niagara Street to its junction with Lakeshore Road, and turn right. McNab Road (Firelane 14) is the third road on the left after passing over the canal bridge at Lock 1. There is a Church on the corner, in the trees.

Wren House

The *Wren House* is located in the heart of the pretty town of Niagara-on-the-Lake on a parcel of land once owned by John Barker, a prominent town politician during the 1830's. Believed to be built in 1838, this bed and breakfast home is located one and a half blocks from the unique main street with its quaint shops; and only minutes walk to the Shaw Theatres.

Each of the pretty guest rooms furnished with antiques and soft colonial colours are spacious and inviting.

A sumptuous breakfast is served in the lovely dining room complemented on cooler mornings by a glowing fire. Fresh seasonal fruits, home-made baked goods, specialty dishes and friendly conversation with your congenial hosts make breakfast a pleasant experience.

Guests may relax in the comfortable guest lounge where refreshments and home-made cookies are offered, a warm welcome after a day of sightseeing and shopping, or perhaps as you prepare for an evening at the Theatre.

Niagara-on-the-Lake is steeped in history, as it is one of the oldest towns in Ontario (formerly Upper Canada). This is where the United Empire Loyalists came first in the 1780's and a focal point of the War of 1812-1814.

Niagara-on-the-Lake has become famous as the home of professional theatre on three stages; the impressive Shaw Festival Theatre; the historic Court House Theatre and the Royal George Theatre, a refurbished early nineteenth century movie house. April to November, these theatres are a showcase for plays by George Bernard Shaw and his contempories.

From the *Wren House* one can also make day trips to places of interest on the Niagara Peninsula including St. Catharines, Niagara Falls and many historic sites.

WREN HOUSE B.&B.

Kim and Phil White
278 Regent Street, Box 1684
Niagara-on-the-Lake, Ontario
L0S 1J0
(416) 468-4361

Season: All year
Rates: Single $70 - $80 Double $75 - $85
Types of Accommodation: 2 Queen, 1 Twin
Bathrooms: En Suite and Shared
Breakfast: Full
Special Information: Non-smoking home; No guests' pets please; Central air-conditioning; Children Meghan and Hilary in residence; Children welcome if all three guest rooms are booked
Directions: Take the QEW to Niagara Falls, Exit Highway 55. Turn right on Queen Street and turn south on Regent Street. One and a half blocks from Queen Street.

The Union Hotel B&B

Entering *The Union Hotel Bed and Breakfast* is like going back 150 years. Peter and Debbie Karges have painstakingly restored their historically designated home to its original condition. The exterior clapboard, decorative wood trim, cast iron latches, wide plank floors, and tin room signs are just a few authentic details that reflect the life style of the past that was prevalent in Upper Canada in the 1830's. Period furniture, vivid historical colours, coal oil lamps illuminating the dining area also re-capture the days of yore. The old hotel even has a ball room, and it too may someday be restored.

The Karges do provide modern amenities, of course, as seen in the luxurious bathrooms on the guest floor. The three guest rooms are each named and are decorated beautifully. For instance, the "Governor Simcoe Room" has a four-poster suite adorned with elegant lace shams and a satin comforter. The "Joseph Van Norman Room" is equally as beautiful, also with a four-poster and a touch of Victorian lace. The "Eva Brook Donly Room" is the most delicate; a quaint pink room with dried flowers, antique quilts and a 1920's white cast iron and brass bed for single occupancy.

The full gourmet breakfasts are served with the influence from the the early 1800's. Breakfasts could consist of home-made breads, muffins, pastries and jams. Entrees may include cognac paté crepes, zephurs, smoked salmon, and baked pancakes with fresh fruit.

The *Hotel* has an upper balcony; a good place for sipping lemonade. Normandale is right on the Lake Erie shore, so guests can relax on the sandy beach, stroll along the trout stream; or in cooler times, warm their feet by the fire or read a book in the bright, cosy parlor.

Peter and Debbie Karges
Main Street, Normandale
Mailing Address:RR1, Box 38
Vittoria, Ontario
N0E 1W0
(519) 426-5568

Season: All year
Rates: Single $35 - $45 Double $65
Types of Accommodation: 1 Single, 2 Double
Bathrooms: 2 Shared
Breakfast: Full
Special Information: Adult guests only please; No guests' pets please; Non-smoking home; Good location for bird watchers, cyclists and hikers
Directions: From Simcoe go south on Highway 24. Turn left onto Fisher's Glen Road. Proceed through the hamlet of Fisher's Glen to stop sign. Turn left and down the hill into Normandale. Turn left at stop sign and proceed to second building on left.

Gosford Place

Gosford Place is a quiet country haven, a few minutes north of Brockville, surrounded by lawns, and acres of trees. To describe the interior of this 150-year old farm home needs phrases that might be considered a contradiction in terms like "artistic sophistication" and "down home comfort", or "the old wood stove" and "luxuriously modern", which only goes to prove that *Gosford Place* is a mellow blending of the old and the new!

Guests have a choice of bedrooms, with period furnishing, or you may choose to stay in the suite comprising a private bath and a sitting room. For more privacy and longer stays the Log Cabin Guest House is available, a separate country retreat. In the morning Eileen serves a generous country style breakfast.

Gosford Place has a heated inground pool where guests may take a plunge or just relax at the pool side. Winter offers cross-country skiing followed by a hot drink by the woodstove, a quiet relaxed time over a picture puzzle, or a game of bridge. Caspar and Eileen speak both English and French.

The countryside is a good area for jogging, walking or cycling along country roads; there are country auctions and local Church suppers to attend. Fine dining is as close as Brockville and other nearby towns; Caspar and Eileen will be glad to help you locate the places you want to explore.

The St. Lawrence River and the Thousand Islands are minutes to the south. The Ivy Lea Bridge to the United States is half an hour west; and the Ogdensburg Bridge to the United States is half an hour east; just before Upper Canada Village at Morrisburg, which is a reconstructed Nineteenth Century Ontario village in action. Kingston is one hour west; Montreal is two hours to the east.

GOSFORD PLACE

Caspar and Eileen Haupt
RR1
North Augusta, Ontario
K0G 1R0
(613) 926-2164

Season: All year
Rates: Single $60 Double $65
Types of Accommodation: 3 Double, 1 King, and 1 Twin
Bathrooms: 3 Private
Breakfast: Full
Special Information: Children 12 and over welcome; Non-smoking home; No guests' pets please; Two friendly dogs in residence named "Gretchen" and "Mindy"
Languages: English and French
Directions: Exit 698 on Highway 401 at Brockville (North Augusta Road). Travel 13 km north of North Augusta Road (Route 6) to Gosford Road (just past 8th Concession). Turn right and *Gosford Place* is 500 feet on the right.

L'Auberge du Marche

This bed and breakfast is unique in that it originally was two Georgian-style Victorian townhouses that have been completely renovated by Nicole and Jean-Jacques, who had the houses connected by putting double French doors in the central wall. One half has been reserved for bed and breakfast guests; the other half serves as the family home and is where guests are served a full breakfast in the dining room.

The guest side offers a completely private self-contained beautiful white and blue suite on the main floor. This includes a sitting room with a chintz covered sofa, easy chairs and cable TV. There is also a bedroom with queen size brass bed, small kitchen and bathroom, as part of this suite. The second floor has three pretty guest rooms. All the rooms are beautifully decorated and airy.

L'Auberge du Marche has a marvellous location; from here you can walk to everything in the Parliament Hill area: the Byward Market; a plethora of restaurants and little specialty shops; Parliament and the Peace Tower; the National Arts Centre for theatre and Symphony Concerts; and, only one block away, the National Gallery of Canada.

Nicole Faubert and Jean-Jacques Charlebois
87 Guigues Avenue
Ottawa, Ontario
K1N 5H8
(613) 235-7697

Season: All year
Rates: Available upon request
Types of Accommodation: 1 Double, 4 Queen
Bathrooms: Private and Shared
Breakfast: Full
Special Information: No guests' pets please; Kitchen and laundry facilities; Central air-conditioning; Two children in residence
Languages: English and French
Directions: Take Nicholas Street exit from The Queensway (Highway 417). Keep left and take Dalhousie. Turn left on St. Patrick. At next light turn right on Parent. The next street is Guigues Avenue, turn right. *L'Auberge du Marche* is at 87 Guigues Avenue.

Australis Guest House

Carol and Brian Waters have the longest established Bed and Breakfast in the Ottawa area. *Australis Guest House* is situated on a quiet, tree-lined street just one block from the Rideau River and Strathcona Park with its resident ducks and swans. Parliament Buildings are a twenty-minute walk away.

The architect-designed house has leaded windows, fireplaces and oak floors. Beautifully coloured light streams down through the unique eight-foot high stained glass windows overlooking the hall from the stair landing; it was created by artist Petervan Rossun in 1959.

The spacious guest rooms include a private suite with bath; the house is decorated with collectibles that reflect the fact that the Waters have lived in many different parts of the world. Carol and Brian's Australian and English heritages, respectively, combined with their Canadian experience provide a truly international flavour and a comfortable atmosphere.

A hearty delicious breakfast could include home-baked breads and pastries to ensure you start the day right.

Ottawa, of course, is the nation's Capital, and there is much to do and see. Every Spring the tulips (a gift from Holland) make a brillant display along the streets and the Canal. Places to visit include The Parliament Buildings and Peace Tower; the National Gallery; the Canadian War Museum; and the Canadian Museum of Civilization, across the Ottawa River in Hull.

AUSTRALIUS GUEST HOUSE

Carol, Brian and Olivia Waters
35 Marlborough Avenue
Ottawa, Ontario
K1N 8E6
(613) 235-8461

Season: All year
Rates: Single $35 and up Double $50
Types of Accommodation: 2 Queen, 1 Twin
Bathrooms: Private and Shared
Breakfast: Full
Special Information: No guests' pets; No smoking in guest rooms; Sometimes tours given of the City
Languages: English and Olivia speaks French
Directions: Exit Nicholas to Laurier, east 1/4 mile to Marlborough. Free pick-up and delivery from Bus and Train Stations.

Blue Spruces B&B

Pat and John Hunter's beautiful Edwardian home is located in the downtown core of Ottawa. There is a welcoming atmosphere in the comfortable surroundings -- lovely period furniture, oriental carpets and muted richness of pleasing colour.

The guest bedrooms exude the same pleasant feelings; lovely linens, sumptuous comforters and pillows, and, again, period furnishings add to the effect. The bathrooms are luxurious; all three rooms have baths en suite and one special bathroom overlooks the garden.

A full breakfast is served in the dining room.

Blue Spruces Bed and Breakfast is close to Ottawa attractions. Capital Hill, the seat of the government of Canada is minutes away by transit. Ottawa is a city of Tulips in the Spring, a grateful gift from Holland for housing their Royal Family during the Second World War.

Ottawa attractions are many. Some include the national Gallery of Art; the Canadian Museum of Civilization just across the Ottawa River in Hull; the national Museum of Science and Technology; the National Library of Canada; and many restored Historical homes.

Patricia and John Hunter
187 Glebe Avenue
Ottawa, Ontario
K1S 2C6
(613) 236-8521

Fax: (613) 231-3730
Season: All year
Rates: Single $55 Double $65
Types of Accommodation: 1 Double, 1 Queen, and 1 Twin
Bathrooms: 3 Private
Special Information: Children over 10 years welcome; Non-smoking home; No guests' pets; Central air-conditioning; Visa and MasterCard accepted
Languages: English and French
Directions: Take Queensway (Highway 417) to Bronson Avenue. Turn south to Powell Avenue (first light), then east on Powell to Percy (one block), south on Percy to Glebe (two blocks), and then east on Glebe for one half block to 187 Glebe Avenue, on your left.

Constance House B&B

Constance House Bed and Breakfast is a warm and inviting Victorian Heritage (1895) home whose exterior has been lovingly restored, right down to the gingerbreading on the roof and its wrap-around verandah. Inside, the house is a mixture of tastefully decorated high-ceilinged rooms accented by period chandeliers, hardwood floors and modern conveniences. In the entrance hall a hand restored maple staircase leads up to the second level bedroom area while the marble fireplace encourages relaxing in the adjacent sitting room. Guests will enjoy sitting on the porch at the front or a quiet read in the privacy of the enclosed patio.

Every guest room has a washbasin, blow dryer, separate heating controls and terry bathrobes. The bedrooms have antique furnishings and the beds are made up with beautiful linens. The third floor Pine Gallery is a special self-contained suite, with queen size bed, private bathroom with skylight, kitchen facilities, a sitting room, and a private deck and entrance.

Constance House is located in the residential Sandy Hill" area of Ottawa, within walking distance of Parliament Hill, downtown shopping and dining. It is close to the University of Ottawa; the Department of Defence; the bridge to Quebec; the Rideau River and Canal, where every winter Ottawa has the longest outdoor skating rink in the world.

CONSTANCE HOUSE

Esther M. Peterson
62 Sweetland Avenue
Ottawa, Ontario
K1N 7T6
(613) 235-8888

Season: All year
Rates: Single $48 Double $59
Types of Accommodation: 4 Single, 2 Double, 1 Queen, and 1 Twin
Bathrooms: Private and Shared
Breakfast: Full
Special Information: Adult guests only please; Non-smoking home; Air-conditioning
Directions: Take Highway 417 to Nicholas Street (Exit 118), turn right on Laurier Avenue and then 8 blocks to Sweetland Avenue.

Le Gite Park Avenue

The name of the Bed and Breakfast, *Le Gite Park Avenue* is a good indication that your hostess, Anne-Marie, is a French-Canadian and that this is a bilingual home; Irving teaches mathematics at an Ottawa Community College, and grew up in Trinidad.

This 1906 home has been beautifully modernized, but period touches remain in the deep woodwork, plaster ceiling medallions and stairway. The atmosphere of the house is cheerful and light. In the guest bedrooms, pretty prints, lace curtains, duvets and cushions set the tone. Each room has a desk with swivel chair. There is a third-floor suite that can be used separately (as two rooms) or together for families.

Anne-Marie serves a nutritious breakfast in the bright area off the kitchen; Irving contributes as the baker of the homemade (usually multi-grain) bread.

Ottawa is a city of many choices: besides a visit to Parliament Hill there are many National Museums; the National Art Gallery; Historic Residences; the Royal Canadian Mint; the National Art Centre for Theatre and home of the Symphony Orchestra; the Experimental Farm and the Rideau Canal, famous for skating in the Winter time.

Le Gite Park Ave

Anne-Marie and Irving Bansfield
54 Park Avenue
Ottawa, Ontario
K2P 1B2
(613) 230-9131

Season: All year
Rates: Available upon request
Types of Accommodation: 2 Bedrooms and 1 Suite
Bathrooms: Private and Shared
Special Information: MasterCard, Visa and Travellers Cheques accepted; Children welcome
Languages: English and French
Directions: *Le Gite Park Avenue* is located at 54 Park Avenue in a residential area off Queen Elizabeth Drive. Park Avenue is located between Cartier and Elgin.

Haydon House

Haydon House is a quiet, spacious renovated Victorian-era home nestled in a tranquil residential district beside the picturesque Rideau Canal and the scenic Parkway. Its location makes this a perfect place for organizing a skating party in the Winter on the world's longest skating rink -- the Rideau Canal! But if you visit in the summer *Haydon House* has beautiful gardens for you to enjoy.

The Central location couldn't be more convenient as it is only a very short walk to the Parliament Buildings, the National Arts Centre, and many fine shops and restaurants.

Haydon House offers air-conditioned comfort, a private outdoor portico, sitting areas and spacious guest bedrooms. These are decorated with Canadian pine combined with colourful works of art, part of their collection of Canadiana.

There is a fireplace and a fine view of the Rideau Canal from one bedroom and another has a French door opening onto its private verandah complete with hammock.

Mary teaches local history; Andy is a Politican. Between them they can inform and enthuse you about Ottawa -- it's culture, history and current events.

HAYDON HOUSE

Mary and Andy Haydon
18 The Driveway
Ottawa, Ontario
K2P 1C6
(613) 230-2697

Season: All year
Rates: Single $50 Double $65 (includes all taxes)
Types of Accommodation: 2 Double, 1 Twin
Bathrooms: 2 Full Bathrooms and 1 Powder Room
Breakfast: Continental to Full
Special Information: Children welcome; Dog in residence named "Torran"; Air-conditioning; A birders' B&B
Languages: English and French
Directions: From Queensway, take Metcalfe Street Exit. Drive approximately 1 km to Somerset Street. Turn right onto Somerset Street. *Haydon House* is the last house on the left. - OR - Highway 16 becomes Queen Elizabeth Driveway. *Haydon House* is at the corner of Queen Elizabeth Driveway and Somerset. (You will drive under three bridges before you arrive at Somerset Street. Do not drive under the fourth or you will just have passed *Haydon House.*

McFarlane House

McFarlane House is one of a terrace row, built in 1868, that has been declared a Heritage Building, located near downtown in Sandy Hill, only a short walk from Parliament Hill and many of the city's attractions. Lenore and Paul Hunter preserved the house's period character through wide pine plank floors and high ceilings, then furnished it with contemporary comfort.

Guest accommodations are two luxurious air-conditioned suites, each with a private bath, telephone, and cable TV. One suite, on the second floor, features a large bright room with queen size bed and adjoining bath has a jacuzzi and separate double shower. The other takes in the entire third floor and has a divided bath and a small modern kitchen. There are two bedrooms, one with a double bed and the other with twin beds; this suite is very suitable for a family or two couples. Adjoining is a warm, inviting solarium (for winter) and the sun deck overlooking the Gatineau Hills and downtown Ottawa.

Breakfast could be, for example, waffles and maple syrup, or eggs and English muffins; but home-baking and fresh fruit are always a feature.

Lenore and Paul are experienced travellers and are more than happy to take time to explain the opportunities in Ottawa to guests. There is so much to do: good shopping; many National museums to visit; the National Arts Centre for live theatre and symphony concerts; historic homes that are open to public view; and interesting restaurants to try.

McFARLANE HOUSE

Lenore and Paul Hunter
201 Daly Avenue
Ottawa, Ontario
K1N 6G1
(613) 236-0095

Season: All year
Rates: Single $70 - $75 Double $85 - $90
Types of Accommodation: 1 Double, 1 Queen, and 1 Twin
Bathrooms: 3 Private
Breakfast: Full
Special Information: Non-smoking home; No guests' pets or young children; Telephone, colour cable TV and refrigerator in each room; Air-conditioning; Rates reduced by 15% after first night; No GST/PST
Languages: English, French and German
Directions: From Queensway (Highway 417) take Nicholas Exit; turn right at first light (Laurier Avenue); five lights to King Edward, continue through, next left (Nelson); 3 blocks to Daly Avenue; turn right. *McFarlane House* is the second house on the left.

Brae Briar "The Quilt House"

Brae Briar "The Quilt House" Bed and Breakfast is located on a quiet street, but very close to the main route to the Bruce Peninsula (Hwy 6).

This early 1900's home is furnished with antiques and hand-carved furniture. When you arrive a complimentary English afternoon tea is served (from 4-5 pm) either by the fireside or, weather permitting, on the verandah.

The entire second floor is reserved for guests; there is a twin-bedded room, a double-bedded room, and a queen size bedded room -- all the beds, of course, are made up with Elizabeth's home-made quilts. There is a large four-piece bathroom for guest use exclusively, and guests are provided with robes for that trip across the hall.

Gourmet breakfasts are hearty and unique and served in the Victorian dining room. Don makes a tasty cheese souffle, among other delights, and dishes are made more savoury with the addition of herbs from Elizabeth's garden. She even candies viola's to brighten the wintertime selections. Delicious picnic baskets are available by prearrangement for your day-time outing. The *Brae Briar* has central air-conditioning for your warm weather comfort.

This *Bed and Breakfast* is within easy walking distance of downtown. This is a great place for business people to stay who come to town, and since Owen Sound is in the ski belt, the best downhill skiing in Ontario is in this area.

Brae Briar
The Quilt House

Elizabeth and Don Yule
980 3rd Avenue West
Owen Sound, Ontario
N4K 4P6
(519) 371-0025

Season: All year
Rates: Single $40 Double $50
Types of Accommodation: Double, Queen, and Twin
Bathrooms: Shared four-piece
Breakfast: Full
Special Information: Non-smoking home; No guests' pets please; No facilities for small children; Picnic basket available; Reservations recommended
Directions: Located just off main route to Bruce Peninsula on west side of Owen Sound. Please call ahead for detailed directions.

Dundela

Dundela is on a peaceful street in the old west end of Peterborough. Situated on a rise and surrounded by mature trees, this neo-classical style home is airy and comfortable, and Elaine's warmth will make you feel instantly at home.

The two cheery sunrooms, inviting living room; and rec room guarantee that everyone will find a place to relax during their stay. The home is centrally air-conditioned to add to your comfort in hot weather. *Dundela* also offers a large, heated in-ground pool where guests may swim or take in the sun. Children are always welcome.

The guest bedrooms are decorated in a French Country style. The largest room, in rose and blue, with a two-piece bath, has both a single and double bed; good for a family. There is also a single and a double room which share a bath.

Come with a good appetite as Elaine serves a hearty breakfast in the pretty dining room, and hopes there is time for guests to enjoy a leisurely breakfast visit.

Peterborough and *Dundela* are situated in the heart of the Kawartha Lakes country on the Trent Canal system. Some area attractions are the Lang Pioneer Village, and Serpent Mounds. In Peterborough there is the Hydraulic Lift Locks, many nearby restaurants, and local theatre.

Elaine and Jenn Orgill
489 Gordon Avenue
Peterborough, Ontario
K9J 6G7
(705) 743-7228

Season: All year
Rates: Available upon request
Types of Accommodation: Single and Double
Bathrooms: Private and Shared
Breakfast: Full
Special Information: Children welcome; Air-conditioned; Heated in-ground pool
Directions: Go north on Monaghan Road to Woodland Street. Turn left; go west to Gordon Avenue.

PETERBOROUGH (Near Lakefield)
ONTARIO

...is an historic stone
...al homesteads built

...circa 1840, has
...re to create a bed
...nfort for travel-

...th period furnish-
...many-paned windows;
...floors, beautifully refinished; and
gracious central stairs.

Windmere has a family sitting room for an evening of conversation, and beautiful guest rooms. Two have semi-private baths and the "bed-sitting room" has a private bath. For more privacy, there is a self-contained housekeeping "Getaway Suite" available.

A hearty country breakfast, including hot muffins and home-made jams, is served in the breakfast room off the country kitchen.

Guests are invited to take a quiet walk around the grounds and by the pond, breathe the clean country air and just relax -- perhaps on the porch, or in the comfort of their room.

Windmere lies in the heart of the Kawartha Lakes district which offers a wealth of activities the year-round -- fishing and boating; skiing and hiking; galleries and theatre, all just minutes away.

WINDERMERE

Joan and Wally Wilkins
Selwyn, RR3
Lakefield, Ontario
K0L 2H0
(705) 652-6290

Fax: (705) 652-6949
Season: All year
Rates: Single $40 Double $50 - $60 Extra person $10 Self-contained Double Apartment $70
Types of Accommodation: 2 Double, 1 Twin
Bathrooms: 2 Private and 2 Semi-private
Breakfast: Full
Special Information: No smoking; No guests' pets; Central air-conditioning
Languages: English and some French
Directions: North on Highway 28 from Peterborough to Highway 507. North on Highway 507 to Selwyn. At Selwyn turn right and go 500 feet and turn right at the first driveway (20 km from Peterborough).

The Poplars B&B

The POPLARS B.+B.

Jean and Keith Whitney have refurbished and made comfortable their circa 1900 country farm home overlooking the Bay of Quinte at Telegraph Narrows. They are ideally suited for guests in fishing season (pickerel, bass) because they have docking facilities right at the bottom of their property and there is a boat launching facility near by.

The Poplars is air-conditioned for hot summers. The comfortable guest rooms are beautifully decorated; there is one queen en suite room available; children are welcome. Jean serves a generous home cooked breakfast in the cheerful dining room.

Prince Edward county is unique, in that it is bordered on nearly every side by water front. Although it is primarily a farming and fruit-growing area it also offers many recreational opportunities provided by the beaches and park reserves. Sandbanks Provincial Park, with excellent swimming, is only a short drive from *The Poplars*. Two golf courses are nearby.

The Poplars is located in the heart of Loyalist country (where the United Empire Loyalist first settled around 1790) and there are many antique shops and museums located in the area.

Jean and Keith Whitney
RR2
Picton, Ontario
K0K 2T0
(613) 476-3513

Season: All year
Rates: Single $35 Double $40 - $50
Types of Accommodation: 1 Double, 1 Queen, and 2 Twin
Bathrooms: 1 Private En Suite and 1 Shared 4-piece
Breakfast: Full
Special Information: Children welcome; No smoking in guest rooms; No guests' pets please; Air-conditioned; Meals offered on request
Directions: From Highway 401 take Exit 566 and go south on Highway 49 for 7.7 km to the Northport Road. Turn right onto the Northport Road and go 1.5 km to *The Poplars*. (Look for the sign on the north side of the road).

Crabapple Creek B&B

Crabapple Creek Bed and Breakfast is Mary Burfoot's much beloved family home, built in 1930 by her Grandfather for her father and mother. This spacious solid brick home has large, many-paned Georgian style windows, which let in lots of light; beautiful chestnut woodwork and panelling; white oak floors; a cosy library with a fireplace; and comfortable living room, also with a fireplace; both places where guests can relax and read, or visit.

The central hall stair leads to the country style guest rooms. Mary serves an English cooked breakfast with home-made bread and jams in the dining room. There is also a sun or Florida room with a skylight and casement windows facing three directions where guests can lounge.

The secluded location of *Crabapple Creek Bed and Breakfast* makes it an ideal stopover for Birders" or Nature Lovers. Besides extensive lawns and gardens, there is about seven acres of forested area that surrounds the buildings and is bordered by the creek. And a very old Crabapple Tree, for which the B&B gets its name, has been growing along the lane for over 100 years.

Port Dover, very nearby, is an unspoiled historic lakeside fishing town where one can browse through craft and antique shops, visit the Marine Museum, or dine. The Light House Theatre offers excellent professional theatre in the summertime. *Crabapple Creek* is eight km from Hay Creek Conservation Area for good swimming and 40 km from Long Point.

CRABAPPLE CREEK B.+B.

Mary Burfoot
RR2
Port Dover, Ontario
N0A 1N2
(519) 583-2509

Season: All year
Rates: Single $35 Double $40 Twin $50 Family $60
Types of Accommodation: 4 Double, 1 Queen, 1 Twin
Bathrooms: 2 Shared
Breakfast: Full
Special Information: Children and pets welcome; Dog named "Hazel" and 3 Cats named "Toby", "Tabitha" and "Daisy" in residence
Handicapped Facilities: Limited
Directions: *Crabapple Creek* is 5 km south of Highway 3 or north of Port Dover on Regional Road 5.

Colette's B&B

You will enjoy the convenience and comfort of Colette Savary's turn-of-the-century home. *Colette's* is located on tree-lined Market Street, one block from Port Elgin's Main Street and a ten-minute stroll from the beautiful sandy beaches of Lake Huron.

The comfortable guest bedrooms are prettily decorated in country Victorian style. Colette serves a home-style breakfast in her cheerful dining area; a special picnic basket for your outing at the beach or tour of the area is available by prearrangement. Tea, coffee, juice, and a snack is served every evening.

Port Elgin is a busy lakeside town which offers, besides the beach, an excellent marina for sailors, pleasure boaters and deep sea fishermen. Snowmobile and cross-country ski trails make this area a four-season destination.

COLETTE'S B.+B.

Colette Savary
650 Market Street
Port Elgin, Ontario
N0H 2C0
(519) 832-5787

Season: All year
Rates: Single $40 Double $50
Types of Accommodation: 2 Double, 1 Twin
Bathrooms: 2 Full
Breakfast: Full
Special Information: No children under 13; Non-smoking home; No guests' pets please
Languages: English and French
Directions: Travel on Highway 21 of the Bruce Peninsula. *Colette's* is one block east of Port Elgin's main street (Goderich Street).

Amaryllis

The *Amaryllis* has the unique distinction of being the only Bed and Breakfast in this book that can only be reached by boat. You must take the water-taxi from the small village of Rockport or arrange to be picked up by your host, Pieter Bergen, at the town dock. After a pleasant fifteen minute boat ride across the Bay past the islands, you reach the place where the 100 foot-long, double-deck houseboat *Amaryllis* is permanently docked on its own seven and one-half acres island, in the middle of the Thousand Island region.

Originally built as a private hunting and fishing lodge to float around the St. Lawrence, it later became a stationary summertime home. A large verandah deck, living room with fireplace, and dining room overlook the water and forested shores. Guest accommodation includes single, double or twin bedrooms. All look out across the water; each room has its own full, private bathroom. The decor is a mixture of period and contemporary, combined to produce a pleasing comfortable effect. Breakfast is served in the dining room or on the sundeck.

The Island itself is in a semi-wild state; paths wind through stands of white pine and other native trees. Beds of brilliant green moss and wildflowers grow among the pink and white quartz which is part of the area's geology. Deer and many species of fowl including duck, geese, wild turkey, loons, and owls frequent the islands. Fish such as bass, pickerel, perch, and muskellunge swim in the clear waters.

Gourmet meals are available to overnight guests; traditional fish shore dinners cooked over an open fire are frequently held. Island picnics, and private boat tours can be arranged.

This area offers all sorts of water recreation -- boating, sailing, and swimming and there is golfing nearby, on shore of course.

ROCKPORT (East of Gananoque) ONTARIO

AMARYLLIS B.+B.

Pieter Bergan, Janet Rodier
Rockport, Ontario
K0E 1V0
(613) 659-3513

Season: June 1 - October 15
Rates: Available upon request
Types of Accommodation: 3 Bedrooms
Bathrooms: 3 Private
Breakfast: Full
Special Information: No smoking please; Additional Gourmet meals available
Languages: English, French and Spanish
Directions: Transportation by water taxi from Rockport on 1,000 Islands Parkway can be had at Andress Boatworks; or arrange pick up by family boat at slight charge.

Pinescape

Pinescape has a truly magnificent hilltop setting that gives a panoramic view of the Waterloo County countryside. The twenty-five acre site has trails through the woods and pastures for walking or cross-country skiing, and a large inground swimming pool, where guests may relax or swim.

Your hosts, Chip and Gail Hovey, offer a friendly welcome to their spacious colonial style house, with its tall, pillared facade. They offer guest rooms with a double bed and private bath; a firm king size waterbed with four-piece en suite and fireplace; or, for the special romantic occasion, a luxurious large private suite which includes king size waterbed, a steam shower, jacuzzi, TV, and screened porch.

Breakfast can include fresh fruit salad, hearty home-made waffles, and bottomless carafes of beverage. Your hosts are happy to accommodate special requests because of food allergies.

How about picnic lunches, a barbecue, or a fireside bowl of chili? Try a relaxing midday snooze, or an evening of star-gazing in the double rope hammock!

Refrigerator and laundry facilities are available to guests. Transportation and babysitting facilities may be prearranged.

Pinescape is located just one hour from Toronto International Airport, ten or fifteen minutes from Kitchener-Waterloo and universities, theatres, museums, golfing and other Waterloo County fare -- from quilts and buggies to pigs' tails and apple strudel. Stratford, the home of the internationally known professional classical theatre, the Shakespearean Festival, is only thirty minutes away.

ST. AGATHA (West of Kitchener-Waterloo) ONTARIO

PINESCAPE

Chip (F.W.) and Gail Hovey
RR1
St. Agatha, Ontario
N0B 2L0
(519) 886-2995

Season: All year
Rates: $50 and up
Types of Accommodation: 1 Double, 1 Queen, and 2 King
Bathrooms: 4 Private
Breakfast: Full
Special Information: Non-smoking home; No guests' pets please; Air-conditioning
Languages: English and un peu de Français
Directions: From Highway 7 west of Kitchener, go north on Waterloo County Road 12 to third sideroad north of St. Agatha; turn right onto Wilmot 2; drive 2 miles to stone pillars on right hand side, and up the winding driveway.

Avonview Manor

Avonview Manor Bed and Breakfast is well named; beyond the back garden a gate opens onto Riverside Park and from here you can take a pleasant ten minute stroll along the Avon River to downtown Stratford. The lovely sunroom provides a view of the park-like backyard with flower beds and an inground pool. Here, in this cheery room, a full breakfast is served each morning to guests by you hostesses, sisters Lynne and Gail Doupe.

Beautiful leaded and stained glass windows complement the ambiance created by the quarter cut oak panelled woodwork and solid oak staircase. Delicate Murals, painted in the early 1900's, decorate the entrance foyer and stair-well of this gracious Edwardian home.

The guest bedrooms have quilts and furnishings in keeping with the period of the house. There is a large upstairs sunroom too, with windows all around, and, again a view of the Avon; it has four single beds -- good for groups or families.

Stratford, of course, is the home of the Shakespearean Festival; some of the best classical Theatre in North America is performed in three theatres here. People come from all over each year, April to early November, to see Shakespearean works and many others.

Stratford has many interesting specialty shops and boutiques. Gallery Stratford has an ever-changing repertoire of shows. Antique collectors should have a very interesting time around Stratford, and Shakespeare (to the east), and Sebringville (to the west), visiting the many local shops. There are many restaurants in Stratford for fine dining.

AVONVIEW MANOR

Lynne and Gail Doupe
63 Avon Street
Stratford, Ontario
N5A 5N5
(519) 273-4603

Season: All year
Rates: Double $55 plus PST
Types of Accommodation: 3 Queen and 1 Twin (4 beds)
Bathrooms: 2 Shared
Breakfast: Full
Special Information: No guests' pets please; Dog named "Katy" in residence; Guest kitchen with tea and coffee available; Ironing board for guest use; Children over age 8 welcome.
Directions: Follow Ontario Street (the main street) onto Huron Street. Go across the river to the first stoplight. Turn left on John Street. Go 3 blocks to Avon Street. Turn left.

Birmingham Manor

Birmingham Manor's impressive entrance hall has so many things that immediately command one's attention. The magnificent oak panelling, the warmth of the green-tile fireplace; the spacious black and white tile floor which extends into the adjacent music room; a reproduction telephone booth, a built-in deacon's bench with floral tapestry; and, leading upward; the grand oak staircase with a Juliet balcony, to name a few.

The rest of the house echoes this unique first impression of delightful artistic flamboyance. The music room has daring red walls and an ebony grand piano. The den invites casual gatherings and lingering conversation on comfortable upholstered furniture. The dining room, the setting for breakfast and afternoon tea, is damask rose with a plum carpet, and has wainscotting and a fireplace to produce a cheerful atmosphere. Interesting paintings hang in all the rooms.

The upper hall is a continuation of the foyer, with the same "Chelsea Prize" red as the music room; a French period console is centrally located for the early morning coffee to which guests may help themselves.

All the spacious guest rooms have access to their own en suite and each has been named for a British Castle; hence the Windsor, Sandringham, Hampton Court, and Balmoral Rooms. Each room is a delight to the eye as great care again has been taken to create artistic unity. For instance, the Balmoral room, named after the royal summer residence, appropriately reflects eternal summer, in a profusion of ribbons and bows wallpaper pattern. The generous window seat offers the ideal spot to gaze out upon the trees and lawns.

Stratford is the home of the Shakespearean Festival, worldclass professional theatre, including a musical production. The downtown offers interesting shops and fine dining. Lake Victoria and acres of beautiful parkland are right in the heart of the city.

BIRMINGHAM MANOR

J.P. Michaels
240 Birmingham Street
Stratford, Ontario
N5A 2T5
(519) 273-6545

Season: June 15 - October 15
Rates: $89 plus tax
Types of Accommodation: 4 Queen
Bathrooms: 4 Private
Breakfast: Continental
Special Information: No children under 15 years of age; Non-smoking home - smoking on verandah; No guests' pets please; Central air-conditioning
Directions: Take Highway 8 to Stratford (Ontario Street) to Erie Street (left turn) to West Gore (right turn) to Birmingham Street.

Deacon House

Deacon House is located within walking distance of downtown Stratford, restaurants and theatres; it is a turn-of-the-century house that has been designated a heritage home by the Ontario Heritage Foundation. Dr. George Deacon, an early Stratford physician, had the house built in 1907 in an Americanized version of the Queen Anne Style.

You enter *Deacon House* into the spacious, open foyer with beautiful oak panelling, and beamed ceiling, highlighted by an 1870 Quebec pine Deacon's bench! The living room with its attractive and comfortable couches is inviting to guests, who can pause here for a moment during a busy day; in cooler weather a cosy fire crackles in the fireplace.

Guest rooms are on the second and third floors, three with private baths, and the rest with semiprivate. There are claw foot tubs and original wainscotting in two bathrooms, complemented by period decor. The guest rooms are decorated in country style with antique iron and brass, or four poster rope beds. Amish quilts, antique dressers, rag style rugs and whimsical accessories convey nostalgia for yesteryear. All guest rooms have ceiling fans, and all are air-conditioned. A second floor common room is decorated in garden style, created through botanical prints, plants and trellised ceiling. Here guests are tempted by comfortable couches and many books and magazines to relax and browse awhile. The whimsical mood is carried throughout the house by delightful discoveries of many one-of-a-kind stuffed animals, dolls and toys.

A generous continental breakfast is served buffet style in the dining room, which is furnished with an antique corner cupboard, and a flatback displaying a unique china collection. The breakfast offering includes seasonal fruit, home baking, home-made jams, an assortment of cheeses, bagels, croissants, cold cereals, coffee and tea. A guest kitchen with a supply of tea, coffee, cookies, and fruits is available, just beyond the dining room, for guest use.

DEACON HOUSE

Mary Allen and Dianna Hrysko
101 Brunswick Street
Stratford, Ontario
N5A 3L9
(519) 273-2052

Season: All year
Rates: $52 and up plus PST and GST
Types of Accommodation: 5 Double, 1 Queen and 1 Twin
Bathrooms: 3 Private and 2 Shared
Breakfast: Extended Continental Buffet
Special Information: Two cats in residence named "Lucy" and "Offence"; Children welcome on request; All bedrooms air-conditioned
Directions: Take Highway 7 to Nile Street (eastern downtown). Travel south on Nile for two blocks and west on Brunswick for one half block.

Eighteen Waterloo B&B

Eighteen Waterloo is an excellent location from which to walk to Stratford sites and Theatres, a few steps from the river and a couple of blocks from downtown.

This turn-of-the-century yellow brick home has been renovated, furnished with Canadian antiques and comfortable contemporary furniture. Oriental rugs are scattered on the warm hardwood floors and books line the living room walls.

The guest rooms are comfortable and light. Two of the guest rooms have queen size beds and share a bath; the large twin-bedded room has a bath en suite and a balcony with a view of Lake Victoria.

Continental breakfast is served in the dining room or on the verandah with a water view. Bicycles are available for guests to use. The house is air-conditioned.

Stratford is the home of the Shakespearean Festival; people come from all over to view world-class productions presented at three theatres, the Tom Patterson Theatre, the Avon and the Festival Theatre, from May to early November. Plays include Shakespearean works, other plays and a musical.

Downtown Stratford has many shops, boutiques, galleries, and fine restaurants. Gallery Stratford offers changing shows.

Kathy See
18 Waterloo Street North
Stratford, Ontario
N5A 5H5
(519) 271-9653

Season: All year
Rates: $55 and up
Types of Accommodation: 2 Queen and 1 Twin
Bathrooms: Private and Shared
Breakfast: Continental - Full
Special Information: Air-conditioned; Non-smoking home; Children 6 and up welcome; No guests' pets please; Cat in residence named "Bailey"
Languages: English, German and some French and Spanish
Directions: Turn north on Waterloo Street (at Queen's Inn), cross bridge and 18 Waterloo is the third house on the left hand side after the bridge.

Harrington House in the Pines

Only fifteen minutes from Stratford, *Harrington House in the Pines* is an unique house situated on forty-two scenic treed acres in the highlands of Zorra Township. This pine and hardwood forest has cross-country skiing or hiking trails wandering throughout the rolling property and linking up with the Avon Hiking Trail (from Kitchener to St. Marys, 100 km). Wildwood Lake, a conservation area and bird sanctuary, is to the east. The woods are a natural habitat for animals and birds, and a great place for "Birders" to come.

Harrington House, with its dark brown exterior, was constructed to blend into its natural setting. The spacious, open-concept interior comes as a surprise and has been a source of delight for your hosts, Lloyd and Helen, and the many guests who have enjoyed their "getaway" visits. Four ten by eight windows and four large patio doors look westerly into a variety of beautiful landscapes and the distant horizon. The master bedroom has an eight by eight view of this panorama. And every creature comfort is provided by your hosts in this ultra natural surrounding.

The en suite guest rooms have king size beds; the home is air conditioned and dust/pollen/smoke free. A full delicious breakfast is served.

As well as being very close to Stratford and the Shakespearean Festival, *Harrington House in the Pines* is thirty-five minutes from either London or Kitchener, and one and one-half hours from Toronto International Airport. Its natural beauty and quiet makes it a great place for getaway weekends any time of the year!

Lloyd and Helen Davis
RR3
Embro, Ontario
N0J 1J0
(519) 475-4760

Season: All year
Rates: Available upon request
Types of Accommodation: Single, Double, Twin and Getaway Suite
Bathrooms: Private and Shared
Breakfast: Full
Special Information: Central air-conditioned; Dust/pollen and smoke free home
Directions: *Harrington House in the Pines* is located in the scenic highlands of Zorra, *Harrington House* is only 15 minutes from Stratford. Please call for detailed directions.

Three Gables

Built in 1876, *Three Gables in Stratford* is a charming example of the Gothic Revival style, situated centrally in Stratford, exactly one mile from the Festival Theatre.

Three Gables has gracious rooms, high ceilings, with lovely old wood trim and period furnishings. The central staircase curves up to the second level where there are three comfortable guest rooms, and one and a half baths shared by guests only. The second floor reading area has relaxing comfortable chairs where guests can linger awhile and visit. The house is centrally air-conditioned.

Barbara and Ted offer an extended continental breakfast served in the beautiful dining room from 8:00 to 9:00 am.

From *Three Gables* one can easily walk to the river, to Stratford's beautiful Shakespearean Gardens, and downtown, where there are many interesting shops, galleries, and fine restaurants. The Avon Theatre and the Tom Patterson Theatre, a little further east along the river, can also be reached on foot, if you are a walker; and you may even want to walk as far as the Festival Theatre.

There is much to do in the area around Stratford. You may wish to take a day trip to Kitchener-Waterloo, visit the bountiful Farmers' Market there and drive through Mennonite country. Another day trip could be to the lovely little village of Bayfield on Lake Huron. Shakespeare, just ten minutes east of Stratford, is an antique hunter's paradise. Or for more theatre, Canadian plays only this time, a day trip to the little Huron County village of Blyth would be an interesting idea.

THREE GABLES

Ted and Barbara Baxter
122 Mornington Street
Stratford, Ontario
N5A 5G1
(519) 271-1513

Season: All year
Rates: Double $58 and up
Types of Accommodation: 1 Queen, 2 Twin
Bathrooms: Four-piece and Two-piece
Breakfast: Extended Continental
Special Information: Adult guests only please; Non-smoking home; No guests' pets please; Resident dog named "Cashmere"; Air-conditioning
Languages: English and French
Directions: *Three Gables in Stratford* is on the north side of the river, between Waterloo and Huron Streets.

Maple Lawn Farm B&B

Maple Lawn Farm Bed and Breakfast is a mordenized 1837 stone home set among maples on spacious lawns and gardens. The atmosphere is that of a country farm home with comfortable old-fashioned bedrooms and an original three-sided verandah sets this home apart.

There is a craft shop on the premises where guests may browse; a full country breakfast is served in the dining area off the kitchen consisting of home-baked muffins, bacon, eggs, home-made jams and marmalade.

Sydenham is just north of Kingston and the Thousand Island Tourist region. Use *Maple Lawn Farm Bed and Breakfast* as your headquarters for touring this historic old area. At Kingston guests can visit Old Fort Henry and many museums and the restored home of Sir John A. MacDonald, Canada's first Prime Minister. There are tours of the Thousand Islands from Kingston. Kingston is the home of Queen's University.

The Rideau Walking Trail crosses the *Maple Lawn* property and hikers may make arrangements to be dropped off and then hike as far as the farm.

SYDENHAM (North of Kingston) ONTARIO

MAPLE LAWN FARM

Lillian Preslar
Box 19
Sydenham, Ontario
K0H 2T0
(613) 376-3127

Season: All year
Rates: Single $25 Double $40 Twin $45
Types of Accommodation: 3 Single, 2 Queen, and 1 Twin
Bathrooms: 2 Shared
Breakfast: Full
Special Information: Non-smoking home; Children welcome; No guests' pets please; Dog in residence named "Major Pete"; A birders' B&B
Handicapped Facilities: Limited
Directions: Take Exit 613 north of Highway 401, proceed to Sydenham. In the village take Wheatley Street between the two schools, go two blocks to the stop sign, turn right, proceed past IGA and turn right. Proceed 1 km to 12 km sign to Frontenac Provincial Park. Make sharp left turn onto 6 Concession Road. Proceed straight on the road for 1.6 km. *Maple Lawn Farm* is the second stone house.

Blue Shutter Guest Home

A curved red brick drive leads up to the guest entry of this beautifully restored pre-1890 Victorian home. Mature trees and lovely flower beds, lawns and gardens surround the house. Inside, high ceilings, spacious rooms with original wood trim and plaster mouldings, period draperies and furniture all contribute to the splendid traditional elegance. A grand piano sits in the front room; John and Alyson are the family pianists.

Mary Lou serves a hearty breakfast in the dining room; and afternoon tea, with home-made biscuits, on the two-storey gazebo porch at the side of the house. The second storey of the porch serves as the private sun porch for the second floor king bedded suite with whirlpool bath. There is also a twin, king, and queen with en suite washrooms. All the rooms are beautifully furnished and decorated, and air conditioned.

The location of the *Blue Shutter Guest Home* in Tavistock means that it is a short distance from both Kitchener-Waterloo, known for Markets and Mennonite country, and Stratford, renowned for the Shakespearean Festival; professional theatre as good or better than any other in North America.

There are three golf courses nearby for those who enjoy this type of recreation. Shakespeare, the hamlet of many antique stores, is five minutes up the road from Tavistock. There are restaurants in Stratford and Shakespeare for fine dining. Your hosts, John and Mary Lou, will be happy to help plan your local tours.

Stratford has the "Festival" Tavistock has the *"Blue Shutter"* say's Roy Lenard of Chicago.

BLUE SHUTTER GUEST HOUSE

John and Mary Lou Appleton
106 William Street, South, Box 135
Tavistock, Ontario
N0B 2R0
(519) 655-2643

Season: All year
Rates: Single $50 Double $75 Suite with whirlpool $100
Types of Accommodation: 4 Single, 2 King, 1 Queen and 1 Twin
Bathrooms: 4 Private
Breakfast: Full
Special Information: Non-smoking home; Children over 10 years welcome; Air-conditioning
Directions: *Blue Shutter Guest House* is 15 minutes southeast of Stratford. William Street is two blocks west of the traffic lights off Highway 59. *Blue Shutter* is the second house on the right beside the Maple's Home for Seniors.

Idle Inn

The Georgian Bay area is an all-season place to visit; mile after mile of apple blossoms in the Springtime; swimming and sailing in the summertime; fall fairs and apple picking in the Autumn; the best downhill skiing in Ontario in Winter; hiking the Bruce Trail at any time of year. The location of the *Idle Inn Bed and Breakfast* makes it a great place to use as your headquarters for any or all of these activities.

A wonderful turn-of-the-century Victorian-cum-Edwardian home, with wrap around classical verandah, the *Idle Inn* has large sunny rooms with tasteful period furnishings. The upstairs has three comfortable guest rooms and a balcony at the back opening up to a view of the garden. Barb serves a full breakfast in the comfortable dining room. The house sits on a street of mature trees surrounded by a large lawn and flower beds. In summer, hanging baskets and flower boxes bloom profusely all around the verandah.

The town of Thornbury is noted for being central to the area apple harvest; and is located right on the Southern shores of Georgian Bay. From the *Idle Inn* guests can walk everywhere; browse through local antique and craft shops; attend theatre; walk to the water front; or a short distance away there is golfing in the summer or downhill and cross-country skiing in the Winter.

Barb and Dave Collie
74 Bruce Street South
Thornbury, Ontario
N0H 2P0
(519) 599-6505

Season: All year
Rates: Single $40 Double $50 and up
Types of Accommodation: 2 Queen, 1 Twin
Bathrooms: 1 Three-piece and 1 Two-piece
Breakfast: Full
Special Information: Children welcome; Non-smoking home; No guests' pets please
Directions: *Idle Inn* is west of Collingwood and east of Meaford off Highway 26. When you reach the traffic lights at Thornbury (Bruce Street) turn south two blocks to number 74. *Idle Inn* is next door to the Baptist Church, which is on the corner of Bruce and Alice Streets.

The Blue Spruce Manor

The Blue Spruce Manor is a lovely colonial style home located in a wooded ravine setting fronted by a blue spruce, which, planted long ago by the Molnar's, has grown to become the focal point at the front of their home. Electric candles glow in the windows when guests are in residence.

Sylvia Molnar enjoyed her bed and breakfast holidays so much that she and her family decided to open their own home to guests. *The Blue Spruce Manor* motto is that "hosting is offering lovely rooms with special amenities, and breakfasts that guests look forward to in the setting of the warm hospitality of a private home".

Blue Spruce Manor has central air-conditioning and a heated inground pool for guests to enjoy. Tea is provided to guests arriving in the afternoon. A sumptuous breakfast is served at the beautifully appointed table in the formal dining room, or, weather permitting, on the poolside patio. A ribbon bound breakfast menu appears each evening on the bedroom door.

The guest bedrooms at *Blue Spruce Manor* are comfortable and charming, with hardwood floors and attractive decor. The "Victoria Room" has a four poster canopy bed and beautiful bedding.

Tillsonburg is on the Otter River which flows south into Lake Erie. The town's Annandale House Museum was a Victorian mansion, built between 1880 and 1883, and today features changing historical displays and special events. Tillsonburg is an agricultural town with a large shopping area, including craft shops, a large Farmers' Market, and the Dolls in Toyland Shop and Museum. Also worth visiting is the Historic Great Western Railway Station which houses the Baggage Room Craft Shop and Art Gallery.

The Blue Spruce Manor

Sylvia Molnar and Family
51 Parkwood Drive
Tillsonburg, Ontario
N4G 2B7
(519) 842-2910

Fax: (519) 842-2412 (office)
Season: All year, except Christmas and New Years
Rates: Single $40 Double $50 - $55
Types of Accommodation: 1 Single, 1 Double and 1 Queen
Bathrooms: 1 Private and 1 Shared
Breakfast: Full Gourmet
Special Information: Adult guests only please; Non-smoking home; No guest's pets; Schnauzer Dog in residence named "Kringles"; Air-conditioned; Dinner served and picnic lunches with advanced reservations; Special Getaway Weekend package
Languages: English and a little German
Directions: Please phone for directions.

Beaconsfield B&B

BEACONSFIELD B&B.

This large brick Victorian home dates from 1882. Guests have used such terms as "unconventional", "fun", and "artistic" to describe this bed and breakfast -- good words! Katya and Bernie are in the acting and painting arts, respectively, and their interests are reflected in their colourful home, full of art, antiques and collectibles, books and plants.

The guest accommodations are reached by a common hall and are separate from the family quarters. Two side-by-side bedrooms share a bathroom, a sitting room/kitchenette and outdoor deck -- great for two couples travelling together or a family. When the second bedroom is vacant, a couple might have the whole area to themselves!

For Honeymooners or those who desire something special, with total privacy, Beaconsfield offers the third floor "San Miguel Suite" with its own living room, bathroom, kitchenette and sundeck. Bernie's original paintings and Katya's romantic tropical decor were inspired by their love of Mexico where they have spent much time.

A generous breakfast, served in their eclectic dining room, is designed around guests' preferences and may include seasonal treats such as the peaches and raspberries that Katya grows in the backyard. Toronto newspapers, books, maps and brochures are always available, along with personalized sightseeing and restaurant suggestions.

Beaconsfield Bed and Breakfast is on an architecturally historic street, within walking distance of Ontario Place and Exhibition Place; it is half a block from the Queen streetcar and a 10 minute ride to City Hall, the Eaton Centre, SkyDome, CN Tower, Chinatown, and major theatres such as the Pantages, Royal Alex and Elgin Theatres. Along the way is "Queen Street West", an avant garde strip of fascinating one-of-a-kind shops, music and bookstores, trendy boutiques and charming bistros.

Bernie and Katya McLoughlin
38 Beaconsfield Avenue
Toronto, Ontario
M6J 3H9
(416) 535-3338

Season: All year
Rates: Single $55 Double $65 Suite $95
Types of Accommodation: 2 Queen, 1 Twin or King
Bathrooms: 1 Private and 1 Shared
Breakfast: Full
Special Information: Smoking on outdoor decks or verandah; On-site parking; Colour TV; Air-conditioning
Languages: English, Spanish, Slavic languages and some French and German
Directions: From Gardiner Expressway, take either Jameson or Spadina Exits; go north to Queen Street. Beaconsfield Avenue is between Dufferin and Ossington.

Beverley Place B&B

Beverley Place's location is extremely convenient; this 1887 Victorian house is in the heart of the University of Toronto Campus area. William Ricciuto has lovingly put back his home to its original condition restoring and refinishing the beautiful floors, woodwork and banisters, and furnishing the gracious high-ceilinged rooms with antiques and works of art. The living room houses a grand piano for the music lover.

The guest bedrooms are all comfortable and beautifully furnished. There is a Honeymoon or Getaway self-contained suite on the third floor with a deck and private entrance. A full breakfast is served in the glass-walled kitchen overlooking a charming enclosed courtyard. The house is air-conditioned and air-cleaned.

From *Beverley Place* one can stroll to all the downtown Toronto attractions such as City Hall and Law Courts, historic Queen's Park, which houses the Government of Ontario, the Royal Ontario Museum, the Art Gallery of Ontario, Eaton Centre, the Convention Centre, CN Tower, the SkyDome, Harbourfront, Yorkville, the Roy Thomson Hall and several hospitals.

Toronto Transit, close by, will take you further -- to Black Creek Pioneer Village, the Toronto Zoo, the Toronto Island and Canada's Wonderland, to name a few places.

BEVERLEY PLACE

William Ricciuto
235 Beverley Street
Toronto, Ontario
M5T 1Z4
(416) 977-0077

Season: All year
Rates: Single $35 - $55 Double $50 - $65 Self-contained Apartment $75 - $85
Types of Accommodation: 2 Double
Bathrooms: Private and En Suite
Breakfast: Full
Special Information: Restricted Smoking; Air-conditioned; Kitchen and laundry facilities
Directions: Take QEW-Gardiner to Spadina north to Queen Street, then east to Beverley Street and north on Beverley. From Hwy 401 go west to Don Valley South, to Bloor Street West exit to St. George, go south on St. George where it becomes Beverley Street at College.

Burken Guest House

The stone gate posts and ornate street lamps of Palmerston Boulevard are a reflection of the time past when this was an area of stately homes. *Burken Guest House* is one of those homes as shown by the pillared two-storey porch and balcony. Burke and Ken live on the main floor. Guests have a separate front entrance and stairway to reach the rooms on the second and third floor. All the guest rooms are individually decorated and furnished with period decor such as wing-backed chairs, brass chandeliers, and tasteful wallpaper. Every room is equipped with a washbasin and there is a shared guest bathroom on each floor.

Ken and Burke serve breakfast in the second floor dining area which opens out onto a deck and has access to the back garden. There is a guest sitting area and TV lounge on the third floor.

Toronto is a very interesting city to visit and *Burken Guest House* is handy to Toronto Transit. Besides the Toronto Zoo, the Ontario Science Centre, the Royal Ontario Museum, the SkyDome and the CN Tower there are theatres, restored historical homes, China Town, shopping in varied and interesting parts of the city, and a plethora of restaurants of every ethnic variety to choose from.

BURKEN GUEST HOUSE

Kenneth Bosher and Burke Friedrichkeit
322 Palmerston Boulevard
Toronto, Ontario
M6G 2N6
(416) 920-7842

Fax: (416) 960-9529
Season: All year
Rates: Single $45 and up Double $60 - $65
Types of Accommodation: 3 Single, 5 Double
Bathrooms: 2 Shared Bathrooms and 1 Washroom
Breakfast: Continental
Special Information: Non-smoking home; No guests' pets
Languages: English, German, and French
Directions: Two blocks west off Bathurst, four houses north off College.

The English Corner B&B

ENGLISH CORNER B.+B.

This charming Bed and Breakfast is a spacious brick and stucco English Tudor-style home, situated under tall old shade trees on a large corner lot in the Toronto Annex. When you step inside the front door of this sparkling clean home your eye is met by gleaming wood, lovely panelling, light streaming through many-paned windows and the charming decor. There is a large living room with a fireplace and a couple of quiet glassed-in sitting nooks where guests may relax for reading or talk.

The elegant bedrooms echo the charming decor of the first floor, and a delicious healthy breakfast is served at the beautifully-appointed dining room table beside a big bow-window.

The English Corner's Annex location means that it is an area of old Toronto homes, quiet tree-lined streets, yet with easy access to Toronto Transit and the rest of the city. One can walk to much that is close by: the University of Toronto Campus; Casa Loma, a refurbished many-roomed chateau; Bloor Street shopping and a variety of ethnic restaurants. Yorkville, a restored area of unique shops and eating places is a few minutes away. Fred and Carol give their guests careful help finding their way around the city.

Other attractions might be the CN Tower; the Roy Thomson Concert Hall; Ontario Place; and Harbour Front and Toronto Island. Places worth visiting that are a little further away are the Toronto Zoo; the Science Centre, Black Creek Pioneer Village and Canada's Wonderland.

Carol and Fred Hansen
114 Bernard Avenue
Toronto, Ontario
M5R 1S3
(416) 967-6474

Season: All year
Rates: Single $60 Double $75
Types of Accommodation: 1 Single, 2 Double, 1 Queen, 1 Twin
Bathrooms: 2 Shared
Breakfast: Full
Special Information: Adults with children over 12 years; Non-smoking home; No guests' pets; Room air-conditioners
Directions: *The English Corner* is between Avenue Road and Bloor Street. Please call for detailed directions.

Feathers

Feathers is a charming Victorian townhouse located in the Annex district of Toronto, a five-minute walk from the Bathurst Subway Station at Bloor Street. The Annex, just above the University of Toronto campus area, is within walking distance of many Toronto attractions -- the Bloor Street shopping district with its European flavour, numerous excellent restaurants and cafes offering a variety of ethnic cuisine and outdoor seating on tree-lined sidewalks, antique shops, bookstores and live Theatre. Torontonians come to this neighbourhood from all over the city to dine, shop and be entertained. Yorkville is close for art galleries, boutiques and restaurants. The University of Toronto, the Royal Ontario Museum and Casa Loma are all near at hand. The Annex is an architectural mixture of older homes, established trees, and quiet streets.

The guest bedrooms at *Feathers* are decorated with antique furniture and china, oriental carpets and original artwork. There is a colour TV in each room. *Feathers* also offers a getaway self-contained suite with cooking facilities and a separate entrance, ideal for honeymooners and families.

A delicious breakfast of fresh fruit cup, assorted cereals and a variety of rolls, breads or muffins is served in the elegant dining area which is part of the spacious open-concept living room design. *Feathers* is centrally air-conditioned. May is always ready to offer advice about getting around Toronto.

Toronto is a city of Theatre and restored Historical Homes, such as the MacKenzie House which offers a special welcome to tourists at Christmas. One can visit the CN Tower; the Roy Thomson Hall for a Symphony Concert; the Art Gallery of Ontario or the Eaton Centre, to name a few places. Or you can go further afield to the Toronto Zoo, Toronto Island and Canada's Wonderland.

FEATHERS

May Jarvie
132 Wells Street
Toronto, Ontario
M5R 1P4
(416) 534-1923

Season: All year
Rates: Single $38 - $55 Double $50 - $65 Extra person $15
Types of Accommodation: 4 Single, 2 Double, 1 Queen or Twin
Bathrooms: 1 Private and 2 Shared
Breakfast: Continental Plus
Special Information: Children welcome; Well behaved pets allowed but no cats (allergies); Central air
Languages: English, Dutch, French and German
Directions: From Bloor/Spadina intersection go west four blocks to Albany Street. Turn right. Go two blocks to Wells Street. Turn left.

Orchard View B&B

Orchard View, a spacious renovated house, is located in the Yonge-Eglinton area, the hub of Metropolitan Toronto. A quick transit ride takes you to other parts of the city.

Donna and Ken Ketchen's home is airy and bright with two areas for guests -- a double with private bath, and a twin with an adjoining sitting room and shared en suite. In summer there is a third floor balcony at the back, overlooking the small garden, and a lower floor patio where a full breakfast may be served. Off street parking is provided in the backyard. The home is centrally air conditioned.

During the summer a full breakfast is served on the deck.

There is much to do in Toronto; Metro's restaurants offer a world tour of fine cuisine. City transit takes you to the SkyDome, the Royal Ontario Museum, Harbourfront, Casa Loma, the CN Tower, the Art Gallery of Ontario, Chinatown and the Eaton Centre. If you have a car, *Orchard View's* location offers access north to Highway 401 and the Metro Toronto Zoo; the McMichael Gallery, which houses the finest collection of Canada's famous Group of Seven painters; Pioneer Village; and Canada's Wonderland.

Donna and Ken Ketchen
92 Orchard View Boulevard
Toronto, Ontario
M4R 1C2
(416) 488-6826

Season: All year
Rates: Single $50 Double $60 Twin $55 One night surcharge $5
Types of Accommodation: 1 Double, 1 Twin
Bathrooms: 1 Private en suite and 1 Shared en suite
Breakfast: Full
Special Information: Adults only please; Non-smoking home; Central air
Directions: *Orchard View* is one block west off Yonge Street and one block north of Eglinton Avenue. *Orchard View* is just two blocks away from the Eglinton Subway on the Yonge Street line.

Blueroof Farm

The story of *Blueroof Farm* begins with a soldier who died in the war of 1812; his widow and sons were deeded this land, and here they errected a log cabin which still stands as the central part of Kim Ondaatje's country home. For nearly two centuries the cabin had been added onto in both directions. Now, all has been brought together under Kim's direction -- the addition of necessary windows in the right places, and modern touches such as luxurious bathrooms. Primitive furnishings, mostly from Quebec, and some wicker, are just part of the creation of the artistic whole that is the welcome, comfort and delight of *Blueroof Farm* house. Here Kim Ondaatje receives guests from all over the world for bed and breakfast, country retreats, gourmet meals and photography lessons. And here also she raises beautiful Dalmatians.

Blueroof Farm has a fine library of videos and films; day tours of many interesting places in old Eastern Ontario available.

The guest rooms are special environments; perhaps the most wonderful space is the large private suite with a sweeping view of the property, a hidden TV, and woodstove, and a luxurious seven-piece bathroom with a kidney-shaped whirlpool surrounded by tropical plants; Kim calls this the Honeymoon or Getaway Suite.

No introduction to *Blueroof Farm* would be complete without describing the setting, the farm itself. Beyond the lovely old farmhouse, surrounded by trees, ponds, flower beds and lawns, is a road that leads to the swimming place where canoes are moored in summer; and in Winter there is skating on the ponds near the house. Fifteen kms of wilderness trails for excellent walking, snow shoeing, or bird watching lead through rolling meadows, as far as the river, or beyond, to Big Beaver Pond Lake; and on the way to all this you will pass beneath the awesome majesty of the tall maple woods.

BLUEROOF FARM

Kim Ondaatje
Bellrock, RR1
Verona, Ontario
K0H 2W0
(613) 374-2147

Season: All year
Rates: Single $40 and up Double $65 and up (plus GST)
Types of Accommodationa: 3 Double, 2 Queen, and 2 Twin
Bathrooms: 4 Four-piece bathrooms, 2 with jacuzzi
Breakfast: Full
Special Information: Adults only; Friendly Dalmatians allowed in parts of the house; All meals can be provided
Handicapped Facilities: Limited to luxury suite and available for visits of one week or longer
Directions: *Blueroof Farm* is half an hour north of the 401 Highway, and is 37 km from the city of Kingston.

McMullen Farm

McMullen Farm

One can sit in the cool shaded area beside the McMullen's early-Ontario solid brick 1874 farmhouse and enjoy the sweeping, beautiful view of the countryside. Gwen and Glen have been welcoming guests to their home for ten years. *McMullen Farm Bed and Breakfast* is right on the edge of the pretty little village of Warsaw; their lane begins between the millpond and the old red brick United Church.

Glen's herd of Charlois cattle graze in the pastures. There are areas for strolling and skiing; take the Bluebird Trail through the maple bush. The Indian River is adjacent to the farm for fishing, swimming, canoeing, and skating.

The McMullen's, who spent some time in West Africa, have used their memorabilia, collected while in Ghana, as part of their decor -- a foil for the natural pine woodwork.

Breakfast is complemented by Gwen's home baking; it could be muffins or bread, sweetened by honey produced on the farm.

McMullen Farm is close to the Warsaw Caves; the Indian Petroglyphs; Lang Pioneer Village; Curve Lake Crafts and Art Gallery; Peterborough; and a golf course.

Glen and Gwen McMullen
94 West Street
Warsaw, Ontario
K0L 3A0
(705) 652-3024

Season: All year
Rates: Single $30 Double $40
Types of Accommodation: 1 Single, 2 Double
Bathrooms: 1 Private and 1 Shared
Breakfast: Full
Special Information: Non-smoking home; Dinner on request; "Shadow", the dog is in the kitchen
Handicapped Facilities: Bedroom and bathroom on main floor
Directions: Follow road map from Highway 7 east of Peterborough to Warsaw. When red brick United Church on millpond is on right, make left turn up hill. This road becomes *The McMullen Farm* lane.

147

he Doctor's House

Bridie and Joe Tibbetts' bed and breakfast home in the beautiful lakeside village of Wellington was a former Doctor's home. Here they offer traditional "English" hospitality. They have given thoughtful personal attention to details that will make your stay like "family". Bridie was a former Naval Air Hostess and Joe a Rolls Royce Service Engineer, now retired. Bridie is a great cook and will prepare three-course dinners by prearrangement; all prepared with fresh farm produce. Her hearty English style full breakfasts are served in the friendly dining room. Joe makes great home-made beer!

The Doctor's House Bed and Breakfast is an 1867 Prince Edward County heritage home. The Tibbetts have chosen to furnish its spacious, high-ceilinged rooms with comfortable, contemporary furniture -- a nice blending of the new with the old. They love children of all ages and have special facilities for accommodating the physically handicapped. There is a special lounge area with TV and fireplace for guests. There are four double guest bedrooms with the use of two full baths, and one single en suite. All the guest rooms have ceiling fans and all the new beds have orthopedic mattresses.

Prince Edward County is a lovely area with lakeshore on almost all boundaries, lots of white sand beaches and places to swim. In the Spring, the apple orchards are full of blossom and in the Fall it is a great place to "pick your own".

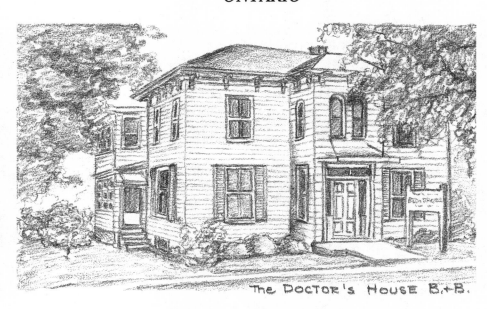

The DOCTOR's HOUSE B.+B.

Bridie and Joe Tibbetts C.E.T.
307 Main Street
Wellington, Ontario
K0K 3L0
(613) 399-2376

Season: All year
Rates: Single $40 Double $50 Family Room $60 Extra person $10 (prices include all taxes)
Types of Accommodation: 4 Double, 1 Single self-contained en suite
Bathrooms: 2 Full Shared and 1 En Suite
Breakfast: Full
Special Information: Non-smoking home; No guests' pets please; Storage area for bicycles
Handicapped Facilities: Wheelchair accessibility ramp and ground floor rooms
Directions: *The Doctor's House* is located in the village of Wellington on the corner of Main Street and West Street, close to all stores and beaches on Highway 33.

Wellington Pottery B&B

Carl Steeves has been creating beautiful pottery in his workshop behind his little shop in the lower level of this house in Wellington for quite a few years now, and Beth has been taking Bed and Breakfast guests, and among other things, also tending the lovely riot of annual flower beds that one can't help admiring when they take the Loyalist Parkway through the little village of Wellington. Wellington fronts right on Wellington Bay, part of Lake Ontario. In summer there are wonderful sandy beaches and quiet roads for cycling; in winter there are good cross-country skiing trails. The village boasts antique, art and craft shops, tea rooms and some good restaurants.

The Steeves home has a welcoming atmosphere with down-to-earth comfort; guests are welcome to relax in the main rooms or on the deck in summer. In winter there is a fireplace to sit by. There are two spacious double guest rooms, one with twin beds and one with a queen size which looks out over Lake Ontario. Guests are invited to join the family at the breakfast table for a full home-cooked meal including home made preserves and hot muffins.

Wellington is in Prince Edward County, known for its parks, lake fronts and fruit-growing climate. In the fall of the year there are many "pick your own" apple places.

WELLINGTON POTTERY B+B.

Carl and Beth Steeves
299 Loyalist Parkway, Box 502
Wellington, Ontario
K0K 3L0
(613) 399-2569

Season: All year
Rates: Single $40 Double $50
Types of Accommodation: 1 Queen, 1 Twin
Bathrooms: 2 Shared
Breakfast: Full
Special Information: Non-smoking home; "Barney", Lab Retriever in residence
Directions: East on Loyalist Parkway (Highway 33) in centre of village of Wellington on lake side. there is a sign on the lawn "Wellington Pottery". Off-street parking.

Spring Street B&B

On entering *Spring Street Bed and Breakfast* you are enveloped by the charm of this 100-year-old home; lovingly maintained and nostalgically decorated, and also by the welcome of your congenial host, Lorrain de Bruyn.

There is original woodwork everywhere, and a fireplace with pine mantel in the comfortable, bright living room, decorated in pastels.

The upstairs, with three pretty, period guest rooms, and a shared bath, is reserved exclusively for bed and breakfast. There are blue, coral, and green rooms, each with either queen or king size beds.

A full breakfast is served, either in the formal dining room, or in the country kitchen. It could be bacon and eggs or something "gourmet".

Westport is a pretty little community with interesting village arts and craft shops. The Rideau Trail leads from here to Foley Mountain. Half a block from *Spring Street Bed and Breakfast* are the Rideau Lakes and Rideau Canal and the village dock.

SPRING STREET
B.+B.

Lorrain de Bruyn
Box 156
Westport, Ontario
K0G 1X0
(613) 273-5427

Season: All year (reservation in winter only)
Rates: Single $30 Double $40
Types of Accommodation: 3 Double
Bathrooms: Shared
Breakfast: Full
Special Information: No children; Restricted smoking
Languages: English and French
Directions: *Spring Street Bed and Breakfast* is situated a half block away from the village dock in the centre of the village.

Bruce Gables

Two of the three large bedrooms have bay windows that overlook the town of Wiarton and the clear blue waters of Colpoy's Bay. Jorn and Elsie Christensen's spacious turn-of-the-century home has been restored to the Victorian splendour that is in keeping with its high ceilings; period fireplace; lovely old wood trim; and original stained glass, including a special "key-hole" styled window. Many of their antique furnishings were acquired during their three and a half year stay in Geneva, Switzerland.

Breakfast is a special affair served in the elegant dining room; some choices are crepes, pancakes, waffles, French toast, Eggs Benedict/Florentine, omelettes, or any style of eggs.

Guests are accommodated in the large, beautifully furnished and decorated bedrooms. They can relax in the spacious living room or in the garden where there are picnic tables and a gas barbecue available for guest use.

Wiarton is known as the "Gateway to the Bruce"; *Bruce Gables* makes a perfect headquarters for exploring the Peninsula. The Provincial Parks are natural habitats for many varieties of birds and animals. Both Georgian Bay on the east, and Lake Huron on the west, offer all water recreations. The Bruce Trail, a naturalist's and photographer's ideal, passes close by. From the high limestone bluffs overlooking the blue water of the many bays and inlets, to the rich green farmlands further south, the Bruce offers some of the most breathtaking scenery in Ontario.

WIARTON (Northwest of Owen Sound)
ONTARIO

BRUCE GABLES

Jorn and Elsie Christensen
410 Berford Street, Box 448
Wiarton, Ontario
N0H 2T0
(519) 534-0429

Season: All year, call in advance for reservations in the winter season
Rates: Single $35 Double $45 - $50
Types of Accommodation: Double, Queen and Twin
Bathrooms: 1 Full and 1 Two-piece
Breakfast: Full
Special Information: Non-smoking home
Languages: English, French, German, Spanish, and Danish
Directions: *Bruce Gables* is located one block north of the gates of Wiarton at 410 Berford which is the Northwest corner of the intersection of Berford and Mary Street. The parking is located off Mary Street.

Reed's Bay B&B

This one-of-a-kind bed and breakfast was formerly a limestone fishing lodge in the early 1900's. It sits only fifty feet from the shoreline of beautiful Reeds Bay, perfectly situated for panoramic sunsets.

Each room has an en suite bath, private entrance, high ceilings, ceiling fans, duvet comforters, and six-foot sliding glass doors onto a balcony overlooking the bay.

A generous continental breakfast may be served outside, weather permitting. Dinners may be pre-arranged.

There is a beautiful beach area for guests to enjoy; the Island is a great place for hiking, cycling, fishing, swimming, windsurfing, picnicking, birdwatching, or just plain relaxing. Ask about the two-night mid-week and longer stay specials.

Wolfe Island is handy to Kingston by free car ferry if you wish to go farther afield for a day tour. This is the Thousand Island area and tours leave from the Kingston waterfront. The city has many historic places and museums to visit. There are many fine restaurants for evening meals.

Wolfe Island is also the "stepping stone" between Kingston and the United States as there is a car ferry that will take you from the Island to New York State.

WOLFE ISLAND (Near Kingston) ONTARIO

REED'S BAY B&B.

Josie Power
Box 125, RR4
Wolfe Island, Ontario
K0H 2Y0
(613) 385-2522

Season: May - October
Rates: Double $70 weekends Double $50 during week
Types of Accommodation: 2 Double
Bathrooms: 2 En Suite
Breakfast: Continental Plus
Special Information: Two night specials during the week and for longer stays; Dinner upon request
Directions: Take the scenic ferry from downtown Kingston to Wolfe Island. Turn right off the ferry, left on Highway 95, right onto Reed's Bay Road. Follow approximately 4.8 km along the shore to Private Road. Turn right and *Reed's Bay B&B* is the second on the right.

Eighty-One Perry B&B

This 1875 Victorian yellow brick, with quoining and tall curved-top windows has been declared a "Designated Property" under the Ontario Heritage Act; it is a unique blend of Victorian charm -- high ceilings, marble fireplace and period furniture, and modern convenience -- one of the three shared guest washrooms has a whirlpool bath. The pretty, comfortable guest rooms give a choice of double or twin beds.

A warm welcome and home-cooking are Linda's specialty. Breakfast is served, either in the eating area of the bright kitchen, or the elegant dining room. Private gourmet candlelight dinners are available by prearrangement; a marvellous idea for an occasion such as a Honeymoon, Anniversary or Birthday celebration!

Guests can relax in the parlour, read or listen to quiet music. The Family Room is available for those who wish to watch TV or engage in board games. When the weather permits, the back garden is a favourite spot for restful moments.

From *Eighty-One Perry* you can easily walk to downtown shopping, the library, the arena, the theatre, or the Art Gallery. The Woodstock Museum is housed in the historic (1853) Old Town Hall, and features Council Chambers restored to 1879.

A short drive accesses the attractions of London, Stratford, Kitchener or Brantford. Your hosts will be pleased to help with points of interest such as local markets, factory outlets, hiking trails and arrange transportation to and from local railway and bus depots.

Linda and Philip Lomax
81 Perry Street
Woodstock, Ontario
N4S 3C4
(519) 539-0692 or (519) 421-0712

Season: All year
Rates: Single $40 Double $45 10% Discount for Seniors and University Students
Types of Accommodation: 1 Double, 2 Twin
Bathrooms: 2 Full
Breakfast: Continental or Full
Special Information: Non-smoking home; Dog named "Belle" in residence; Children welcome; Dinners readily available
Directions: Centrally located in downtown Woodstock, 5 minutes north of Highway 401. To locate *Eighty-One Perry* from the Museum Square on Dundas Street in downtown core, proceed one block west to Perry Street. Turn left (south) and *Eighty-One Perry* is located one and one half blocks on the left side near the crest of a hill.

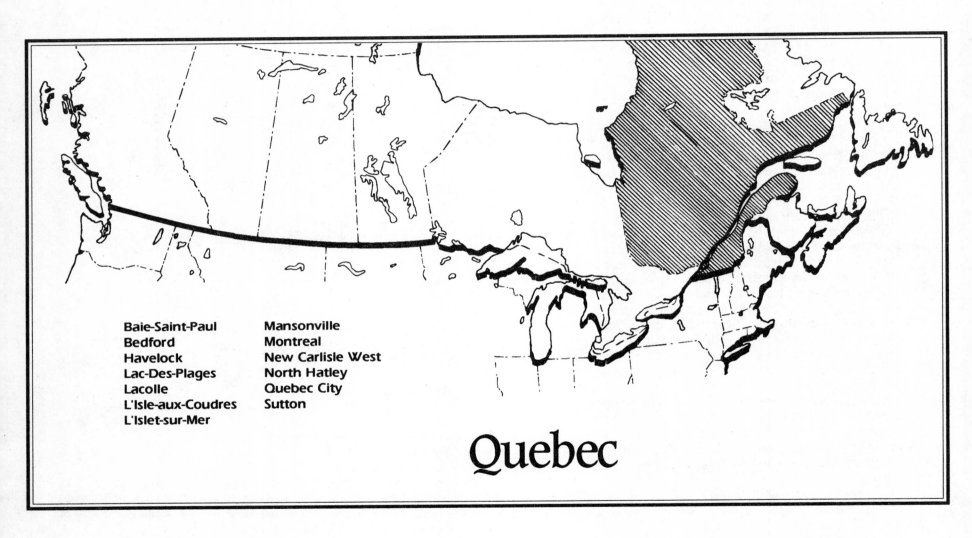

Baie-Saint-Paul
Bedford
Havelock
Lac-Des-Plages
Lacolle
L'Isle-aux-Coudres
L'Islet-sur-Mer

Mansonville
Montreal
New Carlisle West
North Hatley
Quebec City
Sutton

Quebec

La Muse B&B

La Muse Bed and Breakfast is located in the heart of the village of Baie-Saint-Paul in the beautiful Charlevoix region.

This 1881 home offers five beautifully appointed guest rooms and a continental breakfast served in the bright sunroom. The period character of the house is retained by the restoration of the wide wooden plank floors and the preservation of the original architecture. The house is set back on a deep lot and this provides quiet and seclusion. Next door is an art gallery/craft shop where bicycles are available for exploring the Baie-Saint-Paul area.

Baie-Saint-Paul has many interesting craft shops, galleries, fine restaurants and historical sites, including the Maison Rene Richard.

The Charlevoix is an area of stunning natural beauty and abundant vacation surprises. Here, on the north shore of the St. Lawrence River people whale watch for the Great Blue, the largest animal ever to have lived on this planet. There are theatres and summer concerts. Many artists live in the area and so exhibits are plentiful. The Isle-aux-Coudres, the island where Jaques Cartier celebrated the first mass in New France, is just off the shore from Baie-Saint-Paul by car ferry.

LA MUSE

Evelyn Trembley
39, rue Saint-Jean-Baptiste, C.P. 1627
Baie-Saint-Paul, Quebec
G0A 1B0
(418) 435-6839

Season: All year
Rates: Available upon request
Types of Accommodation: 1 Single, 3 Double, 1 Family Room
Bathrooms: 2 Private and 2 Shared
Breakfast: Continental
Languages: French and English
Directions: *La Muse* is 100 km from Quebec City towards Ste-Anne-de-Beaupré, Route 138 East. At Baie-St-Paul, turn right on Route 362, at the church turn left. Or from la Malbaie, Routes 138 or 362 west.

L'Occasion

Margo Chadwick's *L'Occasion Bed and Breakfast* was awarded first prize for "Maison Fleurie" in *House and Gardens 1990-1991*, an attribute to the beautiful gardens that surround this well-kept old country home. A beautiful verandah, and lovely front door are your first impressions of this bed and breakfast.

L'Occasion is located in the heart of Bedford where you can easily walk everywhere. This is a grape-growing area; so there are vineyards nearby. Vermont and Lake Champlain are a short drive across the Border to the United States.

The guests rooms are comfortable and beautifully appointed. Margo serves a delicious breakfast in the front room. Guests may lounge in the living room or outside in the garden, if they wish to take a moment to relax.

Margo enjoys handicrafts and there are handicrafts for sale on the premises.

Bedford is in the Estrie region of Quebec, southeast of Montreal. An area first settled by Loyalists in the 1790's; Estrie is now harmoniously French and English, an area of pretty towns and farms, and historical sites. From antiques to auctions, museums to music, arts and theatre, almost every town like Bedford has something worth stopping for.

L'OCCASION B.+B.

Margo Chadwick
11, avenue des Pins, C.P. 1440
Bedford, Quebec
J0J 1A0
(514) 248-2712 or (514) 248-2271

Season: All year
Rates: $55 and up Additional person $15
Types of Accommodation: 1 Single, 2 Double
Bathrooms: 1 Shared
Special Information: Dog named "Pebble" and Cat named "Charlotte" in residence; No smoking on second floor; Dinner served on request
Languages: French, English, and Spanish
Directions: From Montreal, Highway 10 East, Exit 22, Highway 35 South and Route 133 South. At St-Pierre-de-Véronne, Route 202. In Bedford, first street to the right after railroad track, fourth house on the left.

Stoneboro Farm

As you drive south from Montreal into the region of Monteregie, without fully being aware at first, you are climbing; then all at once you are driving through mile after mile of apple orchards and rolling countryside. When you reach the gates of *Stoneboro Farm*, you will turn and go up once more, as the lane winds up the side of Covey Hill where you discover a lovely old stone Quebec farmhouse, set by a majestic maple, and a panoramic view of the Chateauguay Valley, even as far away as Mount Royal at the heart of Montreal!

Stoneboro Farm Bed and Breakfast is a secluded historic house located on a 100-acres of the rolling hillsides among apple and maple trees. A peaceful brook meanders near the house; there is a swimming pool and deck where guests may relax. This is an excellent place for cycling, or, in the winter, cross-country skiing and sleigh rides.

There is a separate guest entrance and a comfortable guest living room with wood stove were you may relax. There are rooms on the main floor and upstairs, beautifully appointed to suit the period of the home. John and Anne serve a full breakfast with home-baking at the long harvest table in the large kitchen-dining room, or in the sunroom overlooking the valley. Dinners are available on request; and are prepared from organically home-grown vegetables.

Stoneboro Farm is close to all this area has to offer: Park Safari, golfing, the U.S. Border, historic battle sites and museums, and excellent downhill skiing.

STONEBORO FARM

John and Anne Schulman
164 Route 202
Havelock, Quebec
J0S 1E0
(514) 826-0196

Season: All year
Rates: Available upon request
Types of Accommodation: 3 Single, 2 Double
Bathrooms: 2 Shared
Breakfast: Full
Special Information: Non-smoking home; Kitchen and laundry facilities; Air-conditioning; Dinners available upon request
Languages: French and English
Directions: From Montreal on Highway 15 south, take Exit 6 and go west on Route 202 through Hemmingford. Travel another 20 km and look for sign on the left.

L'Auvent Bleu B&B

The *Domaine L'Auvent Bleu* (the Blue Awning Estate) is a comfortable country home situated in the beautiful Laurentian Mountains on the banks of the Maskinonge River. Guests may walk, hike, or cross-country ski right on the property which is a large treed acreage. The river, for canoeing, is a few steps away from the house. There is an in-ground swimming pool behind the house where guests may enjoy themselves. On Lac des Plages guests may wind surf, canoe, and swim. The village of St. Jovite is close for shopping and restaurants. Mont Tremblant, Gray Rocks and Mont Blanc are a 40-minute drive for downhill skiing.

The guest bedrooms each have an interesting country view and offer a good nights rest. There is a solarium where guests may relax and exchange experiences, and visit. Hearty breakfasts are cooked on the wood stove and served in the glassed-in dining area. Cook-out meals can be arranged.

The Outaouais is an area that stretches from the Ottawa River (the name of Ottawa comes from Outaouais) to the Laurentains that surround *L'Auvent Bleu*. Here you can be golfing one day or shopping for souvenirs in historic little nineteenth century towns, and the next be back to nature on the mountain trails.

— L'AUVENT BLEU —

Jean-Francois Boissonneault and Luc Martin
6, chemin Vendée
Lac-des-Plages, Quebec
J0T 1K0
(819) 687-2981

Season: All year
Rates: Available upon request
Types of Accommodation: 4 Single, 4 Double
Bathrooms: 2 Shared, Sinks in all rooms
Breakfast: Full
Special Information: No guests' pets please; MasterCard accepted
Languages: French and English
Directions: From Montreal, Highway 15 North and Route 117 North to St-Jovite, Route 323 South to the interesection with Vendée Road. Or from Ottawa, Route 148 to Montebello, Route 323 North to Lac-des-Plages, 3 km to the intersection of Vendée Road.

L'Aubergine

Your host, Richard Grenier, a former Navy Captain thought it would be fun to have a name for their bed and breakfast that was a play on words. *L'Aubergine* is an *eggplant*, and this shiny purple vegetable has become a decorative element on their sign. Why, you ask? Well pronounce it in French and you have, combined, the French and the English words meaning a place that takes overnight guests! Clever! this sense of fun tells you a lot about the *Captaine* and his wife and their *L'Aubergine Bed and Breakfast*. Entertaining people who will give you a warm welcome to their home!

L'Aubergine Bed and Breakfast is down a short drive set back against a woodlot on spacious lawns fronted by an apple orchard. Nature lovers and birders will love this quiet natural spot. For sailors, the close proximity to Lake Champlain is an attraction. The United States Border is minutes away.

The guest rooms are comfortable and convenient; a lavish breakfast of home-made bread, and fresh eggs is served by your jovial host.

Lacolle is in the Monteregie region, the most southerly part of Quebec, bordered by New York State, U.S.A. Here, the historic Richelieu River and valley links the St. Lawrence to Lake Champlain in the state of New York. Quiet towns, country churches and gracious homes hug the river bank. There are historic sites and forts, notably in Chambly, everywhere. Montreal is only a one hour drive north from Lacolle.

L'AUBERGINE

Richard Grenier
21 Rang Edgerton
Lacolle, Quebec
J0J 1J0
(514) 246-2740

Season: March - December
Rates: Available upon request
Types of Accommodation: 4 Bedrooms
Bathrooms: 3 Shared
Breakfast: Full
Special Information: Non-smoking home; Welcome nature lovers; Cats in residence; Dinner on request
Languages: French and English
Directions: From Montreal, take Highway 15 South to U.S.A. border, Exit 1, Monte Guay, drive 5 km.

Le Gite du Quatuor

Le Gite du Quatuor overlooks the majestic St. Lawrence River, where the tides come and go, on the L'Isle-aux-Coudres. This bed and breakfast gets its name because of the very musical family that is associated with it. Jeannette Moisan's husband plays with the Montreal Symphony; he and their three sons have given Quartet performances on the island. At VEL "O" COUDRES the family rents out some very unique bikes with which to tour the Island -- Mountain bikes, tandems, and quadricycles (these look something like "the surrey" with the fringe on top!) that can accommodate up to six adults and three children. The road around the Island is about 26 km long; just the right length for an enjoyable bicycle tour.

The *Bed and Breakfast*, besides having a marvellous view of ships passing by on the St. Lawrence, is a beautiful spacious brick and frame home with comfortable guest rooms upstairs, also with views, and a special guest lounge area on the first floor looking out on the water. Breakfast is a very special time; Jeannette is a wonderful hostess who makes a breakfast you will never forget. Home-baking is a specialty. Live lobster is available at the family-owned restaurant A La Nage.

L'Isle-Aux-Coudres means Island of Hazel Nuts, because, believe it or not, these are what Jaques Cartier found on the island in 1535 to "write home about". The island is reached by car ferry from St-Joseph de la Rive on the mainand, 19 km after Baie-Saint-Paul. The island was once well-known for ship building. Today the shops and boutiques are an interesting display of the friendly Islanders self-sufficiency. The Island has some very old historical sites for visiting; the ship yard at Saint-Bernard Sur Mer, the church of Saint-Louis; the Museum of L'Isle-aux-Coudres and the double duty water and windmill at Saint-Louis de L'Isle-aux-Coudres.

L'ISLE-AUX-COUDRES (at St-Louis)
QUEBEC

LE GITE du QUATUOR

Jeannette Moisan
217, Chemin des Coudriers
Saint-Louis, Isle-aux-Coudres, Quebec
G0A 1X0
(418) 438-2146

Fax: (418) 438-2261
Season: May - October
Rates: Double and Twin $65 Queen $75 (GST included)
Types of Accommodation: 1 Double, 2 Queen, and 1 Twin
Bathrooms: 1 Shared
Breakfast: Full
Special Information: Adult guests only please; Non-smoking home; No guests' pets please
Languages: English and French
Directions: From Quebec City, Routes 138 east to Baie St-Paul then 362 east to Les Eboulements. Take the ferry (toll free). Once on the island, turn right at the flashing light, drive for approximately 10 km.

La Marguerite

LA MARGUERITE

This spacious, historic 1810 bed and breakfast is located in the heart of L'Islet-sur-Mer, a 300-year-old historic village right on the south bank of the St. Lawrence River.

Your hosts, Marguerite and Denis Caron, have restored their beautiful *manoir* house to period. The wide plank floors, stone walls, and old fireplaces are an echo from Old Quebec; yet *La Marguerite* is delightfully modern in that it offers large comfortable, beautifully appointed guest rooms, each with a private bath. Two rooms have queen size beds.

There is a special sitting room for guests, very comfortably furnished and a lovely garden where guests may sit and relax in the summertime. Breakfast is served in the special, bright dining room. It is both generous and delicious. Guests may choose to begin with cereals and juices of their choice before they are served a full cooked meal.

La Marguerite and L'Islet-sur-Mer are located in Chaudière-Appalaches, a renowned region for its great maple tree forests. The south shore of the St. Lawrence is known for its old rural villages and outgoing people, and well worth discovering. The Appalachian Mountains end here, and the land becomes rolling hills and fertile farmland. Southward are Maine, and New Hampshire in the United States. East of L'Islet-sur-Mer is Saint-Jean-Port-Joli, famous for its wood carving and sculptures. Visit the Musee maritime de L'Islet, a boat museum.

Marguerite and Denis Caron
88, route des Pionniers Est
L'Islet-Sur-Mer, Québec
G0R 2B0
(418) 247-5454

Season: All year
Rates: Single $43 and up Double $53 and up
Types of Accommodation: 1 Double, 2 Queen and 2 Twin
Bathrooms: 5 Private
Breakfast: Full
Special Information: Children welcome; Non-smoking home; No guests' pets please; Air-conditioning
Languages: English and French
Directions: *La Marguerite* is located 100 km east of Québec City. From Montréal or Québec City on Highway 20 Exit at Highway 285 North (Exit 400) travel 4 km through L'Islet Ville to intersection of Route 132, turn right and continue for 1 km to the house on the right side.

La Chouette

La Chouette Bed and Breakfast is near Mansonville tucked in beside the Vermont border and a hour and a half drive from Montreal. It is near Owl's Head, Jay Peak, and Mont Sutton for downhill winter skiing. In fact this B&B gets its name, barn-owl, from its proximity to the Owl's Head mountain which is part of the beautiful view from the windows.

This big white comfortable home with a red roof and large verandah has been renovated with bed and breakfast guests in mind. The guest rooms are clean and bright with country quilts and private baths. A generous breakfast is served in the dining area and there is a lounge where guests may relax after a day of cycling, sight-seeing or skiing.

The terrain in the Eastern Township is suited for cross-country skiing too -- rolling hills through beautiful rural landscapes.

The Estrie (Eastern Townships) are beautiful in other seasons also. In summer alpine nature trails beckon. In autumn the hills and mountain sides are a riot of colour. There are museums to visit, antique shops, craft and artist's boutiques and fine dining to explore in the interesting little villages that dot this area.

LA CHOUETTE

France A. Fortier
560 Rte de Mansonville
Mansonville, Quebec
J0E 1X0
(514) 292-3020

Season: All year
Rates: Single $45 Double $60 Triple $75
Types of Accommodation: 3 Rooms with Single and Double beds
Bathrooms: 3 Private
Breakfast: Full
Special Information: Children welcome; Non-smoking preferred; No guests' pets please; 5 year-old child in residence named Emilie
Languages: French, English, German and a little bit of Spanish
Directions: Take Autoroute 10, Exit 106, Route 245 South to Bolton South and then Route 243 for 6 km. *La Chouette* is on the left hand side.

L'Anse du Patrimoine

On the northern outskirts of Montreal, in Boisbriand, *L'Anse du Patrimoine* (means place of the ancestors) is situated on several secluded acres along the Mille Iles River.

This interesting historic Quebec stone home is nearly two centuries old, and much of its early character has been retained or restored. There are three old fireplaces, and gleaming wide plank floors with beautiful scatter rugs. The house is very comfortable and there are special sitting areas where guests may relax. The guest bedrooms have comfortable county decor. A delicious breakfast is served in the period dining room where guests can enjoy a good visit and exchange information of interest.

L'Anse du Patrimoine is set on spacious lawns and gardens, well back from the street, and surrounded by shrubs and magnificent old trees. Beside the house there is an inground swimming pool where guests may relax and enjoy themselves in the summertime.

There is a Nature Interpretation Center nearby and easy access from here to Montreal International Airport (Dorval or Mirabel). Less than 3 km will take you to a golf course, cultural activities, theatre concerts, and art galleries. Also, *L'Anse du Patrimoine* is a great place to stay while visiting the sights of Montreal. After a busy day of shopping and sight seeing, what could be better than to return to the peace and quiet of this beautiful old Quebec home and its surroundings.

L'ANSE DE PATRIMOINE

Hélène Filion and Émile Bédard
488 Grand Côte
Boisbriand, Quebec
J7E 4H4
(514) 437-6918

Season: All year
Rates: Single $35 Double $50
Types of Accommodation: 1 Single, 2 Family bedrooms
Bathrooms: 1 Private and 1 Shared
Breakfast: Full
Special Information: No guests pets please; Laundry facilities; Air-conditioned
Languages: French and some English
Directions: From Montreal, take Autoroute 15 north or Autoroute 13 north to the Boisbriand Exit. You will exit right on the La Grande Côte. *L'Anse du Patrimoine* is 2 km from either Autoroute.

Chez Alexis

Chez Alexis Bed and Breakfast is an historical "Montreal walk-up" townhouse in the heart of "the Latin Quarter", not far from the intersection of rue Sherbrooke and rue St-Denis. As Sherbrooke Metro Station is two blocks away, a few minutes will take you downtown and to historical Old Montreal.

This elegant greystone residence with traditional slate mansard roof, has a spacious feeling and ambiance created through high ceilings, a combination of comfortable and period furnishings and lovely restored deep wood trim. On the top floor are two large and one smaller guest bedrooms, conveniently and comfortably appointed, where guests, if they desire, may arrange to have a TV and telephone in their rooms, and for longer stays, have use of the main kitchen and laundry. Off street parking is also available.

Chez Alexis is located on a quiet street, close to the Universite du Quebec a Montreal and to Parc Lafontaine, with its lake, jogging trails and ready access to the city's many bike paths. St-Denis Street is a cultural corridor, lined with bistros, cafes, and restaurants offering exotic dining for visitors and Montrealers alike. Each summer the street becomes the home of several popular festivals, among which are the International Jazz Festival, the Just-for-Laughs Humour Festival, and the World Film Festival. Major concerts are held in the Theatre Saint-Denis. The Bibliotheque Nationale du Quebec, built in the Beaux-Arts style in 1915, is number 1700.

Montreal is a cosmopolitan city, where the visitor can experience an international flavour, more so than in any other city in Canada. The *Chez Alexis* hosts, themselves well-travelled, are delighted to share their knowledge of its diversified cultural activities.

Diane-Alexis Fournier
3445 rue St-Andre
Montreal, Quebec
H2L 3V4
(514) 598-0898

Season: All year
Rates: Single $40 Double $65
Types of Accommodation: 2 Double, 1 King
Bathrooms: 1 Shared
Breakfast: Full
Special Information: Children under 12 no charge
Languages: English, French and Spanish
Directions: From Sherbrooke/St-Denis intersection; proceed east; left at third light (St-Andre).

Gite La Douillette

La Douillette (pronounce: "Do-we-yet") means both "cosy" and a comforter in French. In other words, warm and homey. You'll also find this green, renovated Victorian style townhouse clean and cheery. *Gite La Douillette* is located in a residential area just a "stone's throw" from the Berri Metro Station, the hub of Montréal's transport system which provides access to the entire city and suburbs.

Once inside this bed and breakfast you are in for a pleasant surprise; a bright, spacious decor including a charming breakfast nook and lounge where guests are encouraged to relax and curl up with a book from the house library. There are three guest rooms to choose from: the large room, the secluded room and the cosy room. There is also a self-contained suite on the lower level for those who wish to stay longer. The breakfast menu varies daily but not the quality! Fresh food supplies are purchased according to the season at the nearby St. Jacques market.

Gite La Douillette is close to the St-Denis district, the cultural area for the bohemian Montrealer and visitors to the city. Here you'll find restaurants and cafes representing almost every kind of cuisine and boutiques with everything from antiques to avant garde. Also nearby is the Université de Québec à Montréal (UQAM).

Architecturally, Montreal is an interesting city with four centuries of history. Everyone will be celebrating the city's 350th birthday in 1992 with a full slate of events. At walking distance from *La Douillette* is Old Montreal. This restored area with winding narrow brick or cobblestone streets lined with mansard-roofed stone buildings is located right on the waterfront. Dotted with fine restaurants, cafes, boutiques, and galleries, Old Montreal boasts Notre Dame Cathedral and several other historical buildings, all well worth visiting.

Sports fans should visit the Olympic Stadium, whereas music fans might enjoy seeing a show at the Place des Arts complex.

MONTREAL
QUEBEC

GÎTE LA DOUILLETTE

Marie-Carole Daigle
1796 rue Saint André
Montréal, Quebec
H2L 3T9
(514) 526-9595

Season: All year
Rates: Single $40 Double $50 - $60 Additional person $15, special arrangements can be made for groups or longer stays
Types of Accommodation: 2 Double, 1 Triple
Bathrooms: 2 Full (one with a large, relaxation tub)
Breakfast: Full or Continental
Special Information: Children welcome; Non-smoking home; No guests' pets please; Dinners served on request for groups only
Languages: French, English, Spanish and German
Directions: From Berri Metro Station or Voyageur Bus Terminal: Take Maisonneuve Blvd. East, South on Saint-André. By Car: Take Sherbrooke Street East to Saint-André, then go down Saint-André. Look for a green renovated house.

Gite Touristique du Centre-Ville Downtown B & B

Gite Touristique du Centre-Ville is in a small residential area in the heart of downtown that offers friendly accommodation; from here you can walk everywhere. There is limited parking for guests; so be sure and check about this when booking.

This older brick townhouse, has a curved walk-up with wrought-iron railing. The interior gives a feeling of spaciousness, with large living room and fireplace. Guests are served breakfast in the dining room. The guest rooms are large, and clean, with modern decor. Each room has a TV, telephone, radio and ventilation. On the second floor there is a kitchen reserved especially for guest use. There are special rates for longer stays.

Montreal is a cosmopolitan city, with thousands of tempting restaurants in every price range; French haute cuisine, Italian, Greek, Indian, Japanese, and Middle Eastern food, to name a few. In Montreal wherever you walk you will see some enchanting architecture; in particular, stone buildings, mansard roofs and dormer windows, and Montreal's famous winding staircases. Montreal has a profusion of beautiful churches. Don't miss the magnificent neo-gothic Notre-Dame Cathedral near the Place d'Armes. Old Montreal, at the waterfront has been restored and, once again, presents a world of narrow cobblestone streets; but now its ancient greystone buildings house antique shops, cafes and boutiques.

The Place des Arts Complex is home to the Montreal Symphony Orchestra and a year-round schedule of events. Here Montreal international Film Festival attracts big name stars from Europe and the United States when it is held every August.

GITE TOURISTIQUE
DU CENTRE VILLE

Bruno Bernard
3523 rue Jeanne-Mance
Montréal, Quebec
H2X 2K2
(514) 845-0431

Season: All year
Rates: Single $40 and up Double $60
Types of Accommodation: 3 Single, 1 Double, 1 Queen, and 1 Twin
Bathrooms: 1 1/2 Shared
Breakfast: Continental Plus
Special Information: Adult guests only please
Languages: English and French
Directions: On Sherbrooke Street west of Saint-Laurent. Turn on Jeanne-Mance. Which is the same street as Place-des-Arts.

La Maison de Grand-Pre

Get precise instructions, as it is well worth finding *La Maison de Grand-Pré* on rue de Grand-Pré, a quiet little street tucked in behind the busy through streets of the famous St-Denis district of Montreal. Here, in this nineteenth-century French bourgeoise brick Victorian home, with mansard roof, dormed windows, square tower, and walk-up front door you will find warm hospitality and a quiet, cosy atmosphere.

Your host, Jean-Paul Lauzon, a retired professor, has spent a lot of time and care renovating and restoring his home to period ambiance -- hence wood floors, and a nice combination of antiques and comfortable modern furnishings. The comfortable guest rooms open off a hall with old-fashioned painted wooden floors. A generous and varied breakfast is served in the spacious dining area or, in warmer weather, on the glassed-in verandah, with a view of Mount Royal. There is a guest lounge downstairs for relaxing or visiting.

The Laurier Subway Station is two minutes from *La Maison de Grand-Pré*, and a ten-minute ride to the downtown business district.

St-Denis Street is just around the corner; here restaurants, and open door cafes representing almost every ethnic background can be found. Interesting boutiques for shopping dot the area, and here in June and July, the International Jazz Festival is held.

Montreal has much to offer visitors. Old Montreal down by the busy harbour, has been patiently restored to its former world of narrow cobblestone streets, historic monuments and sites, and centuries-old greystone buildings. Today there are antique shops, restaurants, sidewalk cafes and artisans boutiques. Horse-drawn caleches show visitors the sights.

LA MAISON de GRAND-PRÉ

Jean-Paul Lauzon
4660 rue de Grand-Pré
Montréal, Quebec
H2T 2H7
(514) 843-6458

Season: All year
Rates: Available upon request
Types of Accommodation: 5 Bedrooms
Bathrooms: 2 Shared
Breakfast: Full
Special Information: Resident Cat;
Languages: English and French
Directions: From the North, rue St-Denis South. At Gilford, turn right. One hundred feet further, on the corner of De Grang-Pré/Gilford. From the South, rue St-Denis North to St-Joseph, turn right. Turn around the metro station, on Gilford cross St-Denis.

Montreal Oasis

As you cross Sherbrooke Street on Atwater Avenue be ready to turn left. Breslay is the second little street above Sherbrooke and 3000 Breslay is the first house on your left. The entrance door is turquois and there is an evergreen on each side of it, but first, you have to go through a wooden gate.

Lena Blondel's spacious 1920's home is located in what is known as the "Priest Farm District" (once a holiday resort for priests) a beautiful neighborhood of interesting houses, large trees, and pretty gardens in the elegant and safe West End of Downtown Montreal. It has original leaded windows, cathedral ceilings, and furnished with a mixture of modern and Quebecois. Lena, your Swedish hostess, is world travelled and has lived in many countries and on several continents; she loves all kinds of music and art, and her collection of African Art and wood carvings is an interesting part of her home's decor. There are three comfortable double rooms and two bathrooms available upstairs for guests. There is also a powder room on the main floor. A generous and truly gourmet breakfast is a specialty of the house.

From *Montreal Oasis* you can walk to Mount Royal Park, a short hike up the hill to the Museum of Fine Arts and Crescent Street to the Canadian Center for Architecture and the Faubourg to the Montreal Forum which is just a block away. Alexis Nihon Plaza, part of the underground city, and the Metro Station are nearby. The Westmount Galleries, the most exclusive shopping center in Montreal and elegant Greene Avenue is a five minute walk away, as is St. Catherine Street. Restaurants and cafes are plentiful, and Lena can recommend inexpensive, little ethnic restaurants, delicatessens or "Haute cuisine".

Other places of interest that can be easily reached are Old Montreal and the Latin Quarter. Your hostess also represents other quality bed and breakfast homes in the Downtown, Old Montreal, and the Latin Quarter.

MONTREAL OASIS B+B

Lena Blondel
3000 Breslay Road
Montreal, Quebec
H3Y 2G7
(514) 935-2312

Season: All year
Rates: Single $50 - $60 Double $55 - $65
Types of Accommodation: 1 Queen, 2 Twin
Bathrooms: 2 Shared and 1 Powder room
Breakfast: Generous Gourmet
Special Information: No guests' pets; Moderate smoking; Two Siamese cats in residence
Languages: English, French, Swedish and some Spanish and German
Directions: Follow directions to downtown Montreal, then take the Atwater exit and follow Atwater to 3000 Breslay Road, turn left to first house.

Bay View Farm

Bay View Farm offers the comfort and the convenience of direct accessibility from the main highway, yet the tranquillity and beauty of a panoramic seaside location on the Gaspé Peninsula.

The large house was built in the early 1920's by an enterprising businessman-farmer and was finished completely in B.C. fir (in those days, in the area, a sign of prosperity). This original finish still remains unchanged.

Animals are no longer kept on this farm, but there is a small stock on an adjoining property. There are no in-house pets.

Bay View Farm Bed and Breakfast offers five comfortable guest rooms; two with a double bed in each; two with a double and twin bed in each; and one with a double and two twin beds. There are two full shared baths.

A copious gourmet home-baked breakfast is served in the dining room or, if you wish, on the large wrap-around verandah with a beautiful view of the sea. It comprises fruit juice, cereal, bacon or sausage, fresh farm eggs, hashbrown potatoes, whole grain bread and muffins, scones, home-made jams, and fresh fruit from our gardens and orchards in season.

Helen, your hostess, is a Pre-school teacher who enjoys quilting, handicrafts, gardening, and writing. Garnett, your host, is a carpenter-farmer who enjoys "calling" square dances. Their teenage sons enjoy sports, music, and play several musical instruments. The family enjoys being involved in the organization of the Bay View Folk Festival each August, and in Elderhostel Programs.

Visit the local attractions. Share the richness of United Empire Loyalist, Acadian and neighbouring Basque heritages. Relax with your hosts, and walk across the road for a stroll along the beach.

The Gaspé Peninsula has the drama of mountains plunging to the sea; glorious ocean views and huge natural parks.

— BAY VIEW FARM —

Helen and Garnett Sawyer
337 Route 132
New Carlisle West, Quebec
G0C 1Z0
(418) 752-2725 or (418) 752-6718

Season: All year
Rates: Single $25 Double $35 Additional person $10
Types of Accommodation: 5 Double
Bathrooms: 2 Shared
Breakfast: Full Gourmet Home-baked
Special Information: Children welcome; Smoking outside only; No guests' pets please; Light meals on advance request
Languages: English and French
Directions: On the Gaspé Peninsula, if arriving from direction of Percé continue through the village of New Carlisle West. *Bay View Farm* is on Route 132, about 3 km west of the village of New Carlisle, near the Molson Brewery Depot and CNR underpass. If arriving from the west *Bay View Farm* is after Bonaventure and before the village of New Carlisle.

Cedar Gables

Cedar Gables is a large 1890 house located at the lakeside on beautiful Lake Massawippi in the heart of Quebec's magnificent Eastern Townships. A five-minute walk takes you to the fine dining and shopping area of this unique lakeside village.

The house is exquisitely decorated with many antiques and oriental carpets and has three working fireplaces. Ann and Don have a large library of classical and contemporary works, and love classical music -- that's mostly what you'll hear.

Guests are invited to use the whole house, including amenities. These include the lakeside sundeck and docks, canoes and a rowboat. There's good fishing and great swimming in the clean lake waters and great wicker rocking chairs on the porches.

The guest rooms consist of the Suite with king size bed, private sitting room and bath; the huge West Lake Room with king size bed and elegant en suite bathroom; the Canopy Room has a double canopy bed and window seat; this room shares two baths with the East Lake Room, a king, and the Studio, a king, which has a garden view. All the rooms are bright and cheerful with firm, comfortable beds and colourful, co-ordinated linens.

Cedar Gables has the most photographed breakfasts around -- hearty and memorable. In summer it is served on the verandah.

In the Autumn, the hardwoods create a marvellous spectacle. Days are balmy; nights are crisp and cool. In Winter, guests can step out the back door and cross-country ski; or a few minutes drive will take you to alpine skiing. There's an ice skating rink in the village and ice-fishing on the lake. Spring is a favourite time of year. It is quite a spectacle to see the lake's ice depart and the area come back to life. Horseback riding, tennis and golf are minutes away.

CEDAR GABLES --

Ann and Don Fleischer
4080 Magog Road, Box 355
North Hatley, Quebec
J0B 2C0
(819) 842-4120

Season: All year
Rates: Suite $106 Canopy Room $71 East Lake Room $83 West Lake Room $106 Studio $83 (all rates are for two persons, GST included)
Types of Accommodation: 4 King, 1 Double
Bathrooms: 2 Private and 2 Shared
Breakfast: Full Hearty Gourmet
Special Information: Advance reservation suggested; Two week cancellation policy; American Express, Visa and MasterCard accepted; Children over 12 welcome
Directions: From Montreal, take Autoroute 10E to exit 121, Autoroute 55 South. Proceed on 55 to exit 29, route 108E. Proceed to Ste. Cath. de Hatley, following signs to North Hatley. Entering the outskirts of North Hatley, you will come to a stopsign at the lakeside intersection. Proceed on Route 108; *Cedar Gables* is 0.8 km from the stopsign.

B&B Ste-Foy

Monique and Andre Saint-Aubin's two storey stone-faced residence, built in early French-Canadian style, is situated on a tree-lined street in a quiet residential neighbourhood in Ste-Foy, in the western part of Quebec City. They are very close to a shopping centre and the main bus and railway station.

The home is modern and spacious inside. The comfortable guest rooms are on the main and upper level and there are three shared household bathrooms. Monique serves a full, home-cooked breakfast in the family dining room. Though French is the household language, Monique is learning to speak English and doing very well!

There is much to do while you are visiting Quebec; the Saint-Aubin's will be glad to be of help. Sit back and enjoy a caleche ride. Enjoy an outdoor cafe. Take in the aquarium and the zoo. Visit the Old city, the Citadelle and the Plains of Abraham if you wish to steep yourself in history. Laval University and the 100-year-old Assemblee Nationale, Parliament of Quebec are also impressive.

In summer there is the July Summer Festival, two weeks filled with concerts, exhibits and all sorts of lively outdoor entertainment. In winter, there is the February Carnaval de Quebec, eleven days of non-stop winter activities including the famous snow sculptures and festivities in the heart of the Old City. A few minutes outside the city there is downhill skiing at Mont Stoneham and Mont Sainte-Anne. Make *B&B Ste-foy* your headquarters for enjoying Quebec City.

Monique and André Saint-Aubin
3045, rue de la Seine
Ste-Foy, Quebec City, Quebec
G1W 1H8
(418) 658-0685

Season: All year, except December
Rates: Available upon request
Types of Accommodation: 3 Bedrooms
Bathrooms: 3 Shared
Breakfast: Full
Special Information: No guests' pets please
Languages: French and English
Directions: From Montreal, take Highway 20 east to Quebec City and Pierre Laporte Bridge. Exit on Laurier Boulevard. At the first traffic light turn right to rue Lavigerie, and right on rue de la Seine (at second stop sign).

Bienvenue Quebec Sillery

Bienvenue Quebec Sillery is located in a new townhouse development in Sillery, the old established, central area of Quebec City convenient to many attractions. This new, beautifully decorated home offers single and double guest rooms with private baths. There is a comfortable sitting area if you wish to relax. The house is very secluded, set back off the main thoroughfare, yet near bus routes on the Boulevard Laurier -- you are guaranteed a quiet and comfortable stay.

Claude is a marvellous cook and breakfast is a delight. Expect to be treated to some gourmet cooking, whether it be a special omelette, and home-baking, a crepe with maple syrup, or something else, with beverages, of course. In warm weather breakfast can be served on the patio among the flowers.

Lili is an experienced bridge player in case this is your interest too; and she also will be glad to help you plan your stay in Quebec. *Bienvenue Quebec Sillery* is within walking distance of an interesting shopping area and places for fine dining. It is ten minutes to the walls of Old Quebec which has been restored to the original state of the little colony founded by Samuel de Champlain, nestled just below the high escarpment, on the banks of the St. Lawrence. Towering over it is the turreted Chateau Frontenac, well worth a look inside. The Plains of Abraham and the Citadelle fortress are two among many historical sites worth visiting. There are many antique and handicraft shops. Quebec is famous for wood carvings and artisans.

Bienvenue has special winter rates and what better time to come to stay; downhill skiing is only half an hour away. Try Mont Sainte-Anne or Stoneham, where family skiing is a top priority, beginning with free skiing for children six and under. The Carnaval de Quebec, eleven memorable days of festivities for the whole family, is held every February.

Claude Poissant and Lili Perigny
1067 Maguire
Sillery, Quebec City, Quebec
G1T 1Y3
(418) 681-3212

Season: All year
Rates: Single $40 Double $50 - $65
Types of Accommodation: 3 Bedrooms
Bathrooms: Private and Shared
Breakfast: Full
Special Information: Children welcome; Smoking outside; No guests' pets please
Languages: French and English
Directions: Sillery is in the center of Quebec City. Take Boulevard Laurier to Maguire Avenue and turn left. Look for the signs.

Bourgault Centre-Ville

The facade of this century-old three-storey townhouse belies what lies within. Built with the entrance right at the street, you enter into a spacious renovated and restored home with a large bright living area downstairs that opens onto a wonderful backyard, flower garden and inner courtyard where you may relax or have tea.

Your hostess, Ginette will welcome you with coffee, juice, cookies and information about things to do and see in Quebec City. And the location couldn't be better for seeing the attractions on foot: the Old walled city of Quebec; the Museum of Civilization; the Art Gallery; restaurants for every budget and mood; the train and bus stations; the library; Churches; a shopping mall; a public swimming pool; tennis court and parks.

There are single, double and family style guest rooms, all clean and comfortable, all with baths en suite, and some with kitchenettes and balconies.

Breakfast is served every morning at the long table in the dining room looking out on the garden. The menu varies each day: eggs, pancakes, French toast, eggs benedict, muffins, zucchini or banana loaf, fruits of the season including strawberries, raspberries, blueberries, or apples. Full Kitchen facilities are available, including a microwave oven. A washer and dryer, a bike rack, a garage for motorcycles or canoes, a B.B.Q. and a picnic table are available for guests.

Quebec City is also worth visiting in the winter. There is downhill skiing at Stoneham, minutes north of the City and each February Quebec hosts a Winter Carnival, the world's biggest Winter celebration.

BOURGAULT
CENTRE-VILLE

Bourgault Centre-Ville
650, rue de la Reine
Quebec, Quebec
G1K 2S1
(418) 525-7832

Season: All year
Rates: Available upon request
Types of Accommodation: Single, Double and Family Room
Bathrooms: En Suite
Breakfast: Full
Special Information: Full kitchen available for guest use; Laundry facilities; B.B.Q. and picnic table for guest use
Languages: English and French
Directions: Very near Old Quebec City. Please call for directions.

Fleet's B&B

The Fleets have been welcoming bed and breakfast guests to their home for many years, and Marie-Paule and Stuart will give you a warm reception at their two-storey residence on a quiet street in Sillery, the prestigious old established residential area of central Quebec City, close to Laval University. The house has a deck overlooking a beautiful back garden.

The entire second floor is for guests only, and there are three bathrooms shared by guests. The rooms are comfortable and nicely appointed.

A full breakfast with home-baking is served either in the dining room, or out on the patio, weather permitting.

Stuart is a leaded glass artist and his works, installed in some of the windows of the house, are quite beautiful.

It has been written that a visit to Quebec City, especially Old Walled Quebec is "a trip back through time". The old stone buildings, towered over by the Chateau Frontenac are restored to 300 years ago. The heart of Vieux-Quebec is the beautiful Place d'Armes. The Citadelle and the Plains of Abraham are historical sites also worth visiting.

Fine dining, shopping, galleries, antique hunting at flea markets or in second hand shops, are other ways to spend your time in Quebec. In winter, downhill skiing is as close as Mont Stoneham or Mont Sainte-Anne.

Stuart and Marie-Paule will be glad to advise you about what to do and see in Quebec.

FLEET'S B&B.

Stuart and Marie-Paule Fleet
1080 Holland Avenue
Sillery, Quebec City, Quebec
G1S 3T3
(418) 688-0794

Season: All year
Rates: Available upon request
Types of Accommodation: 1 Double, 2 Queen, and 2 Twin
Bathrooms: 3 Shared
Breakfast: Full
Special Information: No guests' pets please; Dinners available on request; Laundry facilities
Languages: English and French
Directions: Take Pierre Laporte Bridge, turn right on Blvd Laurier and 2 km to Holland Avenue, then turn left.

Willow House B&B

Willow House Bed and Breakfast or *La Maison des Saules* (its French name) is a beautiful old Loyalist home with a warm and friendly atmosphere situated on the edge of Sutton in view of a running brook and a pond. Yet it is within walking distance of the town centre.

Willow House has homey, pleasant rooms and furniture, guest rooms are well furnished and comfortable. Your friendly hostess, Pat LeBaron serves breakfast, including home-baking, either in the friendly kitchen or the more formal dining room with its interesting corner fireplace. Surrounded by large trees, *Willow House* has an enclosed porch where guests may relax in warmer weather. Afternoon tea and home-made breads and muffins are served to guests.

Sutton is an interesting place with an Art Gallery, boutiques, a library, antique stores, craft shops and fine restaurants. This is an environment where many artists and artisans have chosen to live. The town lies at the foot of Mount Sutton ski hill where guests can participate in either cross-country or downhill skiing in the Wintertime. The Vermont border is less then half an hour away. There are places to golf and horseback ride in the area. Brome Lake is not far away for boating and swimming.

There is public transportation from downtown Montreal to and from Sutton. In the Autumn gorgeous colour covers the hills around Sutton.

— WILLOW HOUSE B&B

Pat LeBaron
30 Western Avenue, Box 906
Sutton, Quebec
J0E 2K0
(514) 538-0035

Season: All year
Rates: Available upon request
Types of Accommodation: 1 Double, 6 Twin
Bathrooms: Shared
Breakfast: Full
Special Information: Air-Conditioning; Children welcome; Dinners available on request; Laundry facilities
Languages: English and French
Directions: From Montreal, take Eastern Township Auto Route 10 and Exit 60 onto Highway 139 to Sutton. Turn right off Principale at Foyer Sutton to Western Avenue.

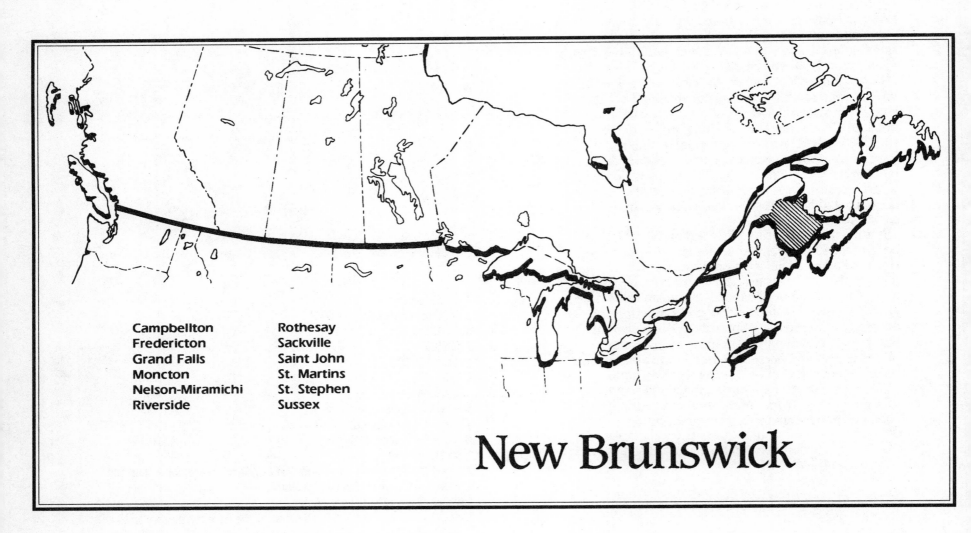

Campbellton
Fredericton
Grand Falls
Moncton
Nelson-Miramichi
Riverside

Rothesay
Sackville
Saint John
St. Martins
St. Stephen
Sussex

New Brunswick

Aylesford Inn

The *Aylesford Inn* is a fine example of New Brunswick's late Victorian architecture. Built at the turn-of-the-century by John Murray-MacLean, this warm gracious, Four Star bed and breakfast home has elegant stained glass, elaborate woodwork, and built-in cabinets with leaded glass doors -- features that allow guests to enjoy the ambiance of yesteryear. Imagine taking morning or afternoon tea or coffee by the warmth of the fireplace, or in summer, on the verandah, or in the beautiful gardens in the shade of chestnuts and lilacs.

The guest bedrooms are all decorated in a Victorian theme and invite you to enjoy the style of the Victorian Era. Mornings welcome you with the aromas of a home-made breakfast, including several gourmet delights, and plenty of coffee or herbal teas.

There is a gift and craft shop on the premises where guests may browse. English and French are spoken.

Campbellton is located at the western end of the Baie des Chaleurs. Sports fishermen from around the world fish the famed Restigouche River and its tributaries for Atlantic salmon. In fact, an eight and one half metre model of this game fish and lighthouse dominate the waterfront park, where visitors may ride on a replica of a steam locomotive, or enjoy a walk. Nearby, Sugarloaf Provincial Park offers many outdoor activities. The Restigouche Art Gallery, featuring regional works; and the Golf and Country Club are accessible to visitors.

Campbellton is just across the Van Horne Bridge from Quebec and the Battle of the Restigouche National Historic Park.

— AYLESFORD INN —

Richard and Shirley Ayles
8 MacMillan Avenue
Campbellton, New Brunswick
E3N 1E9
(506) 759-7672 or (506) 759-7007

Season: All year
Rates: Available upon request
Types of Accommodation: 6 Double, 1 Single
Bathrooms: 1 Private and 2 Shared
Breakfast: Full
Special Information: Breakfast served 8:00 to 10:00 am; Check out time 11:30 am; MasterCard, Visa and Amercian Express accepted; TV in guest rooms
Languages: English and French
Directions: *Aylesford Inn* is in Campbellton on Route 134, exit at Arran Street and take second left, which is Macmillan Avenue.

Carriage House B&B

This three-storey Victorian mansion in picturesque downtown, Fredericton, was built in 1875 by Harry Beckwith, owner of a large lumbermill. He later became the Mayor of Fredericton.

Carriage House is furnished in antiques; and has a Three Star rating; guests have the use of the library, television, and laundry facilities. Guest rooms reflect taste and charm; private and shared bathrooms are available.

Delicious homemade breakfasts are served in the solarium; pots of cheery geraniums and a garden view add to the meal's enjoyment. Additional meals are available by reservation.

Carriage House is adjacent to "The Green" which offers walking and biking paths along the Saint John River. A five minute walk takes you to the Farmer's Market, the Provincial Legislative Building, the Art Gallery, the Playhouse, many fine restaurants and craft outlets. Kings Landing, a 1780-1830 recreated village, Woolastook Park and golfing are only half an hour drive by car.

Carriage House is open year around and if you choose to visit in winter it is just one hour to excellent skiing at Crabbe Mountain; special off-season rates are offered during November through February. *Carriage House* makes a splendid base for exploring the area.

– CARRIAGE HOUSE B+B –

Joan and Frank Gorham
230 University Avenue
Fredericton, New Brunswick
E3B 4H7
(506) 452-9924

Season: All year
Rates: Single $44/$54 Double $49/$59 Additional Adult $15
Types of Accommodation: 6 Double, 4 Twin
Bathrooms: 2 Private 3-piece and 3 Shared 4-piece
Breakfast: Full
Special Information: Children welcome; Dinners offered on request; Air-conditioning; Irish Setter Dog named "Jake" and Cat named "Puzzle" in residence; Children in residence named Katherine and Alex
Directions: Trans Canada Highway Forest Hill Exit (295), Fredericton Centre.

Maple Tourist Home

Maple Tourist Home Bed and Breakfast is a charming 1930's home with verandah, and sun-porch situated on a quiet, large lot in Grand Falls, New Brunswick.

There are three comfortable guest rooms. The Romeo and Juliet Room has a private balcony, ceiling fan and four-poster; the Iris Room has a queen size bed, ceiling fan, radio and sink; the Blue Room has twin beds, a lover's seat, ceiling fan, coloured TV and sink. All the rooms have handsome hardwood floors and private baths.

Guests can relax in the cosy lounge with a TV or, for quiet reading, the living room. The unique continental breakfast consists of juice, home-made jams, muffins and toast. Your hostess can converse in both French and English, and tea and coffee are served on your arrival.

Maple Tourist Home Bed and Breakfast is within easy walking distance of restaurants, gift shops and the magnificent Gorge and Falls. For here at Grand Falls the Saint John River drops a dramatic 75 feet and has created a mile long gorge with fascinating wells-in-the-rocks. Interpretative displays explain the effect of the action of the falls on the surrounding terrain. Stairs provide access into the gorge and walking trails offer a variety of vantage points for viewing the falls. The town is also an important agricultural centre for Victoria county, and each summer a festival pays tribute to the major crop, potatoes. An 18-hole golf course, and outdoor swimming pool, tennis courts, and the United States border are all within a mile radius.

MAPLE TOURIST HOME

Edwina Ethier
142 Main Street, Box 1587
Grand Falls, New Brunswick
E0J 1M0
(506) 473-1763

Season: All year
Rates: Double $45 Twin $50
Types of Accommodation: 1 Double, 1 Queen and 1 Twin
Bathrooms: All private
Breakfast: Unique Continental
Special Information: Non-smoking home; No guests' pets please
Directions: *Maple Tourist Home* is located in Grand Falls, one mile off the Trans Canada Highway at Exit 76.

Bonaccord House

Bonaccord House is a lovely, three-storey 1880's residence, painted yellow. The double living room, complete with fireplace and bay window offers a convivial atmosphere in which to meet fellow guests or just relax and read. Guest rooms are furnished with taste and elegance and offers three private bathrooms. In summer, enjoy a morning coffee or afternoon tea on the lovely front verandah; in winter, beside the fire.

Make *Bonaccord House* your base, and, following a delicious full breakfast, stroll in the park or go shopping at Champlain Place, the largest shopping centre east of Montreal. Promenade by the river, see a movie, or dine in any of Moncton's nicest restaurants. Enjoy everything the downtown has to offer.

Bonaccord House has a Three Star rating and offers the business person interesting, affordable accommodation. Telephones are available for all rooms and a fax machine keeps you in touch with your office. Audio visual aids are available also. What better place to meet your colleagues than in the double living room. Nutrition breaks feature Jeremy's home baked muffins, and arrangements can be made to serve a luncheon in the dining room.

Bonaccord House is open year round, welcomes holiday guests, and offers the discerning business person a comfortable, elegant and affordable alternative.

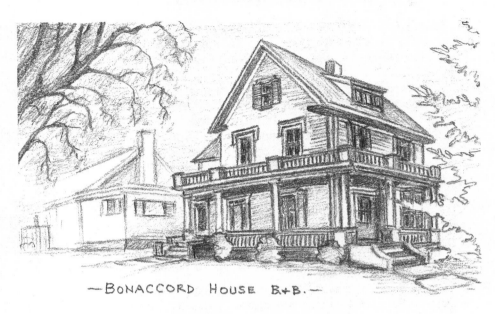

— BONACCORD HOUSE B+B. —

Patricia Townsend and Jeremy Martin
250 Bonaccord Street
Moncton, New Brunswick
E1C 5M6
(506) 388-1535

Fax: (506) 853-7191
Season: All year
Rates: $35 and up
Types of Accommodation: 4 Queen, 1 Twin
Bathrooms: 3 Private and 1 Shared
Breakfast: Full
Special Information: Non-smoking home; Children welcome; No guests' pets
Languages: English, French and some Spanish
Directions: Bonaccord Street intersects both Mountain Road and Main Street. To reach Mountain Road take the Magnetic Hill turnoff. To reach Main Street take the Airport turnoff.

Governor's Mansion

This 140-year-old mansion, former residence of a New Brunswick Lieutenant Governor, sits on a spacious ten acres of lawns and gardens facing the Miramichi River and the historic Beaubear Island National Park.

Governor's Mansion Bed and Breakfast is elegantly furnished with outstanding period pieces; the mansion has spacious high-ceilinged rooms with chandeliers and fireplaces. The music room houses a unique Steinway grand piano, originally imported from Germany, for guests to enjoy. Guests are welcome to browse the well-stocked library. The second floor glassed-in balconies provide spectacular river views. Breakfast is served in the dining room, and afternoon tea and scones in the Tea Room.

Governor's Mansion and the town of Nelson-Miramichi are located across the Miramichi River from Newcastle and close enough to the ocean to enjoy the invigorating salty Atlantic breezes. And this tends to remind one that this a richly historic area where the Tall Ship Era began in 1765, with the building of the first schooners.

Upriver there is salmon fishing; down river deep sea fishing on local lobster boats. Canoes and motor boats are available for rental.

In summer there are many local Festivals and an ocean playground with wharves, lighthouses and fishing villages nearby.

Governor's Mansion is close to a Championship Golf Course; tennis; nature trails for hiking; clamdigging; birdwatching; swimming at the *Mansion's* private beach; bicycling; surf boating; Heritage Home Tours; Historic sites; ten magnificent examples of church architecture; and Micmac Indian Interpretative Lectures (1,000 B.C.)

GOVERNOR'S MANSION

Rev. Charles Mersereau
River Road
Nelson-Miramichi, New Brunswick
E0C 1T0
(506) 622-3036

Season: All year
Rates: Available upon request
Types of Accommodation: Single, Double and Dormitory
Bathrooms: Shared
Breakfast: Full
Special Information: Non-smoking home; Canoes and motor boats available
Directions: *Governor's Mansion Inn* is directly opposite Beaubear's Island National Historic Park, opposite Newcastle on Miramichi River. Call for further directions.

Cailswick Babbling Brook B&B

This century old Three Star Victorian home is surrounded by running brooks, trees, flowers and spacious land where one can relax and enjoy the beauty of nature. At *Cailswick Babbling Brook Bed and Breakfast* overlooking Shepody Bay, guests can experience pleasant, comfortable accommodation and are welcome to spend some quiet time with a book in front of a fire, or watching television. Families with children are welcome.

Country style breakfasts are served in our newly renovated, spacious kitchen. Lunch and Dinner are available by prearrangement.

Guests are invited to use the large patio; this is a good place to have a visit with fellow travellers. English and French are spoken.

Cailswick B&B is a short drive to Hopewell Cape Rocks, Fundy National Park, Moncton, Chignecto Bay, Fundy Bay, a Bird Sanctuary, hiking, cross country skiing, and all the area attractions close by.

Your hosts, Hazen and Eunice Cail, offer warm and friendly hospitality at *Babbling Brook*, where they enjoy their many guests from across the country.

CAILSWICK BABBLING BROOK B.B

Hazen and Eunice Cail
Riverside, Rte. 114,
Albert Co., New Brunswick
E0A 2R0
(506) 882-2079

Season: All year
Rates: Available upon request
Types of Accommodation: 2 Single, 4 Double
Bathrooms: 2 Shared
Breakfast: Full
Languages: English and French
Directions: Coming from Moncton follow Route 114 to Riverside. From Sussex On Highway 1 take Highway 114 and follow all the way through Fundy National Park to Riverside.

Shadow Lawn Country Inn

~ SHADOW LAWN COUNTRY INN ~

Looking for something out of the ordinary, then *Shadow Lawn Country Inn* may just be the answer. Lovingly restored to its former splendor this Three Star Inn offers guests a choice of bedrooms, all tastefully decorated, and furnished with antique beds and dressers, featuring private baths, high ceilings, and hardwood floors. The Honeymoon Suite offers a romantic retreat with its four-poster canopy bed, crackling fire, and luxurious bathroom.

The intimate dining room overlooks spacious grounds and provides superb food. Greet the morning with freshly brewed coffee served with a delicious breakfast. Main courses for dinner include such specialities as Atlantic Poached Salmon, Cornish Hen, Chicken Cordon Bleu and Beef Wellington for example.

Shadow Lawn Country Inn is an ideal setting for business seminars. The conference room can accommodate up to thirty people and a facsimile service is available. Special arrangements can be made also for secretarial service and audio-visual equipment.

For relaxation, nearby recreational facilities include an excellent 18-hole golf course and tennis courts. The Kennebecasis River is within walking distance and there are mooring facilities at the Rothesay Yacht Club. Located in the quaint town of Rothesay, thirteen kilometres from the city of Saint John, and only ten minutes from the Airport, *Shadow Lawn Country Inn* has much to offer.

Patrick and Margaret Gallagher
3180 Rothesay Road, Box 41
Rothesay, New Brunswick
E0G 2W0
(506) 847-7539

Season: All year
Rates: Double $58 - $85
Types of Accommodation: 8 Guest Rooms (King, Double, Queen or Twin beds)
Bathrooms: 8 Private 3-piece
Breakfast: Full (not included in Room price)
Special Information: Conference Room for up to 30 people; Dining room can accommodate 75 - 150 people; Perfect place for romantic dinner for two to a wedding reception or a business luncheon
Languages: English and French
Directions: *Shadow Lawn Country Inn* is located in the quaint town of Rothesay, 13 km from the city of Saint John, only 10 minutes from the airport.

The Different Drummer

At the *Different Drummer Bed and Breakfast* you can enjoy the comforts and convenience of modern living in a restful and homey atmosphere. Attractive bedrooms, each with a private bathroom, are furnished with antiques and period furniture much as they would have been at the turn-of-the-century. In the parlour and adjacent sunroom guests may chat, browse through a well-stocked library of books and magazines, watch colour TV, or just sit back and relax.

Every morning, from 7:30 to 9:00 a.m. complimentary continental-plus breakfast is served in the sunny dining room. Enjoy home-made bread, muffins, and jam, local honey, and fresh-ground coffee or an array of teas.

This spacious Victorian home, with four bedrooms in the main house and another four in the Carriage House, is set in the midst of an acreage of landscaped shaded gardens, open to guests. *The Different Drummer* is an easy ten minutes' walk to restaurants, craft shops, churches, stores, Mount Allison University, the Owens Art Gallery, and the Sackville Waterfowl Park, with its 2 km of boardwalks giving visitors a unique close-up of marsh life.

The old Sackville Harness Shop, located on West Main Street, just minutes away welcomes visitors. There, stepping back in time to a Nineteenth-Century setting, you can see horse collars and harnesses still being made by hand for customers throughout North America and overseas. A short drive to the east is Fort Beausejour (1751), a National Historical Site. From the Fort, there is a panoramic view of Chignecto Bay, and the vast Tantramar Marsh, which the Acadians reclaimed from the sea almost three centuries ago. To the west is the Kellior House Museum (1813) and the Bell Inn (1811). Nature lovers will appreciate the fact that the Tantramar Marsh is one of Canada's best wetland bird habitats.

~ THE DIFFERENT DRUMMER ~

Georgette and Richard Hanrahan
82 West Main Street, Box 188
Sackville, New Brunswick
E0A 3C0
(506) 536-1291

Season: All year
Rates: Available upon request
Types of Accommodation: 4 Bedrooms in the Main House and 4 in the Carriage House
Bathrooms: All private
Breakfasts: Continental
Special Information: No smoking; No guests' pets please; Visa and MasterCard accepted;
Directions: *The Different Drummer* is located at 82 West Main Street across the street from the Sackville Hospital. Take Exit 541 from Highway 2 (Trans Canada Highway) and go straight ahead at the traffic light on Route 106. Please call for brochure or detailed directions.

Country Wreath 'N' Potpourri

This charming heritage home has been restored with loving care by Rubye Haines, to create a display of warmth and character. The three-storey house welcomes you from the moment you enter; spacious rooms, finished wood floors that glow in the candlelight, and a delightful aroma of homemade potpourri wafts throughout. Relax in the blue living room where you can read the paper or chat with new friends; the cheery kitchen is decorated in red and white, with dried herbs hung from the ceiling.

Enjoy a restful night in the "Welcome Friends" Room with its four-poster bed, decorated in ivory, forest green and dusty rose or have pleasant dreams in "Sunshine Hearts", a cosy room tucked away on the third floor, featuring a double bed and quaint chapel window.

Wake up to a full gourmet breakfast served on the eight foot pine table in the forest green and pink dining room. Linger over coffee and plan you day's activities.

Country Wreath 'N' Potpourri Bed and Breakfast is situated five minutes from the heart of downtown: it has a great location for shopping, good restaurants, craft outlets and a stroll through the square. The Martello Tower, Old City Market, Digby Ferry, the Reversing Falls, and Cherry Brook Zoo are a short distance. Rockwood Park, located a quarter mile away, offers hiking, swimming, an 18-hole golf course, or a walk around Lily Lake.

A stay at *Country Wreath 'N Potpourri* is a memorable experience for the traveller.

COUNTRY WREATH 'n' POTPOURRI

Rubye Haines
125 Mount Pleasant Avenue North
Saint John, New Brunswick
E2K 3T9
(506) 636-9919

Season: All year
Rates: Single $45 Double $49 Rollaway $10 (No tax)
Types of Accommodation: 2 Double
Bathrooms: Shared 4-piece
Breakfast: Full
Special Information: Non-smoking home; No pets please; Children welcome
Directions: Exit 112/113 off Highway 1. *Country Wreath 'N' Potpourri* is located on the hill opposite the City Centre, a ten minute walk. Located five minutes from the Digby Ferry.

Cranberry's B&B

Cranberry's Bed and Breakfast is situated on a tree-lined boulevard in the heart of Saint John, minutes from King's Square, City Market, the central business core, and uptown shopping.

This house design appeared on the cover of the Boston Architectural Digest in 1879. Today it stands as one of the elegant old homes on the city's "Victorian Stroll".

Step inside this Three Star brick residence and feel the enjoyment of its gracious living. Distinctive features include high ceilings accentuated by gold leaf plaster mouldings, six white marble fireplaces, four of which are operational, and an abundance of rich hand-hewn oak trims, embellishing all levels. During the summer months you can step out onto the back patio and enjoy, not only a feeling of solitude, but the delight of a kaleidoscope of flowering wallpots.

The upper floor has two guest rooms, one a twin-bedded room; the other a four-poster, double bedded room, with an operating fireplace. *Cranberry's* also offers a private suite with its own kitchen and living room which is very comfortable for guests planning longer stays.

The Red Room offers a crackling fire where one can curl up with a book, watch television or share travelling experiences with other guests. Breakfast is served by candlelight; is there any other way to start your day? Home baked items, complemented by fruit, cereal, juice and beverage are breakfast fare.

Since 1988 *Cranberry's* has had the ongoing pleasure of hosting guests from around the world, and they look forward to being your "home away from home".

— CRANBERRY'S B.+B. —

Janice S. MacMillan
168 King Street East
Saint John, New Brunswick
E2L 1H1
(506) 657-5173

Fax: (506) 634-8990
Season: All year
Rates: $45, $50 and $65 Additional person $10, GST applicable
Types of Accommodation: 1 Double, 1 Twin
Bathrooms: Shared
Breakfast: Full
Special Information: Non-smoking home; Cat on premises
Directions: Please phone ahead for detailed directions.

St. Martins Country Inn

You will feel very welcome at the *St. Martins Country Inn*, a restored 1857 Queen Anne Home. Part of the original land grant awarded by the Crown in 1796 to David and Rachel Vaughan, United Empire Loyalists, the home itself was constructed by David's son, Captain William Vaughan. The *Inn* is a replica of a villa they had seen on the French Riviera, and is the only one of its kind in North America!

The guests bedrooms are decorated in pretty Victorian or cosy country style, each with a private bathroom. All the rooms offer seascape or lush forest views. Early risers can help themselves to coffee and tea in the guest kitchen nook. A full country breakfast greets you in the morning, and after a day of exploring, you may return for a candlelight dinner of fresh salmon served in the Victorian dining room, made cosy by a crackling fire. Those late-to-bed guests can enjoy a glass of wine or tea in the Victorian parlour while relaxing in a chair pulled close to the fire or next to the bay windows overlooking the sea.

Once a bustling shipbuilding town, that launched more then five hundred ships between 1805 and 1880, St. Martins is now a tranquil fishing Port. Lobster and scallop boats chug slowly in and out of the tiny Harbour, with its twin covered bridges. History is captured in the St. Martins Museum, the library and the gingerbread clapboard homes that grace the shore.

St. Martins Country Inn offers friendly, helpful service that is not intrusive -- their home is your home.

ST. MARTINS (East of Saint John)
NEW BRUNSWICK

— St. Martins Country Inn —

Myrna and Albert Leclair
General Delivery
St. Martins, New Brunswick
E0G 2Z0
(506) 833-4534

Fax: (506) 833-4722
Season: All year
Rates: $57 - $80 (Rates do not include GST or Provincial Sales Tax)
Types of Accommodation: 12 Queen
Bathrooms: 12 Private
Breakfast: Full
Special Information: Sorry, no pets; MasterCard and Visa accepted; Check-in time from 3:00 to 6:00 pm; Winter rates are 20% off regular prices
Directions: Please call for detailed directions.

Blair House

Enjoy English Bed and Breakfast, with that special personalized hospitality at *Blair House*, built during the 1850's. *Blair House* is a spacious elegant mansion overlooking the international heritage river St. Croix at St. Stephen -- the Eastern most USA-Canadian border crossing.

Betty, your hostess, offers morning tea or coffee on fine bone china in your room and there are bedtime beverages, cookies and conversation in the guest living room -- "a most relaxing way to begin and end the day". A full English breakfast, including home-made preserves and honey, is presented on fine damask in the sunny dining room. Guest bedrooms are spacious with en suite bathrooms and fans.

Blair House Bed and Breakfast is seven hours from both, Halifax, Nova Scotia and Boston, Massachusetts, and at the hub of the "Quoddy Loop"-Fundy Isles international coastal attraction. Here twenty-eight foot Atlantic tides surge in twice daily.

The Grand Manan Island Ferry is 45 minutes away. There are three golf courses located nearby. Ask your hosts about canoeing, kayaking, cycling, and other interesting opportunities.

BLAIR HOUSE

Betty and Bryan Whittingham
38 Prince William Street, Box 112
St. Stephen, New Brunswick
E3L 2W9
(506) 466-2233

Fax: (506) 466-5636
Season: All year
Rates: Single $40 Double $50 Twin $53 Extra person $10
Types of Accommodations: 2 Double, 1 Twin, and Family Suite
Bathrooms: 3 Private 4-piece
Breakfast: Full
Special Information: Non-smoking home -- upstairs deck for smokers; No guests' pets
Directions: *Blair House* is 1/4 mile east of Highway 1. From USA, take right at first traffic light. From Canada, take left at third traffic light. *Blair House* is the third house after the Christ Church.

Dutch Valley Heritage Inn

Leave home and "come home" to *Dutch Valley Heritage Inn* when you are visiting southern New Brunswick. You will feel at home in this comfortable spacious, lovingly restored 1810 heritage home -- a unique example of Federal architecture with added Gothic embellishments.

Four bedrooms are furnished in rare New Brunswick Empire and Victorian style antiques each with private bath. Relax with a soothing cup of herbal tea and enjoy a good book in the front room or conversation with fellow travellers in the "Keeping Room". Slip into a hot bubble bath in an antique tub before retiring.

After a quiet country night, enjoy a full health-conscious breakfast, served family style, with fresh ground coffee and local "King Cole" tea.

Dutch Valley Heritage Inn is in the Dutch Valley farming area -- only two miles from Sussex. Nearby is the Sussex Golf and Curling Club, covered bridges, cycling and hiking trails, and in town, quaint shops. You can establish your "home base" at *Dutch Valley* because we are within 45 minutes of Fundy Park, St. Martins, Moncton, and Saint John -- all exceptional day trips, and, for skiers, only seven minutes from Poley Mountain.

You may arrive a stranger, but you will leave a friend whether you stay one night or longer.

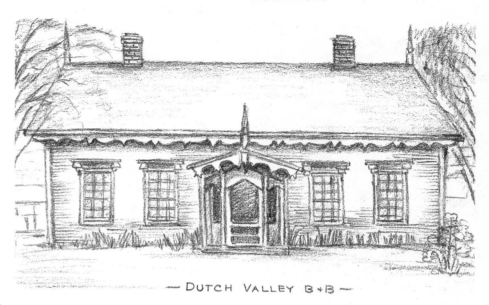

— DUTCH VALLEY B+B —

Vickey and Lawson Bell
RR4
Sussex, New Brunswick
E0E 1P0
(506) 433-1339

Fax: (506) 433-4287
Season: All year
Rates: Single $45 Double $55 Extra person $10
Types of Accommodation: 4 Double, 4 Twin
Bathrooms: 4 Private
Breakfast: Full Home-cooked
Special Information: Non-smoking home; No guests' pets please; Cat in residence; Dinners offered on request
Directions: Nearing Sussex, follow ski signs to Poley Mountain or call from town.

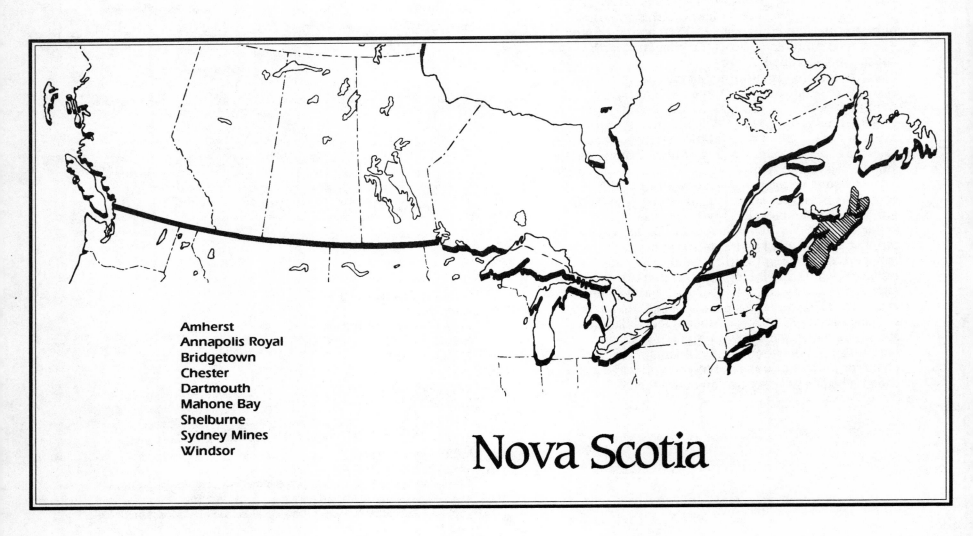

Amherst
Annapolis Royal
Bridgetown
Chester
Dartmouth
Mahone Bay
Shelburne
Sydney Mines
Windsor

Nova Scotia

Amherst Shore Country Inn

If you are looking for a secluded "comfortable country" place, right on the ocean on the Northumberland Shore then the *Amherst Shore Country Inn* is the answer. The *Inn* is situated along route 366 halfway between Amherst and Pugwash in the farming community of Lorneville. It is also handy to the Cape Tormentine, New Brunswick Ferry to Prince Edward Island.

"Quality is stressed here, and warm service. And the staff here seem to hold the same level of pride in quality that I do. I think that's what makes us special" says Donna Laceby, mother of five children, all of whom help in the operations at *Amherst Shore* and at the Blomidon Inn in Wolfville, Nova Scotia, also owned by the Laceby's and which also has that special "Laceby touch".

At *Amherst Shore Country Inn*, a converted two-storey farmhouse, every room is different, yet all seems to blend. Most of the furniture is refinished antiques, and quilts made by Donna Laceby top the beds. Paintings sent as gifts from guests and relatives line the walls. There are two guest rooms upstairs with private baths, and two on the lower level with a private bath and private entrances.

A special feature of the *Amherst Shore Country Inn* is the four-course fixed price meal; this dining room has been rated "as one of the best in Nova Scotia". The first person to book sets the menu for the evening from the Laceby master list. The meal includes soup, salad, choice between two entrees -- meat or fish -- and dessert. There are also wonderful homemade breads. Breakfast is just as special!

AMHERST SHORES COUNTRY INN

Donna Laceby
RR2
Amherst, Nova Scotia
B4H 3X9
(902) 667-4800

Season: May 1 - Mid-October
Rates: $69 and up
Types of Accommodation: 4 Double or Queen (also a Twin bed in 3 of the rooms)
Bathrooms: 4 Private
Breakfast: Full
Special Information: Dinner at 7:30 by advance reservation only; Own Blomidon Inn in Wolfville
Directions: *Amherst Shore Country Inn* is 32 km (20 miles) from Amherst on Highway 366 on the Northumberland Strait. Please call ahead for detailed directions

Bread and Roses

Bread and Roses Country Inn is dedicated to the concept that people require not only the basic essentials of life, but beauty and inspiration as well. This term came from a poem by James Oppenheim, written in 1912, after a banner carried by striking women textile workers saying "we want bread *and* roses".

This restored Victorian mansion was constructed by Italian craftsmen in 1882 in the Gothic Revival style. You enter *Bread and Roses* into a central hallway, panelled with fine woods -- mahogany, oak, ash and tiger maple, and a beautiful wide staircase lighted by a large Church chandelier. This dramatic use of contrasting woods sets the tone of the house, the gracious hospitality and warm welcome that make guests feel at home.

The antique-filled guest bedrooms, all with private baths, range from grand and dramatic to small and delicate. Breakfast includes wonderful home-made granola, brown bread and jams, porridge, bacon and eggs, served with brewed Columbian coffee in the charming, spacious dining room.

Both the parlour and dining room have exquisitely tiled fireplaces. Evening tea served in the parlour by the fire is conducive to interesting conversation with people who have been to all parts of the globe.

Annapolis Royal was founded by the French under Samuel de Champlain in 1605, fifteen years before the Pilgrims landed at Plymouth. It is noted for the beautiful Annapolis Royal Historic Gardens, the scenic Waterfront and boardwalk, Fort Anne, numerous historic buildings, museums, and many parks.

BREAD and ROSES COUNTRY INN

Don and Jeannie Allen
82 Victoria Street, Box 177
Annapolis Royal, Nova Scotia
B0S 1A0
(902) 532-5727

Season: All year
Rates: $55 - $75 plus taxes
Types of Accommodation: 4 Double, 2 Queen, and 3 Twin (with Double beds)
Bathrooms: 9 Private
Breakfast: Full (moderate charge)
Special Information: Non-smoking home; No guests' pets please; Cat in residence named "Sammy"
Handicapped Facilities: Limited -- 2 Double bedrooms on main floor
Directions: Two and a half hours by car from Halifax via Highway 101 or Route 1. Two hours from Yarmouth via Highway 101 or Route 1. Half an hour from Digby and Ferry to Saint John. Two hours from Lunenburg via Highway 8. Please call for detailed directions.

The Queen Anne Inn

The Queen Anne Inn built in 1865 is a superb example of Second Empire architecture; the house is surrounded by shaded lawns and mature trees including a number of stately old elms, and located virtually across the street from the delightful Annapolis Royal Historic Gardens.

Leslie J. Langille, your host, has restored the house to its original Victorian grandeur. The large entrance hall with a grand staircase, the fine interior woodwork of oak, ash, and walnut are all in the best Victorian style. The elegant antique furnishings reflect the gracious atmosphere of the Nineteenth Century. Guests may wander through the three sitting rooms and on cool evenings relax in front of the fireplace and enjoy a cup of tea or coffee (perked decaffinated), fresh cookies and conversation.

A full breakfast including freshly-squeezed orange juice and toasted home-made brown bread is served in the elegant dining room furnished with period mahogany and Eighteenth Century English porcelain between 8:00 and 10:00 each morning. All the gracious guest rooms have private baths.

Queen Anne Inn is located within walking distance of fine restaurants, shops and the waterfront. Annapolis Royal is the birthplace of Canada, in that it was founded in 1605 by the French under Samuel de Champlain on the Annapolis River.

Other places to visit in the area are Fort Anne, a national historic site, the King's Theatre, many heritage buildings, and the waterfront promenade overlooking the Annapolis Basin and the village of Granville Ferry, one of the most scenic areas of Nova Scotia.

— QUEEN ANNE INN —

Leslie J. Langille
494 Upper St. George Street, Box 218
Annapolis Royal, Nova Scotia
B0S 1A0
(902) 532-7850

Season: All year
Rates: Double $50 - $80
Types of Accommodation: 6 Double, 4 Twin
Bathrooms: All Private
Breakfast: Full
Special Information: No smoking; No guests' pets; Resident Cat
Directions: *Queen Anne Inn* is on the main street (St. George) across from Annapolis Royal Historic Gardens.

Chesley House B&B

Chesley House, a lovely Queen Anne style house, was built in 1903 by a well known merchant in Bridgetown in the verdant Annapolis Valley. The Valley is one of the most celebrated apple-growing regions in the world. A trip through the countryside during apple blossom season (late May or early June) or to enjoy the brilliant fall colours is memorable. Located at the head of navigation on the Annapolis River, Bridgetown was an important ship-building centre. Many historic stately homes built by ship-builders and sea captains, on treelined streets, reflect this ship-faring past.

The house boasts a splendid staircase leading to spacious comfortable bedrooms, both twin and double. A reading area and a charming salon, in which guests are invited to read or visit, complete the picture.

A full breakfast includes home-baked goods and preserves, as well as fresh fruit in season. Your hosts, Lorelei and David, are well travelled, and enjoy sharing ideas and impressions with guests. Lorelei speaks French, Spanish and some Italian; David's forte is expatiating on political and historical issues.

Chesley House is a short distance from Canada's oldest European settlement, Annapolis Royal, home of Port Royal and Fort Anne, both National Parks. View the fascinating tides of the Bay of Fundy from nearby hiking trails or picnic grounds, visit the local museums, craft stores and farmers' market. Dine on lobster or scallops before visiting King's Theatre. A visitor would be well entertained for many days in this picturesque and historic area. Come and be welcomed.

-CHESLEY HOUSE-

Lorelei Robins and David Shepherd
304 Granville Street, Box 134
Bridgetown, Nova Scotia
B0S 1C0
(902) 665-2904

Season: All year
Rates: Single $28 Double $38 Twin $40
Types of Accommodation: 1 Single, 1 Double, 1 Queen, 2 Twin
Bathrooms: 1 Shared
Breakfast: Full
Special Information: Children welcome; Non-smoking home; Dinners available with advance notice; Evening tea always offered; Rock-Hounding Beach nearby
Languages: English, French, Spanish and Italian
Directions: Coming from the East, take Bridgetown Exit from Highway 101. From the West Route 1 comes straight into town and becomes Granville Street.

The Mecklenburgh Inn

Suzan Fraser chose the name *Mecklenburg* for her bed and breakfast Inn because this was the earliest known name for the body of water, known today as Mahone Bay, on which the town of Chester is situated.

The Inn is a three-storey structure with two covered balconies offering ocean views. The large and informal dining room usually has a crackling fire in the fireplace as a focal point. The breakfast table is the original cutting table used by Ida Mac-Neil, niece of the Robinson sisters who had the house built in 1890. Miss MacNeil operated a millinery, yarn and woolens shop on the premises until it was purchased by Suzan Fraser in 1990.

The Mecklenburg Inn is charmingly decorated with painted period furniture and local artists' works. The spacious and bright guest rooms are delightful and each is named after an island in Mahone Bay. "Mrs. Finney's Hat" and "Gooseberry" are furnished with early Nova Scotia painted furniture.

Suzan trained as a "Cordon Bleu Cook" at the school in London, England. She has travelled extensively and chose to return to Chester where she was born, in order to share her home, interests and her knowledge of the Bay area with her guests.

After a delicious breakfast around the big table, Chester has many delights for visitors to explore, including an 18-hole golf course; craft and gift shops; and sailing. Instruction is available at the Chester Yacht Club; Chester Race week, the largest sailing regatta in the Maritimes, is held in mid-August.

— MECKLENBURGH INN —

Suzan Fraser
78 Queen Street
Chester, Nova Scotia
B0J 1J0
(902) 275-4638

Season: June 1 - October 31
Rates: Single $50 Double $59 Extra person $20 (plus 10% Sales Tax and GST)
Types of Accommodation: 3 Double, 1 Twin
Bathrooms: 2 Shared
Breakfast: Full
Special Information: Picnics packed on request; Smoking on balcony
Directions: Please call ahead for detailed directions.

Riverdell Country Inn

RIVERDELL

Riverdell, nestled among the trees beside a babbling brook, offers you Four Star executive luxury complete with modern, spacious rooms decorated with antiques and collectibles. There's space to relax by the fireplace with a book, or birdwatch from the sunny Florida room.

The large guest rooms offer you a choice of private and semi-private baths. In addition the charming suite, with double whirlpool bath and handmade quilts, keeps guests warm and cosy.

Your day begins with breakfast in the bright Florida room where you can birdwatch while enjoying apple crepes, blueberry pancakes topped with Nova Scotia maple syrup, or other selections, including home-made breads, muffins and preserves.

All this is within minutes of downtown Dartmouth and Halifax. Bedford Basin offers beautiful sailing and boating. The twin cities which are steeped in history are placed on opposite sides of one of the world's finest harbour and a regular passenger ferry service connects the two downtown areas. Several interesting museums are within walking distance, as are fine shopping areas, and specialty stores, many of which feature Atlantic handicrafts. Excellent restaurants offer seafood and gourmet dishes before you treat yourself to top entertainment for your evening out.

Not far away you will discover quiet fishing villages and unspoiled beaches. Your hosts are knowledgeable and would be delighted to help you plan your itinerary. With so much to see and do *Riverdell* makes a fine base for your visit to Dartmouth and Halifax.

Clare and Isabel Christie
68 Ross Road, RR3
Dartmouth, Nova Scotia
B2W 5N7
(902) 434-7880

Season: May 1 - October 31 (other times by advance reservations)
Rates: Each person $30 - $45 Extra person $25
Types of Accommodation: Large bedrooms and 1 Suite
Bathrooms: Private, Semi-private and Suite has double whirlpool
Breakfast: Full
Special Information: No guests' pets please; No smoking; Not suitable for small children
Directions: *Riverdell* is located just off Dartmouth's main street travelling to the Eastern shore or beginning of Marine Drive. Ross Road joins Highways 207 and 7 (107). From Cape Breton look for Little Salmon River Bridge just before Ross Road. Ten miles from Halifax city centre (less by ferry); 20 minutes from the Airport.

Sterns Mansion Inn

Sterns Mansion Inn is a restored century home located on a quiet, residential tree-lined street, six minutes from downtown Halifax. *Sterns Mansion* was awarded a Four Star rating by Nova Scotia Tourism.

The Victorian decor is reminiscent of a bygone era -- stained glass, brass chandeliers, period furnishings all contribute to this ambiance.

The guest bedrooms have private baths stocked with a full range of all-natural *Nu-Skin International* amenities; some have jacuzzi spas en suite. All the rooms have colour cable TV.

Guests are invited to join in evening tea and sweets. Morning beverage is made available to the guest rooms. Later a candlelight breakfast extravaganza with a menu offering over forty breakfast choices is served in the elegant dining room. Or, for the Honeymooners-at-heart, Breakfast in Bed is available.

Dartmouth, founded in 1750, is steeped in history and offers interesting museums, fine shopping areas, and excellent opportunities for recreation.

Halifax, the capital of Nova Scotia, has all the top entertainment and a waterfront area that is a prime example of the blending of the old and the new. The wooden buildings and fine stone structures of 18th-century Halifax stand in harmony with the contemporary. Harbour tours and boat trips are offered day and night, including sailings aboard the famous *Bluenose II*. There is a regular passenger ferry service between Dartmouth and Halifax.

STERN'S MANSION

Holly and Bill DeMolitor
17 Tulip Street
Dartmouth, Nova Scotia
B3A 2S5
(902) 465-7414

Season: All year
Rates: $55 - $100
Types of Accommodation: 6 Guest bedrooms
Bathrooms: 6 Private
Breakfast: Full
Special Information: Non-smoking home; No guests' pets please; MasterCard and Visa accepted
Directions: Take Route 118 to Victoria Road and turn left (south). Go through 2 sets of lights, then take first left on Tulip Street and look for sign.

Longacres B&B Inn

Longacres Bed and Breakfast Inn sits on fifteen secluded scenic acres on the crest of a hill at the northern boundary of the historic and beautiful town of Mahone Bay. Built prior to 1800 the home still retains its pioneer character, even though dormers and a new wing have been added. Fine woodwork, the large original fireplace with massive mantel, bake oven and panelled side doors, one with the traditional Christian cross, the parlour with built-in corner cupboard, and the front door with a reeded centre band are some of the house's original features.

Flower gardens, mature ornamental trees, large lawns, a pond and old pasture (where pheasants thrive) surround the house; mature oaks, and pine trees form a natural park-like setting which extends, along with a walking trail for guests, a quarter mile to the shore of the Mush-A-Mush River.

A delicious home-baked breakfast is served in the warmth of the original old kitchen. The guest bedrooms, reached by traditional and quarterturn stairways, are quaint and comfortable, each with a washroom. There is a gift shop on the premises where guests browse through unique local handicrafts.

Mahone Bay, with its three famous beautiful Churches along the shore, is close to Peggy's Cove and Lunenburg. It is known as a craft and antique centre, and the town has many fine restaurants and museums, ocean views and river fronts, which are a photographer's paradise.

LONGACRES B+B

Ross and Sandy Hayden
Box 93, Clearland Road
Mahone Bay, Nova Scotia
B0J 2E0
(902) 624-6336

Season: All year
Rates: Bay Room: Single $50 Double $60 Triple $70
Sage Room: Single $40 Double $50
Mint Room Single $45 Double $55 Triple $65
Types of Accommodation: Bay Room: Queen Bed with 3-piece washroom Sage Room: 2 Twin beds with 2-piece washroom Mint Room: Queen bed with 3-piece washroom
Breakfast: Full (All you can eat)
Special Information: Children welcome; Non-smoking home (smoking allowed only on verandah and parking area); No guests' pets
Languages: English and some French
Directions: From Highway 103 take Exit 10 and turn right on Highway 3 to Mahone Bay, between the three churches and Kedy's Landing drive up the hill on the road beside the Tourist Bureau. *Longacres* is the large secluded cape cod home behind the long white picket fence.

Cooper's Inn

-COOPER'S INN-

The Cooper's Inn is situated on Shelburne's restored historic waterfront. Built in 1785 by a blind loyalist merchant, George Gracie, it has been home to mariners, ship builders, Esquires, Coopers, and now Innkeepers. The house was restored in 1988 by your hosts Cynthia and Gary Hynes, and provides warmth and welcome as a fine Country Inn. The charming rooms all have private baths, water views, and are furnished with antiques.

Your hosts, Cynthia and Gary, also own and operate The Cooper's Restaurant. The restaurant is acclaimed for its gourmet cuisine and friendly candlelight ambiance. It offers regional cuisine, fresh local produce, and tempting desserts.

The town of Shelburne is nestled into a shore, strewn with lighthouses, unspoiled sand beaches and Cape Islander lobster boats. Settled in 1783, Shelburne once rivalled Boston as the most important port in North America. Today it is a sleepy town, enjoyed for its rich heritage, clean environment, and various recreational opportunities.

A sunset stroll provides visitors with unequalled views of the world's third largest natural harbour and restored waterfront. Shelburne also makes a fine base for exploring the area's beaches, fishing villages, craft shops, and museums.

The *Inn* is within easy reach of Riverside Golf Course, and, for history buffs, a detailed walking tour guide book is available from the local Tourist Information Centre on Dock Street.

Gary and Cynthia Hynes
36 Dock Street, Box 959
Shelburne, Nova Scotia
B0T 1W0
(902) 875-4656 or Check Inns 1-800-565-0000

Season: May 1 - Thanksgiving
Rates: Available upon request
Types of Accommodation: 2 Double, 1 King
Bathrooms: 3 Private
Breakfast: Full
Special Information: No guests' pets please
Directions: *Cooper's Inn* is located on the harbour in South Shore village on the Lighthouse Route.

Toddle In

Toddle In is an early 1800's American Colonial home that underwent major renovation during the Victorian period with the addition of side bays and a turret. During the early 1900's a shop was introduced into the original dining and kitchen areas.

Today, it features four bedrooms with private and shared baths. The spacious smoke free rooms have period furnishings. In the evening guests can relax on the balcony or stroll along the waterfront, a few steps away, along historic Dock Street.

The *Toddle In* dining room offers "down east" cooking and the Curiosity Shoppe, on the premises, has an unique collection of local crafts and giftware from around the world.

Shelburne is an old "Loyalist Town"; many people come here to trace their roots. It was settled in 1783, when about 3,000 Loyalists arrived in thirty ships from New York, establishing an instant boom town in the wilderness. They chose the location because of the superb natural harbour. Many of Shelburne's homes date from this Loyalist Period and a walking-tour guidebook is available. The Ross-Thomson House, built by Loyalists in 1784, is now a Provincial Museum and features artifacts, furniture, china and paintings dating to Colonial times. The David Nairn House Museum, 1787, specializes in Loyalist genealogies and exhibits.

This area has lovely white sand beaches, golf courses and yacht racing, many places for fine dining, and much more.

SHELBURNE (East of Yarmouth)
NOVA SCOTIA

~ TODDLE IN ~

Anthony Caruso
Box 837
Shelburne, Nova Scotia
B0T 1W0
(902) 875-3229

Fax: (902) 875-3629
Season: All year
Rates: Single $25 Double $35 Twin $35
Types of Accommodation: 4 Guest bedrooms
Bathrooms: Private and Shared
Breakfast: Full
Special Information: Breakfast served 8:00 to 10:00 a.m.; The Tea Room is open 11:00 a.m. to 7:00 p.m.
Directions: *Toddle In* is just one short block from the Tourist Bureau and beautiful Dock Street, which runs along the edge of Shelburne Harbour.

Gowrie House

Gowrie House, a Georgian style home built in 1825 by the Archibald family, was named after the village of Blair-Gowrie, Scotland. A Century and a half later, Clifford Matthews and Ken Tutty purchased Gowrie House; they have carefully redecorated and furnished their home with fine antiques and art. The result is an atmosphere of comfortable elegance.

In 1982 *Gowrie House* opened its first guest rooms to the travelling public, and catered its first private dinner party for guests. Since then, its reputation has steadily grown. Today it is recommended in *Where to Eat in Canada* as "what may be the best kitchen on Cape Breton Island", and by the Boston Globe as "a museum showpiece" where "dinner is, quite simply, Heaven". *Gowrie House* was awarded the Food Service Award for 1991 by the Tourism Industry Association of Nova Scotia.

Besides the spacious guest rooms in the house, there is also a "Garden House" providing four suites complete with fireplaces, private baths, and balconies upstairs overlooking the beautiful flower garden.

The central location of *Gowrie House* makes it a perfect base for exploring Cape Breton, and its proximity to the Ferry Terminal, a pleasant stopover en route to and from Newfoundland.

Cape Breton is famous for the Cabot Trail, one of the most beautiful drives in North America; and the Cape Breton Highlands National Park, the largest remaining protected wilderness and wild animal habitat in the province. The Fortess of Louisburg, a National Historic Park is within 45 minutes. But most important of all, people come to *Gowrie House,* to experience the food!

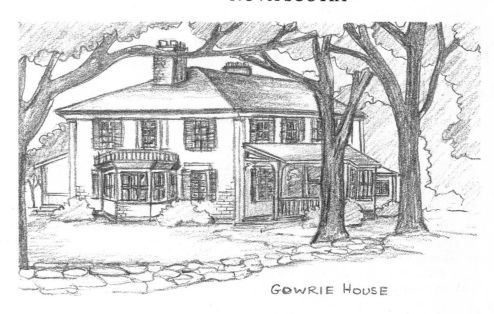

GOWRIE HOUSE

Clifford Matthews and Ken Tutty
139 Shore Road
Sydney Mines, Nova Scotia
B1V 1A6
(902) 544-1050

Season: All year
Rates: Single $48 - $65 Double $58 - $75 Suites $110 - $125 Extra person $12
Types of Accommodation: 6 Large bedrooms and 4 Suites
Bathrooms: In House bedrooms have shared baths, Garden House Suites have private baths
Breakfast: Full Gourmet
Special Information: Dinners served June 1 - September 30; Visa and MasterCard accepted; No smoking in rooms; Pets with permission
Directions: Follow Highway 105 east. Take Exit 21 and follow Highway 305 north to Sydney Mines - 3 km to *Gowrie House.*

Clockmaker's Inn

You will receive a warm welcome at this grand Victorian house, built in 1894, and furnished with antiques. The *Clockmaker's Inn* has a relaxed atmosphere and is situated in an historic town, Windsor, Nova Scotia, right at the gateway to the Annapolis Valley.

There are four spacious guest rooms, decorated with hand-paintings; a large stained glass window; and parquet stairs and floors. A delicious home-baked breakfast is served.

Relax in front of the Victorian fireplace, curl up with a book or watch television. During the winter or summer enjoy the sunroom and verandah.

The *Inn* is open year round and close to local and Haliburton (Sam Slick) museums, Fort Edward Blockhouse, and windsurfing on Lake Piziquid. It is a short drive to the Tidal Bore, Halifax, Peggy's Cove, Grand Pre National Park, and beautiful Mahone Bay.

Windsor is famous for its participation in the World Pumpkin Festival held annually on Thanksgiving Day in October. Some of the world's largest pumpkins are grown in and around Windsor. Visit us in winter and ski at Martock.

The hosts at *Clockmaker's Inn* are very proud of their Three Star rating and would be pleased to assist you with your travel plans.

— CLOCKMAKER'S INN —

Veronica and Dennis Connelly
1399 King Street, P.O. Box 42
Curry's Corner, Windsor
Hants Co., Nova Scotia
B0N 1H0
(902) 798-5265 or Check Inns 1-800-565-0000

Season: All year
Rates: Available upon request
Types of Accommodation: 4 Guest bedrooms
Breakfast: Full
Special Information: Visa accepted
Directions: *Clockmaker's Inn* is located at the junction of Route 14 to Chester. Please call for detailed directions.

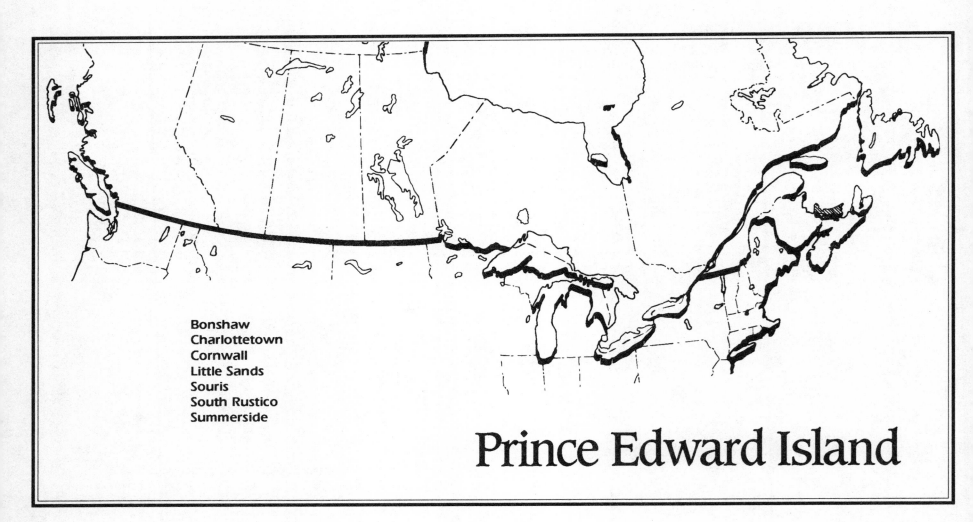

Bonshaw
Charlottetown
Cornwall
Little Sands
Souris
South Rustico
Summerside

Prince Edward Island

Strathgartney Country Inn

Strathgartney was built circa 1863 for Robert Bruce Stewart of Perthshire, Scotland. Four generations of Stewarts resided here until the early 1960's. Then the homestead was sold and operated as a Heritage Museum. The present owners purchased *Strathgartney* in 1986 and opened its doors as a Country Inn.

Set in thirty acres of pastoral countryside and gardens it has been designated as a Heritage property and has earned a Four Star Rating. Each guest room is finely appointed and offers you a beautiful view of the Northumberland Strait or the surrounding countryside. The Royal Stewart Suite is furnished with fireplace, jacuzzi and is the Inn "treasure".

The Country Hearth dining room offers a complimentary buffet breakfast to guests, and in the evening dinner is available to non guests also. The food, prepared by a gourmet chef, may include fresh seafood dishes, and vegetables right from the garden.

During selected weeks in July, August and some weekends in Autumn, creative workshops are available, offering nature photography, sketching, water colours and creative writing. These are provided with the support of the Centre of Creative Arts at Holland College.

The *Inn* is located in the heart of the South Shore where you can enjoy the Island's warmest air and water temperatures north of the Carolinas. Hence their motto "Warm Tidings". Secluded beaches, sea-side villages, and Heritage parks are yours without crowds and congestion. The *Inn* is just minutes away from Charlottetown, the theatre production of *Anne of Green Gables*, Summerside, Cavendish, and principal entry points of the Marine Atlantic Ferry at Borden, and Prince Edward Island's main airport.

BONSHAW (West of Charlottetown)
PRINCE EDWARD ISLAND

— STRATHGARTNEY COUNTRY INN —

Gerald and Martha Gabriel
RR3
Bonshaw, Prince Edward Island
C0A 1C0
(902) 675-4711

Season: May 1 - October 31
Rates: Available upon request
Types of Accommodation: 10 bedrooms
Bathrooms: 7 Private, 2 Share, and Suite has jacuzzi
Breakfast: Buffet
Special Information: Non-smoking home; No guests' pets; Dinner available
Languages: English and French
Directions: Located on the Trans Canada Highway and 18 km west of Charlottetown. Please phone for detailed directions.

The Duchess of Kent Inn

The Duchess of Kent Inn is a charming and elegant 1875 designated Heritage home, now a Three Star Bed and Breakfast Inn located in the heart of downtown Charlottetown, the capital of Prince Edward Island and the birthplace of Confederation.

This Victorian clapboard and shingled Inn features a three-storey "turret" corner, antiques, collectibles and fireplaces. The *Inn* has eight charming guest rooms including a third floor two bedroom suite, all with period furnishings. Guests are welcome to use a fully equipped kitchen offering complimentary tea, coffee, and hot chocolate.

Within a one block walk, you can explore Province House, the museum dedicated to the meeting place of the Fathers of Confederation in 1864, Confederation Centre of the Arts, home of the long running musical, *Anne of Green Gables*, the art gallery, shops, restaurants and churches. Waterfront walks, scenic Victoria Park, guided walking and double-decker bus tours are also nearby.

— DUCHESS of KENT INN —

Sharyn Dalrymple
218 Kent Street
Charlottetown, Prince Edward Island
C1A 1P2
(902) 566-5826

Season: Early May - Late November
Rates: $40 - $55
Types of Accommodation: 8 Bedrooms including a Suite
Bathrooms: Shared -- 3 full bathrooms and 2 half bathrooms
Breakfast: Continental Plus
Special Information: Non-smoking home; No guests' pets please; Bicycle storage; Phone available for guest use; Complimentary tea, coffee, and hot chocolate; Air-conditioning on third floor
Languages: English and some French
Directions: *The Duchess of Kent Inn* is 1 1/2 blocks east of University Avenue on Kent Street in downtown Charlottetown.

Chez Nous

Welcome! Bienvenue! to the ♡ of Prince Edward Island at *Chez Nous Bed and Breakfast*. Nestled among tall birches and mature maples, this secluded retreat is just ten minutes west of Charlottetown, at Cornwall.

This very spacious charming country home will make you feel welcome at once. The elegant, yet cosy decor, the living room with fireplace, and the solarium, the care taken in furnishing guest bedrooms, all reflect the loving warmth that is epitomized by the "heart" motifs of *Chez Nous'* decor.

There are four spacious guest rooms, each with a private three-piece bath, cable colour TV and telephone. The extra special mattresses guarantee a superb night's sleep. A bountiful complimentary breakfast is served in the lovely solarium - dining room to enhance your early morning appetite. For other meals the much-acclaimed Bonnie Brae Restaurant is only a few minutes away.

One of the best things about *Chez Nous*, besides its quiet seclusion, is its proximity to Charlottetown. The capital of Canada's smallest province calls itself the birthplace of Canada; here in September 1864 the Fathers of Confederation met for the first time; therefore; there are many interesting heritage buildings and museums. Interesting too, is the Confederation Centre of the Arts; covering two downtown blocks, it contains a memorial hall, theatre, art gallery and a provincial library. It is here each summer, since 1964, that the Charlottetown Festival has played to sold-out audiences with its classic production of *Anne of Green Gables*.

CORNWALL (West of Charlottetown)
PRINCE EDWARD ISLAND

— CHEZ NOUS —

Sandi and Paul Gallant
Route 248 (Old Ferry Road)
Cornwall, Prince Edward Island
C0A 1H0
(902) 566-2779

Season: June 1 - October 31
Rates: Available upon request
Types of Accommodation: 4 Bedrooms
Bathrooms: 4 Private
Breakfast: Full
Special Information: Babysitting; Laundry arranged; Stay two nights and the third at half price
Languages: English, Spanish and some French
Directions: Located west of Charlottetown on scenic drive off Trans Canada Highway 1. From Cornwall, take Highway 248 (Ferry Road) and look for house on left with pickett fence.

Bayberry Cliff Inn

Bayberry Cliff Inn, named for the bayberry bushes growing along the cliff edge, is situated at the top of a rugged forty-foot redstone cliff, and overlooks the Northumberland Strait.

Nancy, a marine painter, and Don, a retired teacher, moved two post and beam barns to the site in 1982, and renovated them to create their five-level home, with windows from all eight rooms capturing the magnificent ocean view. Antiques, hand-made furniture, quilts, paintings, rustic beams, and loft sleeping areas add to the Inn's uniqueness. Nancy and Don are especially proud of their new Honeymoon Suite with brass bed, private bath and a large deck. Marine murals depicting the 1800's cover the walls. Guests enjoy a full breakfast served family style.

Outside, there is a tree loft, stairs to the shore, and innertubing and snorkeling equipment to use while swimming.

Nancy's paintings are featured at a former guests' new folk art gallery, the "Compass Rose Studio" nearby.

Bayberry Cliff Inn is handy to restaurants, and local activities.

Thirty-five wild flower species are right outside the *Inn*; Nancy and Don have a large library and video selection for quiet times. Seals, porpoises, the ferry, cruise ships, and even whales can be seen from the balcony.

One guest's comment says it all: "We wish we had come here first." Why don't you? Nancy and Don will give you a warm welcome.

BAYBERRY CLIFF INN —

Don and Nancy Perkins
RR4, Little Sands
Murray River, Prince Edward Island
C0A 1W0
(902) 962-3395

Season: All year
Rates: Available upon request
Types of Accommodation: 8 Bedrooms
Bathrooms: Private and Shared
Breakfast: Full
Special Information: No guests' pets; Non-smoking home
Directions: From Wood Islands Ferry turn right on Route 4 (East) and follow 8 km to house on right.

Matthew House Inn

The *Matthew House Inn* invites you to bed and breakfast in spacious comfortable guest rooms, each with its private bath and Victorian ambiance. Also, you may relax beside the fire in the parlour overlooking the harbour or enjoy Cable TV or a film in the study. Guests are welcome to use the spa and exercise room. A gift shop on the premises invites you to browse through local handicrafts.

Delicious complimentary breakfast starts the day; gourmet lunches and candlelight dinners are available by prearrangment and box lunches packed for your beach adventure are a specialty of *Matthew House*. Ask about the "Romance" and "Escape" packages. Choose an idyllic picnic spot at an ocean-side park or sample delicious local sea food at the excellent area restaurants.

The Ferry Dock for Magdalen Island is only a few minutes away and *Matthew House* is in a quiet area, yet close to the centre of Souris. There is so much to do in the area that you'll want to spend several days; your hosts at *Matthew House* will be very glad to help you plan your holiday. There are miles of white sandy beaches to explore along the coastline, and museums, including the famous Basin Head Fisheries Museum, historical sites and arts and crafts places in the area.

Special trout or tuna fishing tours, or Harbour Cruises can be arranged. There is much here for the photographer -- wildlife, shorebirds and seals.

The churning tides of Northumberland Strait and the Gulf of St. Lawrence meet at East Point where the lighthouse stands, a vista unsurpassed anywhere in the Maritimes.

— MATTHEW HOUSE —

Linda Anderson and Emma Cappelluzzo
15 Breakwater Street, Box 151
Souris, Prince Edward Island
C0A 2B0
(902) 687-3461

Season: June 1 - October 1
Rates: Double $48 - $85
Types of Accommodation: 8 Double
Bathrooms: Private
Breakfast: Full
Special Information: No guests' pets please; Gourmet or box lunches and candlelight dinner by prearrangement; Reservations are suggested
Languages: English and limited French
Directions: From Charlottetown, take Highway 2 to Souris. In Souris, follow signs to the *Matthew House Inn*, harbourside at 15 Breakwater Street.

Barachois Inn

BARACHOIS INN

The fifteen room *Barachois Inn* was originally the Victorian mansion built in 1870 for local merchant, Joseph Gallant. Mr. Gallant was a man of considerable importance in his community which is reflected in the house he built.

The *Inn* is located in historic South Rustico on the North Shore of Prince Edward Island; one of the oldest settlements in Prince Edward Island, Rustico was established by the Acadians in the early 1700's. Across the street is the St. Augustine's Church built in 1838, and the Farmer's Bank Museum built of Island sandstone, which operated as a bank between 1864 and 1894.

Barachois Inn has been restored to its former graciousness; the rooms are furnished with period pieces and works of art. There are four guest rooms with private baths; two have sitting rooms, and all have wonderful views.

You can enjoy a quiet evening walk on the shore or relax with a book in the living room. There is golfing, horseback riding, deep sea fishing, clam digging, swimming, windsurfing, tennis, hiking, biking, craft shops, theatre and excellent dining nearby.

The *Inn* is centrally located on the Island, perfect for day trips to any location in the province. The National Park and the beaches are nearby. Cavendish, the home of L.M. Montgomery's, "Anne of Green Gables" is close to South Rustico, and Charlottetown, the capital of Prince Edward Island, and the Birthplace of the Confederation of Canada, is 28 km away.

Judy and Gary MacDonald
Box 1022
Charlottetown, Prince Edward Island
C1A 7M4
(902) 963-2194

Season: May 1 - October 31
Rates: $75 and up
Types of Accommodation: 4 Double
Bathrooms: 4 Private
Breakfast: Full
Special Information: Non-smoking home; No guests' pets please; Suitable for older children; Dogs and Cats on premises
Directions: *Barachois Inn* is located just off Route 6 on Route 243, in South Rustico, Prince Edward Island.

Silver Fox Inn

The *Silver Fox Inn* is named after the fur industry that brought fame and fortune to Prince Edward Island in the early part of this century. Built in 1892 as a private residence, it was designed by the famed architect William Critchlow Harris. For nearly a century, proud owners have carefully preserved the beauty of the spacious rooms with their fireplaces and fine woodwork.

Combining modern comfort with the cherished past, the *Silver Fox Inn* offers accommodation for twelve guests. Its six bedrooms, each with a private bath, feature period furnishings. Breakfast is served in the dining area.

The quiet location of the *Silver Fox Inn* is convenient to Summerside's business and shopping district. You may park your car and take a historic walking tour. Summerside is the Island's second largest community. Fiddling and step-dancing contests, harness racing and lobster suppers are highlights of an annual mid-July Carnival. Located right on Bedeque Bay, part of the Northumberland Strait, the town has a Harbour and marina. There are historic churches, a museum, theatre, a craft centre, and a "Tour the Island" Visitor Information Centre. Beaches, tennis, golfing, and shopping are nearby.

SILVER FOX INN

Julie Simmons
61 Granville Street
Summerside, Prince Edward Island
C1N 2Z3
(902) 436-4033

Season: All year
Rates: Single $50 - $55 Double $55 - $60
Types of Accommodation: 3 Double, 2 Twin
Bathrooms: 6 Private -- 2 with a tub and 4 with a shower
Breakfast: Continental Plus
Special Information: Adult guests only; Smoking in public areas only; No guests' pets please;
Directions: In Summerside, Granville Street is north off Water Street (the main street in the town).

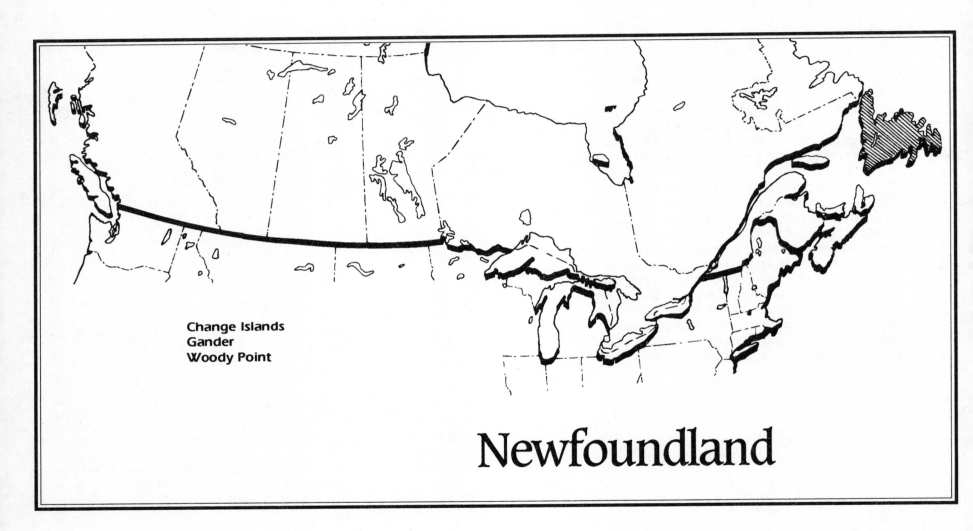

Change Islands
Gander
Woody Point

Newfoundland

Seven Oakes Island Inn

Seven Oakes Island Inn is a 100-year-old historic home with a surrounding balcony overlooking the ocean. From here, guests can whale watch or view icebergs, in season.

Guests can relax by an open fireplace in their bedroom, in the dining room or parlour. Besides breakfast, Newfoundland meals are served in the new spacious dining room.

The bedrooms all have radios, and besides regular bathrooms and showers, a whirlpool bath is available. Three lovely self-contained guest cottages are located at the ocean front. Breakfast includes home-made breads and preserves. Complimentary tea, coffee and cookies are available.

There are hiking areas nearby. Rowboats are available. Boat charters, cod jigging, and sightseeing trips can be arranged on request.

The Change Islands are located in Notre Dame Bay, between Twillingate and Fogo. Little has changed here since the last century -- there have only been motor vehicles on the Islands since 1965, but all the roads are paved! The architecture and lifestyle reflect an earlier era; white painted, narrow clapboard homes sit in tidy green gardens. Fishing stages and stores, painted in the traditional red ochre colour, hug the shore. Small boats chug in and out the harbours. There's even a general store where you can buy the makings of a picnic, and an almost abandoned community at Puncheon Cove that's a perfect place to eat it.

— SEVEN OAKES —

Beulah and Eddie Oake
Box 57
Change Islands
Notre Dame Bay, Newfoundland
A0G 1R0
(709) 621-3256 or (709) 635-2247 (off season)

Season: May - October 31
Rates: Available upon request
Types of Accommodation: 4 Bedrooms and 3 Self-contained Cottages
Bathrooms: All private
Breakfast: Full
Special Information: Non-smoking home; Meals served at extra cost; Laundry service; Row boat available
Directions: Take the Gander Bay Road, Route 330, to Gander Bay. Turn left to Route 331. Turn right at Stoneville, Route 335, to Port Albert and Farewell. - OR - Take the Trans Canada Highway, Route 1, to the Notre Dame Junction, Route 340. Turn right past the Lewisporte Mall to Boyd's Cove. Turn right on Route 331. Turn left at Stoneville, Route 335, to Port Albert and Farewell. Then a short ferry ride will land you on Change Islands.

Cape Cod Inn

The *Cape Cod Inn Bed and Breakfast* was originally a family home built in 1983 by the Kuta's. Now, Margaret and Roy offer their home as a warm and friendly place for bed and breakfast guests. Built in modern Cape Cod style, their home sits on spacious grounds with a large back lawn and gardens.

Guests can watch remote controlled television in the privacy of their bedroom; or join others in the family room around the woodstove. A quiet time of reflection can be spent on the sheltered patio deck overlooking the landscaped yard.

During your summer holidays, the *Cape Cod Inn* can be used as your home base while touring. Gander is centrally located and many guests like to take day long trips visiting the smaller coastal communities and islands, returning to the *Cape Cod Inn* in the evening.

In the winter months, central Newfoundland is a winter wonderland with ice fishing, cross-country and downhill skiing and snow mobiling, all within driving distance of the *Cape Cod Inn*

The Atlantic Canada grading authority recently rated the *Cape Cod Inn* among the top Bed and Breakfasts in Newfoundland.

A full breakfast is served by your hostess each morning and tea and coffee are served each afternoon. Various "traditional" Newfoundland and Canadian meals are prepared upon request.

Gander is the home of the Gander International Airport. Established in 1930 as a strategic military base, Gander now has a museum depicting Gander's aviation history. Gander features a full complement of retail and shopping centres; a convention centre for up to 1,000 people; and a cultural programme designed to please all tastes.

CAPE COD INN

Margaret and Roy Kuta
66 Bennett Drive
Gander, Newfoundland
A1V 1M9
(709) 651-2269

Season: All year
Rates: Single $40 Double $55
Types of Accommodation: 4 Double
Bathrooms: 2 Private and 2 Shared
Breakfast: Full
Special Information: No guests' pets please; No smoking in bedrooms; Lunch and dinner offered with 2 hours notice; Reservations suggested
Languages: English and French
Directions: Turn off Trans Canada Highway at Cobham Street by G.E.O. garage. Turn right on Bennett Drive to #66. One minute from Trans Canada Highway.

Victorian Manor

Victorian Manor is a 1920 home built in a Victorian style at Woody Point in Gros Morne National Park. The house is set well back from the road on a large area of land, very private, but part of Bonne Bay.

The *Manor* still contains many interesting artifacts from the turn-of-the-century lifestyle of Newfoundland. The guest rooms are spacious and comfortable. Breakfast is served in the sunporch or the dining room.

Drive to the end of Trout River and embrace the awe-inspiring scenery of Trout River Pond. From the beach of the little pond, one of the hills resembles an elephant's head -- a most intriguing sight!

There is a swimming area nearby and the Green Gardens Hiking Trail. There are cross-country ski trails at Lomond and the *Manor* is approximately ninety kilometers from Marble Mountain, a downhill ski resort. A tour Ferry Boat links you to the northside of Gros Morne National Park.

There is also a guest house for complete privacy with its own jacuzzi en suite. Great for honeymooners!

VICTORIAN MANOR

Stan and Jenny Parsons
Box 165
Woody Point, Newfoundland
A0K 1P0
(709) 453-2485

Season: All year
Rates: Single $36 Double $40 - $45 Efficiency Units $49 - $65 Guest House $85
Types of Accommodation: 4 Efficiency Units, 1 Single, 3 Double
Bathrooms: 1 Shared and Guest House has Jacuzzi en suite
Breakfast: Continental
Special Information: Restricted smoking; No guests' pets allowed; Children welcome
Handicapped Facilities: Limited
Directions: At Deer Lake on Trans Canada Highway 1, take Route 430 to Wiltondale (31 km), then take Route 431 (33 km) to Woody Point. The *Manor* is located in Gros Morne National Park at Woody Point.

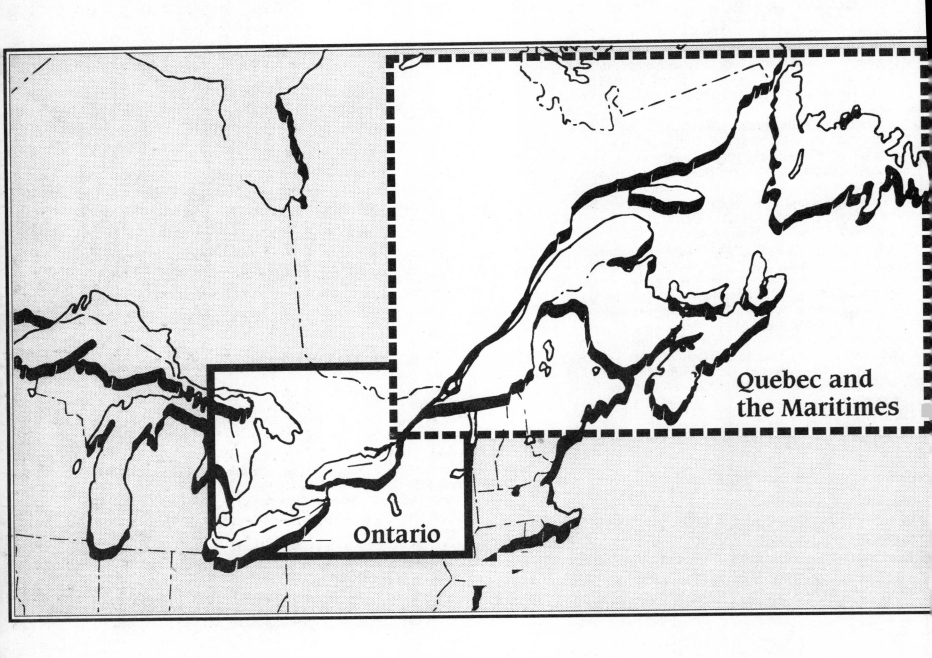

Quebec and
the Maritimes

Ontario